T0333427

POLITICAL ISSUES FOR THE TWENTY-FIRST CENTURY

Political Issues for the Twenty-First Century

Edited by
DAVE MORLAND AND MARK COWLING
University of Teesside

ASHGATE

Published by
Ashgate Publishing Limited
Gower House
Croft Road
Aldershot
Hants GU11 3HR
England

Ashgate Publishing Company
Suite 420
101 Cherry Street
Burlington, VT 05401-4405
USA

Ashgate website: http://www.ashgate.com

British Library Cataloguing in Publication Data
Political issues for the twenty-first century
    1. International cooperation 2. Great Britain - Politics and
    government - 1997- 3. Great Britain - Foreign relations -
    1997- 4. European Union countries - Politics and government
    - 21st century
    I. Morland, Dave II. Cowling, Mark
    320.9'41'0905

Library of Congress Cataloging-in-Publication Data
Political issues for the twenty-first century / edited by Dave Morland and Mark Cowling.
    p. cm.
    Includes bibliographical references and index.
    ISBN 0-7546-1903-6
    1. Political science--Philosophy. 2. Great Britain--Politics and government--21st century.
    3. Monetary unions--European Union countries. 4. European Union. 5. North Atlantic
Treaty Organization. 6. Globalization. I. Morland, David. II. Cowling, Mark.

JA71.P617 2004
320--dc22

2003062014

ISBN 0 7546 1903 6

Printed and bound in Great Britain by Antony Rowe Ltd, Chippenham, Wiltshire

Contents

PART III: EUROPEAN AND GLOBAL ISSUES

List of Contributors

Charlotte Bretherton is Senior Lecturer in International Relations/European Studies at Liverpool John Moores University. Her research interests are currently focused on the external policy of the European Union, broadly conceived. She also has an interest in the gender dimensions of global environmental politics. Recent publications include 'Gender mainstreaming and EU enlargement: swimming against the tide', *Journal of European Public Policy* 8 (1) (2001) and 'Movements, networks and hierarchies: a gender perspective on global environmental governance', *Global Environmental Politics* 3 (2) (2003).

John Carter works at the University of Teesside. He has research interests in social theory, anarchism and the new social movements.

Andrew Cottey is a Lecturer in the Department of Government, University College Cork. His major area of interest is NATO and the evolution of its role following the end of the Soviet Union.

Mark Cowling is Reader in Criminology at the University of Teesside. His previous publications include: *Approaches to Marx* (edited with Lawrence Wilde), Open University Press, Milton Keynes, 1989; *The Communist Manifesto: New Interpretations* (edited), Edinburgh University Press, Edinburgh, 1998; *Date Rape and Consent*, Ashgate, Aldershot, 1998; *Marxism, the Millennium and Beyond* (edited, with Paul Reynolds), Macmillan, 2000; and *Marx's Eighteenth Brumaire: (Post) Modern Interpretations* (edited, with James Martin), Pluto Press, 2002.

Professor Howard Elcock was educated at The Queen's College, Oxford. He has taught at the Universities of Hull and Northumbria, UK and at Fredonia State College, USA. He has lectured at many other universities and colleges in Europe, Asia and North America. He has numerous publications on local and regional government, public administration and policy analysis. He is at present engaged in a study of local councillors and elected mayors in Northern England.

John Gibbins is a Principal Lecturer in Research Management in the School of Social Sciences and Law at the University of Teesside, and a member of Wolfson College Cambridge. He recently published *The Politics of Postmodernity*, a book on value change and political futures with Bo Reimer. He has written extensively in the fields of political and social theory, but is currently working in the fields of criminology, social epistemology and the history of university curriculum, focused at Cambridge University.

Julian Gough is a Principal Lecturer in Economics at the University of Teesside specialising in business economics. Julian was formerly Senior Economic Analyst at British Gas plc 1984-95, and prior to that a lecturer in economics at Cardiff Business School. His main research interests are in business economics, economics of financial institutions, regional economics, and European integration.

Stephen James is a Senior Lecturer in Economics at the University of Teesside. He has published on UK macroeconomic policy, labour market policy, financial markets and the Single European Market and Single Currency. Current research interests include the relationship between banking, financial markets and the development of the iron and steel industry in the nineteenth and early twentieth centuries.

Dave Morland works in the Sociology section at the University of Teesside. He has published widely on anarchism and is developing research interests in technology and the sociology of football.

Andrew Shepherd is studying toward a PhD in the School of Social Sciences and Law at the University of Teesside. Andrew's research examines contemporary views and experiences of New Labour's communitarian welfare paradigm and its 'civic society' objective in the Teesside area.

Brian Vale is a post-graduate student at the University of Teesside.

List of Abbreviations

ABM	Anti-ballistic missile
ACM	Anti-capitalist movement
BIC	British-Irish Council
CAP	Common Agricultural Policy
CEEC	Central and East European Countries
CFA	Communauté Financière d'Afrique (African Financial Community)
CFE	Conventional Armed Forces in Europe
CFSP	Common Foreign and Security Policy
CSCE	Conference on Security and Co-operation in Europe
DEFRA	Department for the Environment and Rural Affairs
DGs	Directorates-General of the European Commission
DUP	Democratic Unionist Party
EC	European Community
ECB	European Central Bank
EMU	Economic and Monetary Union
ESCB	European System of Central Banks
EU	European Union
FARC	Revolutionary Armed Forces of Colombia
FRU	The British Army's Force Research Unit
G8	Group of Eight leading industrialised economies
GATT	General Agreement on Tariffs and Trade
GORs	Government Office of the Regions
IMF	International Monetary Fund
ICTs	Information and communication technologies
INTERREG	EU Inter-regional programme
IRA	Irish Republican Army
IT	Information technology
NACC	North Atlantic Co-operation Council
NAFTA	North American Free Trade Agreement
NATO	North Atlantic Treaty Organisation
OECD	Organisation for Economic Co-operation and Development

PfP	Partnership for Peace
PIRA	Provisional IRA
PSNI	Police Service of Northern Ireland
PUP	Progressive Unionist Party
QMV	Qualified majority voting
RAPBs	Regional Advisory Planning Boards
RDAs	Regional Development Agencies
REPCs	Regional Economic Planning Councils
RMA	Revolution in military affairs
RUC	Royal Ulster Constabulary
SDLP	Social Democratic and Labour Party
STV	Single Transferable Vote
SWP	Socialist Workers Party
TEC	Treaty establishing the European Community
TMD	Theatre missiles defences
TQM	Total quality management
TUC	Trades Union Congress
UDA	Ulster Defence Association
UDCs	Urban Development Corporations
UFF	Ulster Freedom Fighters
UN	United Nations
US	United States
UUP	Ulster Unionist Party
UVF	Ulster Volunteer Force
WEU	West European Union
WMD	Weapons of mass destruction
WTO	World Trade Organisation

List of Tables

1 Introduction

DAVE MORLAND AND MARK COWLING

Why this Book?

Political and social speculation is not an uncommon event at the turn of a century. Imagine then the intellectual frenzy engendered by the onset of a new millennium. Academe has long been buzzing to the sound of the 'post' discourses. Participants and progenitors are too numerous to mention here. Suffice to say that debates on post-industrialisation, post-materialism, post-structuralism and postmodernism are both vigorous and extensive. Accompanying this flurry of theoretical imaginings and suppositions were a set of more hard-hitting accounts that represent the end of the battle of ideologies and the commencement of a new political world order. The closing of the twentieth century, then, induced a chorus of speculative political analysis about the future. Whilst not wanting to demean these various developments, the editors of this book remain convinced that there are a series of enduring political issues that are so deeply rooted in historical political structures that they will not dissolve and cannot be dissipated either by the advent of new millennium or by the growth of a so-called postmodern world.

It is not that the editors completely reject the value of some of the 'post' literatures. We are both deeply sceptical, however, about announcements of a new world order. Experience informs us that the collapse of the bipolar ideological struggle between Soviet communism and US neoliberalism has created a number of political vortices and vacuums that are presently being contested at both a local and global level. Pre-eminent among the contenders for power is nationalism. The consequences of this have already been felt in the Balkans and elsewhere. And it is not simply the demise of one world superpower that results in new political struggles emerging after decades of suppression. Rather, the triumph of US neoliberalism and the prospect of renewed American imperialism, whether at a political, cultural or economic level, has ignited the fuse of Islamic resistance in many parts of the world. Symbolically, the consequences of this have far outweighed anything the Cold War had to offer. For the first time in a long time the US took a direct hit on its homeland territory on 11 September 2001. It is difficult to underestimate the importance of the attack on the former World Trade Centre in New York. One thing that is clear is that the attack has reverberated across the globe, with direct military intervention by the US and its allies in Afghanistan and Iraq to date, with the prospect of further consequences in countries such as North Korea and Iran, to name but the most obvious.

The implications of such actions are equally unambiguous within individual nation states. Relations between some European states and the US, for example, have become strained over the US-led military intervention in Iraq. It has been estimated that somewhere between one million to one and a half million people marched through central London in early 2003 to protest against the impending war. That US foreign policy does not occur in practice in a political void is hardly a revolutionary thought. However, the attack on the twin towers and the subsequent US reaction does illustrate that there remain a number of interconnected political issues that will remain live for many decades to come: viz, ideological politics and resistance to forms of ideological politics.

But this is not a book about global politics as such. In recognising the global, national and local interconnectivity of such events as described above, the purpose of the book is to provide a collection of accessible and informative essays on contemporary developments and future issues in politics, broadly conceived, but with a UK focus where appropriate. Having established the intention of this volume it is worth pointing out at the start that some of the contributions in this collection of essays pursue a more general agenda than others. Whilst some chapters focus in a very tight way on an issue that directly affects UK politics, others, particularly some of the theoretical essays, raise issues that, whilst they may provide an informative backdrop to events in the UK, are much broader in scope.

The Structure of this Book

It would be foolish to believe that a single text could effectively represent the entire array of political issues that will remain or perhaps become significant over the next few decades and beyond. Rather this collection confines itself to offering a sample of investigative essays that address some of the major political issues that will remain prominent for the foreseeable future.

The text is divided into three sections that reflect what the editors believe to be some of the most important historical issues and contemporary developments in politics. Generally speaking, all of the contributions to this work may be read from a UK perspective. To be sure, some of the theoretical chapters transcend the limitations of UK politics and portend trends that know no state boundaries. But many of the other essays here have an obvious concern with UK politics, either on the domestic or international front. Part I concerns itself with political theory and political philosophy. There are three contentious accounts here.

In the first substantive chapter of this book Gibbins examines the question of philosophical foundations. Do concepts like truth, right and knowledge possess solid foundations? If not, what are the consequences for politics and philosophy? In a wide-ranging review Gibbins analyses a number of key issues. To begin with a sketch is offered of what an anti-foundationalist politics and philosophy might look like. Here communitarianism is explored by focusing on its conception of morality grounded in communities of agents, with accompanying community-based anthropological and ontological foundations. Similarly, the role of traditions in our intellectual heritage is considered through the writings of MacIntyre, Rorty and Walzer. The second part of this chapter examines the issue of truth and foundations in more detail, evaluating the arguments against foundationalism with reference to Wittgensteinian philosophers. Following this, the chapter looks at the role of metaphor and supervenience, and how the latter supports the anti-foundational argument. Gibbins concludes this opening part of the book by contending that the state and modernity reached their zenith in the late nineteenth century. What we now need, he suggests, is a language of time as an antidote to the language of permanence and space. Such a language would help us make sense of the decline of the nation-state, the restructuring of classes and cultures and the deterioration of the Newtonian-Cartesian world picture.

Following this opening chapter, Carter offers a contentious analysis of the decline of the old left and the apparent victory of the free market. He explores the historical backdrop that led to the rise of New Labour, but also witnessed the emergence of a more dynamic progressive force – the anti-capitalist movement (ACM). In short, Carter's claim is that in dispatching the old left to oblivion the forces of the free market have provided an opportunity for a movement that is potentially more powerful and effective than that which preceded it. In the first part of this chapter the major events and theories of the past are surveyed to reveal how New Labour was born.

Here notions of flexible specialisation, the flexible firm and postmodernism are considered, together with some of the leading theoretical resources drawn upon by the party. The chapter then illustrates some of the similarities between New Labour and the former Conservative governments under Thatcher and Major. In particular, New Labour's adoption of flexible labour markets, managerialism and public-private partnerships are key for Carter. Finally, the chapter analyses the nature of the emerging ACM, tracing its roots back to thinkers like Debord, and its more recent resonances in Klein. In doing so it demonstrates how the ACM has an international character and identifies the forces of globalisation as important targets for resistance. Additionally, it informs the reader how the ACM is mainly a fluid network of co-operative movements that roughly adhere to a core of common principles.

This first section of the book closes with another contentious contribution. Morland's chapter proposes that it is time to resurrect the term totalitarianism. The reason for this is that contemporary society is on the verge of degenerating into a mode of socio-cultural totalitarianism. This mode of totalitarianism is the product of a long process of technological and scientific developments. Today, the potential for the development of a socio-cultural totalitarianism is disseminated by contemporary information and communication technologies (ICTs), which form the nucleus of a new surveillance assemblage. By drawing principally on the work of Lewis Mumford, but also others, it is argued that ICTs facilitate a convergence of the social, the cultural and the economic that establishes a new totality, a rhizomatic network of digital nodes and interconnections that constantly monitor and deterritorrialise the individual into a series of digital dopplegangers. In the process, the individual's dominion of privacy is obliterated by an omniscient, omnipotent system that leaves her/him not only depoliticised and voiceless, but helpless in face of a dominant techno-scientific myth. Fuelled by this myth and nurtured by capital, this rationale or technique is in danger of begetting a new form of totalitarian society.

Morland suggests that the term totalitarianism can be meaningfully employed in a new direction. It is contended that one of the most important benchmarks of a totalitarian state, for example, has always been the disintegration of the barrier between the public and the private, the invasion of that supposedly inviolable sphere of privacy and self-concerning action which the state has no right to interfere with or encroach upon, is viciously trampled upon by totalitarian regimes. The chapter continues by demonstrating how society in the twenty-first century is perilously close to penetrating that sphere again, and is steadily eroding our defences against this invasion of our private lives. One of the key factors in this assault is the rise of a dominant techno-scientific myth. This is not a recent event, for as history reveals this myth has inhabited human culture, with periodic reversals such as the medieval era, since the dawn of civilisation. The chapter concludes by employing some of the post-structuralist thought of Deleuze and Guattari to illustrate the impending danger of a new socio-cultural totalitarianism.

The second section of the book is devoted to an examination of three important areas of present UK politics. All of them have been slowly unfolding over recent years, but none have concluded their journey across the twenty-first century political landscape. Indeed, it is unlikely that any will do so shortly, and it is possible that the issues at stake here have consequences that last well into the future.

This section begins by examining the rise of New Labour in Britain and the development of the Third Way. Here, Shepherd offers an account of the development of the Third Way that is set within the context of a supposed decline of ideological politics – at least within the UK. In the opening part of the chapter, Shepherd provides a history of the development of the Third Way by way of a tour of the party's recent history from the 1980s forward. The commitment to modernisation made under Neil Kinnock and John Smith is examined in some detail, before proceeding to the leadership of Tony Blair.

Having provided the historical backdrop to changes within the party and its principles, Shepherd then goes on to analyse the central ideas of the Third Way. Key here are the Christian and ethical socialism that Blair draws from earlier figures, such as Tawney, together with the inherent pragmatism that New Labour has adopted in the face of seemingly insurmountable obstacles like globalisation. However, Shepherd contends that it would be wrong to argue that New Labour has abandoned ideology entirely. There still are differences between left and right in UK politics. New Labour may have moved onto new political terrain, but it is not without principle. More importantly, it is, according to Shepherd, a return to some traditional roots and ideas that will see New Labour dominate the UK political landscape for some time to come.

One of the most difficult and impassioned issues in the UK constitutes the materials for the second chapter in this middle section of the book: the issue of Northern Ireland. In his historical introduction to this issue, Cowling concentrates on the major background considerations that will influence developments in Northern Ireland over the next few years. After offering an informative historical backdrop to recent events the chapter proceeds by discussing the major parties and organisations involved, arguing that they make better sense if it is assumed they represent two nations. The crux of Cowling's argument is that there are four main issues that are likely to dominate the next few years: the limited value of the Good Friday Agreement to Northern Ireland's Protestants, decommissioning, demographics and the role of cross-border institutions. By investigating each issue in turn the dynamics of this issue are clearly mapped out for the future. In the longer term it is suggested that the evolution of the Republic into a more affluent and secular society and the deepening of the European Union may somewhat defuse the issue of the border.

The final chapter in this section focuses on regionalism. Here Elcock furnishes the reader with a brief historical introduction to regionalism in the UK. This early stage of the chapter focuses on the Thatcher regime before examining the fate of regionalism under New Labour. The progression to devolution in Scotland and Wales is analysed, as is the case for regional government in England. At this juncture Elcock addresses some of the major issues at stake. These include democratic accountability; local co-ordination of planning and policies; the allocation of resources; and the existence of a democratic deficit.

After examining the history and future prospects for further regionalism within the UK, Elcock then moves on to the international arena. Here the focus begins with Europe. Issues of language and culture are explored, before moving further afield to North America and consideration of economic factors in the drive for regionalisation in New York state. Elcock concludes by suggesting that there is a growing demand for regional government throughout the western world. More importantly perhaps, the rise of the international trading blocs, like the EU and NAFTA, has unleashed accelerating demands for autonomy and representation from minority identities and cultures across the globe.

The final section of the text is devoted to an examination of issues of growing significance in both a European and a global context. The implementation of the Euro has potentially massive implications for Europe's standing as a world financial superpower, especially in light of the EU's imminent expansion. Moreover, the issue of a single European currency is still considered too hot to handle by the present government. Having pledged to hold a referendum on whether the UK should join the single currency, New Labour remains reluctant to commit its credentials on this matter. The role of NATO has also come under increasingly close scrutiny over the past few years. In particular the Alliance has been forced to reassess itself in light of the re-emergence of ethnic conflicts in the Balkans and the wars in Iraq. Perhaps the most talked-about issue recently has been globalisation. The consequences of a pursuit of neo-liberal economic policies across the globe are discussed here, and help to illustrate the importance of this issue within the anti-capitalist movement discussed by Carter in the first section of the book.

The launch of the Euro has been a central feature of the development of the EU in recent years. In their chapter Stephen James and Julian Gough explain the economic effects of the single currency and examine some of its political implications. Euro membership, they demonstrate, affects all major aspects of policy from public spending and taxation decisions, to labour market policy and social protection. They start by describing the transition to the Euro. They note that the EU developed from free trade area to customs union to common market. The Euro takes the EU well on the way to a fourth stage of economic union in which the nations complete the integration by becoming a single economy with common monetary arrangements and enhanced fiscal arrangements, i.e. becoming in some sense a federal entity. The currency was introduced without a referendum in any member state except France, but despite lukewarm public support and an initial slide against the dollar, it thus far commands a high and increasing level of public acceptance. They move on to discuss the framework within which the European Central Bank operates, concluding that despite working tolerably well up to now it has major shortcomings in the three areas that are generally regarded as crucial for the legitimacy and efficient operation of institutions in democratic societies – democratic control, accountability and transparency. Turning to economic policy they are concerned that there is insufficient convergence between the national economies for a single rate of interest to make sense. Thus, for example, the small Irish economy is left to overheat because the German economy is in recession. They look at various possible remedies, concluding with a discussion of the possible role of labour market flexibility.

What about the Euro and enlargement? The new members from Eastern Europe are liable to strain EU budgets and exacerbate the division between an inner core of Euro-zone members and a less central group. Historically both the EU and monetary unions generally have been seen as a way of promoting harmony and preventing wars between nations, making this last issue very important. In a final exchange the two authors disagree about the role of the Euro as a stable currency, one fearing that the exacerbation of a two track Europe already mentioned may lead to instability and disintegration, the other arguing that the stabilizing effect of the Euro is so crucial that it trumps all other possible problems.

For EU watchers and international relations observers generally one of the most fascinating developments in recent times has been the emergence of the EU as a major player in world politics. With the decline of the Soviet Empire and the shift from a world dominated by bipolar military superpowers to one increasingly characterised by competing economic and trading blocs, the question of whether the EU is an international actor *sui generis* is addressed by Charlotte Bretherton in Chapter 9, *Economic and Monetary Union: Implications for the European Union's Global Role.* One of the central questions posed is to what extent the EU enjoys autonomy from its Member States. In sketching out the historical backdrop to the EU's emergence onto the global stage, Bretherton suggests that in trade and environmental policy, for example, competence is divided between the Commission and Member States. And whilst the Nice Treaty has extended the role of QMV, it remains uncertain, she argues, what the future holds. Whatever the future brings, Bretherton contends that the EU's prominence as an international actor will depend on its presence and its capability.

Employing these concepts to appraise the future prospects of the EU, Bretherton argues that the EU's presence is essentially a function of its being. Accordingly, presence is related to the EU's internal policy developments and will manifest itself through enlargement, the CAP, the single market and the Euro. Underlying this analysis, however, is the explicit recognition that the EU's presence will be as much to do with the reaction of third parties, particularly the US, as it is to do with the EU's own policy developments. The capability of the EU is considered in relation to a number of key issues: a commitment to overarching values and principles; an ability to identify priorities and construct appropriate policies; a capacity to negotiate with other parties; and the power to produce and implement policy instruments. Bretherton observes that to date there have been difficulties associated with the consistency in which Member States adhere to EU policies, and problems of coherence that derive from the internal policy processes of the EU itself. Despite these troubles, Bretherton concludes that at present the EU's greatest area of capability lies in its economic policy instruments. This does not mean, however, that the EU is yet a major actor on the world's financial stage, even if it has occupied the role of major opponent to the US in global environmental and economic negotiations.

The changing international security context has presented a number of dilemmas for NATO. In Chapter 10 Andrew Cottey considers how NATO has responded to events after 11 September 2001. In particular, he scrutinises the divisions between Europe and the US, and questions what role awaits NATO in the future. Situating his analysis within the historical context of post-Cold War international relations, Cottey questions whether NATO's *raison d'être* has crumbled along with the Berlin Wall, or whether we are beginning to witness a realignment of NATO around concerns over the proliferation of weapons of mass destruction. If so, does this mean that the 'war on terrorism' will become the central focus of US foreign policy in the twenty-first century, or are non-military risks, such as climate change, as likely to be incorporated onto the international security agenda?

Cottey notes that there have been two recent historical challenges to NATO's existence and credibility, and one significant challenge that lies ahead. The first of the recent challenges is to do with enlargement and centres on NATO's response to demands for membership of the Alliance by East European states. Here Cottey outlines the build up to NATO expansion in 1999, and illustrates the reasons behind the continuing uncertain relationship with Russia. The second trial that faced NATO in the 1990s was the war in the Balkans. The conflict in the former Yugoslavia represented a major threat to NATO's credibility. Cottey adumbrates how NATO responded to this and assesses the significance of NATO's controversial series of airstrikes in the Kosovo crisis. Accordingly, the willingness of European countries to undertake collective military action without the US, which has not occurred since World War Two, is appraised. The final dilemma facing NATO surrounds the increasingly different strategic interests of the US and EU states. As the US and Europe maintain differing perceptions of the Israeli-Palestine problem, and the US continues to wage war against international terrorism, Cottey assesses whether NATO is becoming progressively more irrelevant from the US perspective to address issues like the proliferation of weapons of mass destruction. Whatever unfolds within the next few years, Cottey contends that the long-term future of NATO is marked by uncertainty.

In our final chapter Brian Vale discusses globalisation. He links its current form, at least, to increasing Third World poverty. The mechanism for this increase is the use of neoliberal economic policies, economic globalisation, free trade, deregulation, privatisation, the opening up of local markets in the Third World to transnational corporations, structural adjustments through the International Monetary Fund and World Bank and the cutting back of social welfare subsidies. Given that 1.2 billion people live on less than $1 a day this issue is arguably the most important in the book. Because the rich nations provide the agenda for international meetings, for example on affordable drugs, debt reduction or pollution, this is leading not just to moral and humanitarian questions but also to a possible rationale for terrorism. Vale summarises the debate on globalisation. His own position is that he is a 'pessimistic Transformationalist'. He considers that economic globalisation has widened and deepened, reaching across the globe, but is having negative effects on Third World poverty. Having identified the main features of globalisation, Vale focuses on the neoliberal ideology which currently pervades the IMF and the World Bank, the major institutional aspects of globalisation seen from the Third World. He concludes by arguing that their policies have exacerbated poverty since around 1980.

PART I
THEORETICAL ISSUES

2 Political Philosophy without Foundations and Anti-Foundational Politics

JOHN GIBBINS

At the foundation of well-founded belief lies belief that is not founded (Wittgenstein, 1979).

Looking backward, critics of Modernity proclaim or regret (it is not clear which) the absence of any established foundations for contemporary thought. Their observation is accurate: the dream of *foundationalism* – i.e., the search for a permanent and unique set of authoritative principles for human knowledge – proves to be just a dream, which has its appeals in moments of intellectual crisis, but fades away when matters are viewed in a calmer and clearer light (Toulmin, 1990, p. 174).

Introduction

My two critics of foundationalism were divided by half a century but shared an answer to a question that has divided intellectuals in the west for over two thousand years, namely, does knowledge, truth and right; do human actions, social behaviour and structures have solid, indubitable and permanent foundations? Can we justify our knowledge and moral claims? If not, what does this entail for politics and philosophy? As Raymond Plant puts the matter, how can we do, 'Political Philosophy on Dover Beach?' (Plant, 1991, pp. 320-375). My short exploration of both questions and answers must, because of the focus of this book, focus on modern debates and on political thought, behaviour and institutions. However, the debate is informed by, and has implications for other disciplines, practices and structures, such as those around science, mathematics, history, philosophy, criminology, sociology and social policy where claims for disciplines having foundations have been rife (Harris, 1986; Hertzog, 1985). For convenience this argument takes it that the case for discoverable foundations is known or easily knowable, but that the case against is less widely known and accepted. I will adjudicate on the case against foundationalism rather than the case for, the case that western knowledge has severe problems in self-justification (Chisholm, 1982). My case that western culture has severe problems in self-justification can be found in other places (Gibbins and Reimer, 1999; Gibbins, 1999).

The chapter has five parts, the first explains what is at stake and what is entailed for politics and philosophy in accepting anti-foundationalism; the second unpacks the core questions, and the range of traditional answers; the third looks at the current and focused philosophical debates over anti-foundationalism and the key issue around which debates must hinge, supervenience. This section will look briefly at the arguments of Richard Rorty, Alasdair MacIntyre and Michael Walzer which though narrowly focused, were the prompt for the wider debate. The fourth brief section moves from philosophy to historiography and politics itself, by asking the related question of relativism raised by Toulmin. Can one argue that the foundations of contemporary politics in the west, such as nation state, class, family and ideology, can be pictured as themselves breaking down, and whether anti-foundational theory and practice are symbiotically related? The concluding section deals with the implication of the hypothesis that political science, like all disciplines and knowledge-claiming discourses, has no indubitable or agreed foundations, and argues that, while political theory and practice must change, that there is still a valuable and workable role for a non-foundational philosophy and politics in the future. No building on earth has foundations that can hold up its superstructure against all physical and human threats, yet however temporary the edifice, we can still build, benefit from and enjoy the artefacts created, and so for political science.

What is At Stake in this Debate?

While I focus on political knowledge here, at stake are numerous matters of great import to contemporary intellectuals, disciplines, politicians and citizens. These have been reduced to eight core areas, or levels, where legitimation crisis is entailed by negative answers. Only the answers to question 3 were the original matter of the anti-foundational debate, and will hence attract major attention, but I want to go further.

Table 1 Questions of Foundations and their Inferences

Questions asked	*The problem entailed for politics*
1) Can we trust as legitimate and true, our own perceptions, beliefs and *claims to knowledge*?	If not, how do we proceed to think, judge, converse, and exert the will to act? Can we ever act with confidence in political life?
1b) Do words have an essential and definable meaning, or are meanings plural and related to context?	If words have no shared meaning, how can we justify the truth or right of statements?
2) Can we ever trust our *moral and value* judgements as providing good grounds for conviction?	If not, how can moral discourse be anything more than personal or group preferences or interests? How can we know if one moral claim is better than another?
3) Justification - Are *academic discourses* privileged in some way by providing valid justifications, e.g. proof or verification made by method, evidence or argument?	If not, why should politicians, experts and citizens take note of political science and theory?
4) Are there any fundamental grounds or *structures underpinning and directing human activity*, behaviour and institutions?	If theory cannot identify the grounds that direct action and behaviour, why should society invest in discipline training in universities?
4b) Are academic *theory and practice* linked? Does policy entail sound theorization?	If there are no infallible links between theory and practice, why bother with theory?
5) Can we trust our *political leaders* and political bodies, such as *political parties*, movements to function as prescribed? Can we	If not, who do we trust? Are we defenceless in the face of demagogues and demagoguery? How could we articulate and

know the veracity of their claims?

aggregate divergent interests and values without intermediary political bodies and leaders we trust?

6) Can we ground the legitimacy of our *institutions*, such as the constitution, the criminal justice system, and parliaments?

If not (if there are no foundational legal norms, or 'ground norms' (Kelsen), how can we legitimately rule on disputes, impose punishments, uphold the law? How could the police and courts justify their actions?

7) Can we trust the legitimacy of that most *sovereign* of all political bodies, the *Nation State*, as possessing the monopoly of the legitimate use of force within a given territory (Weber)?

If sovereignty of the Nation State, is dead or dying, how can we have any political or moral order, and the components for a just and effective international order? Who or how can we exercise power or authority?

8) Can we trust our *meta-political* beliefs, or 'grand theories' of the west (which are used to legitimate local, national and international governance) as well grounded and privileged? Are our beliefs in liberal freedoms, human rights, parliamentary representative democracy, the rule of law, contract and consent, firmly grounded and privileged?

If not, how can we ever justify regional political order, let alone a just international order? If not, how can we ground and justify imposing the will of such bodies as Parliaments, the European Community, the United Nations, on bodies as diverse as the Taliban, Serb nationalists, Saddam Hussain and Columbian drugs cartels?

The right-hand column lists the key questions that anti-foundational political science must answer, and with some urgency. If the anti-foundationalists are right, our most cherished beliefs about our selves and the public world are not firmly grounded, not justified by present means.

What follows is ironical, namely, that at precisely the time when western language and institutions are on the verge of imperial conquest, and diverse cultures suffer imbrications and amalgamations, that what we should abandon in the west, is confidence in our privileged cultural institutions and world view, or *geist*. With postmodernism so with anti-foundationalism, 'the owl of Minerva takes flight at the approach of dusk' (Hegel). Stephen Toulmin has correctly judged one valid response to this dilemma, but we should retrace some steps and come to our own conclusions.

So What? What Follows for Politics and Philosophy if the Anti-Foundationalists are Right?

Politics

If there are no foundational universal political principles and institutions we have to either change our political practices or re-establish them on contingent and particular grounds (McGuinness, 1993; Ingram, 1995). Richard Rorty has achieved the second by re-grounding liberal democracy on pragmatism (Rorty, 1979; 1982). Liberal democracy works – judged as a practice it passes muster working for citizens, businesses and diverse multi-cultural groupings. Liberal democracy allows a sensible balance between individualism and the needs of social cohesion. If no group or ideology can ever claim a monopoly of wisdom or right, then defending the freedom of individuals and the conditional authority of majorities is sensible. It is noticeable that Rorty is often associated with Oakeshott and MacIntrye on pragmatism and the value of traditions. If there are no *a priori* principles upon which to operate deductively, then the choice is either rationalism in politics, or the attempt to live according to ideology and technique, or traditionalism – carrying on the evolution of long-cherished beliefs and re-enactments. To Burke, conservatives, pessimists and the cautious, these prescriptions on the value of tradition had reactionary merits, but to others they have reformist potential. Traditions may be revolutionary, radical, socialist, republican, feminist and Green as well as conservative and nationalist.

But the opponents of anti-foundationalism in political theory save most invective to attack not only its conservative implications, but its communitarian and nationalist associations. If there is no *a priori* right way to live, is there not a green light for any group to flourish without need for justification? The answer is yes, flourish, and no, you must provide justifications. Justifications may need rules and standards, but these do not have to be foundational, absolute and universal. Most anti-foundationalists have explored the leads indicated by difference, distinctions and diversity and are trying to produce a new political justice for such a diverse order (Young, 1990; Connolly, 1991; Weeks, 1994). Indeed this takes us to the radical side to the anti-foundationalist agenda which I want to explore here, the advocacy of new politics, of expressivity, spontaneity, networking, direct action, new social movements, new values and re-setting the boundaries (Gibbins, 1979; Beck, 1997; Gibbins and Reimer, 1999; Yeatman, 1994).

One popular theoretical antidote to anti-foundationalism has been communitarianism, that proposes we can only understand and direct our behaviour morally if we imagine ourselves as intrinsically situated in communities of agents. The latter accepts that there are no transcendental universal criteria of right and the good, and goes further, to accept the relativity to our situatedness of all such criteria and conceptions. However, this conclusion is derived from a holistic anthropological argument that conceives of mind, human nature and rules of right as products of the language, form of life and goings on of discrete communities. The loss of transcendental foundations for truth and right are then compensated by the certainty of anthropological and ontological foundations for our thinking, being and acting in the practice of community (Sandel, 1982; Taylor, 1989; Ingram, 1995; Cutrofello, 1998; Plant, 1991, pp. 324-375). In one sense this view supports a kind of sociological foundationalism, but on the other buys moral security at the cost of a vicious form of communal relativism and communal exclusion and rivalry. But the Wittgensteinian strength of the communitarian argument has obliged some political theorists to transform the political question from 'are there any foundations'? to 'how can different communities sharing the same space come to any moral, political and legal agreements, when there are no possible transcultural criteria of justification'? (Gibbins and Reimer, 1999, pp. 155-166). Communitarianism will not do to answer this second question, because each space in the world has arbitrary horizontal lines (boundaries) that are as arbitrary as its vertical lines (foundations). In contemporary politics most boundaries are contested, and each space is inhabited by more than one community (Palestinian/Jew; Catholic/Protestant; Catalan/Castilliano). Postmodernism, cosmopolitanism, multi-culturalism and pluralism are amongst the theories that offer answers to our new question.

Philosophy

If the anti-foundationalists are right, then philosophers and theorists have three key options open to them. The first is psychological, and involves developing a 'coping strategy' of some sort, a way of living with insecurity and contingency. Such coping strategies were developed by Diogenes, Sextus Empiricus, Lucretius, Seneca, Schopenhauer, Heidegger and Sartre, Baudrillard and Lyotard. Most of eastern philosophy, such as Buddhism, Taoism, follows this tradition of coming to terms with endless flux and contingency. A second, option is to develop some cynical critical posture that amounts to continual carping and deconstruction, always being in negative mode, parasitical on the positive affirmations of others to undermine. This we see in the work of many of the French philosophers such as Derrida, Lacan, Deleuze, and Lyotard. The third strategy is 'to work harder at inventing footholds upon which we can re-build justification in theory and practice', if not foundations. This is the option that Rosenau associates with the 'affirmative postmodernists' and which Bo Reimer and I have argued in *The Politics of Postmodernity* (Luntley, 1995, pp. 219-224).

In this view the many types of foundationalism offered in western philosophy were brave, though in the end, failed attempts to ground thought and action. They have had largely beneficial social and psychological effects in providing essential preconditions for exploring thought and action, above all providing some existential and metaphysical security and order, as many have so effectively illustrated in intellectual history (Wolin, 1961; Voegelin, 2000; Gunnell, 1987; Pocock, 1972; Letwin, 1965). The effectiveness of traditions has been best explained by Michael Oakeshott and Alasdair MacIntyre as being largely due to their inherited rather than taught nature, and their capacity to provided continuity through time, and order during change, continuity through discontinuity, and fixity during temporal flux (Oakeshott, 1962; MacIntyre, 1981). Traditions do not have to be true to be effective, they do not need to be grounded in reality, they only need to be re-enacted, respected and revered. The many, discordant and incommensurable traditions, positions, and theories that make up the canon of western philosophy are in fact examples of such traditions. At any one time most are discarded but they form a heritage, a store or stock of thinking that may be visited in times of crisis (MacIntyre, 1981). Traditions provide the 'standard accounts' of how things are from the vantage points of groups of scholars (Toulmin, 1990, pp. 12-22) or 'paradigms' (Kuhn, 1970).

The collective traditions make up the canon of the western intellectual tradition. Made up at any time of beliefs and values, some held to be verified and established beyond doubt, intellectual and discipline traditions litter history like boulders on a mountain side, apparently impervious but the detritus of evolutionary and human forces. The history of any discipline is the history of discarded and disproved beliefs, truths, and traditions about itself and how it works. In retrospect, the history of science, for instance, is a history of how scientists and historians evolved their tradition, developing what was entailed but often getting it wrong. Knowing this the affirmative postmodernist can work, like a conservator, on surveying the intellectual ruins for intact and durable resources that can be reclaimed for present and future use, knowing full well their fallible and fragile status, but confident that they can serve some potential and useful service. The affirmative philosopher is an eclectic, forming divergent sources into new shapes that serve particular purposes, such as justification, proof, argumentation, discourse, polemic, computation, explanation or understanding. Unable to explore without some firm footings, some taken-for-granted propositions, some agreed vocabulary and language, the affirmative, like the Victorian, John Grote, takes from traditions what is available and serviceable, what best works to produce desired outcomes, and then explores their potential (Grote 1865, 1876, 1901; Gibbins 1989, 1998c). If all else fails the affirmative can, as Hobsbawm suggests, 'invent traditions' and ('invent the self'), propose and defend propositions and arguments, coin a new vocabulary or discourse, which is exactly how disciplines do develop in times of crisis (Kuhn 1970). An invented tradition is a narrative, an imaginative account of what we are, how things are and how we ought to be. We have moved in Postmodernity from politics based upon tradition to one based upon narrative.

If our argument is right then contemporary philosophy seems inclined towards postmodernism, indeed, anti-foundationalism is the epistemology of postmodernism and Postmodernity (Gibbins, 1999; Bauman, 1987; 1991; 1992; 1997). Some traditions of philosophy become relegated to the museum. Both rationalism and empiricism become grounded whales of intellectual and cultural history, museum items, as neither can justify their claims to indisputable, necessary major and minor premise. Empiricism and materialism are also fatally damaged, because the privileged existence of their foundations in sense data, qualia, sense impressions, matter or epiphenomena of matter, are all unsustainable. Other philosophic positions can be surveyed for their restorative potential. Idealism best fits this category as some have shown (Plant, 1991; Rorty, Skinner and Schneewind, 1984; Gibbins, 1989; 1998). If the ideas, thought, mind, experience, thinking and concepts that ground idealism are considered as themselves in historical flux, as Hegel, Croce and Oakeshott conceived, then the acceptance of the propositions that there are no longer any defensible cases for privileged beliefs, no absolutely certain propositions, becomes the invitation for a new dialectical advance, a new tradition, or epoch in social and cultural thinking (Gibbins, 1997).

Another beneficiary of the anti-foundational turn may be new subject areas such as *social epistemology*. Its originators, such as Steve Fuller and Alvin Goldman have responded to the decisive attacks on the privileged foundations given in individual experience, by transferring attention to the foundations or practices of relative social experience (Goldman, 1999; Fuller, 1986; 1999). If what is taken as true, as knowledge, is a contingent relative construction, perhaps we can find, 'ways that human knowledge can be increased via social transactions, whatever the starting point happens to be, (Goldman, 1999, p. vii). 'Social practices can make both positive and negative contributions to knowledge rather than subvert it', and social epistemology seeks to answer, the 'main question for veritistic epistemology is: Which practices have a comparatively favourable impact on knowledge as contrasted to ignorance?' (ibid., p. 5). Goldman, however, believes that there may be some good practices that are universal and transcultural, making him a foundationalist by belief and self-selection. His first chapter entitled 'Epistemology and Postmodern Resistance' exposes anti-foundationalist 'veriphobia' to critique (ibid., pp. 7-40). Such views are open to sustained attack (Pelleker, 2000). However, *Social Epistemology: The Journal of Knowledge, Culture and Policy*, makes no such judgement and contains explorations of how we can do epistemology without privileging any specific individual foundations. Education, and the university in particular, once sovereign in the manufacture of knowledge are near terminal decline (Delanty et al., 1998a). Knowledge is produced and consumed in various ways, contexts and for a wide variety of purposes, with no institution privileged. Linda Alcoff argues for a kind of 'epistemic coherentism' and Michael Lynch calls for a 'pluralistic position on truth' in which justification is context dependent (Alcoff, 1996; Lynch, 1998, pp. 224-5). Others have spoken of replacing the study of human nature with the study of the invention of selves, of replacing the study of the foundations of politics with 'the reinvention of politics', and the study of the foundations of ethics with 'invented moralities' (Luntley, 1995, pp. 197-224; Beck, 1997; Bauman, 1993; Weeks, 1995).

Three philosophical positions have surfed the new post-analytic anti-foundational tide to positive effect: American Pragmatism as exhibited in Richard Rorty, Richard Bernstein; William Quine, Hilary Putnam and Donald Davidson; European and American Phenomenology, Hermeneutics, Existentialism and Post-structuralism of Zygmund Bauman and Fred Dallmayr; and worldwide Postmodernism of William Connolly, Francois Lyotard and myself. All show that philosophy and theory can be continued to good effect within the conversation that is philosophy, without the belief in universal and absolute foundations, a claim now defended in several good surveys of the contemporary terrain (Bernstein, 1976; 1991; Rajchman and West, 1985; Baynes, Bohman and McCarthy, 1987; West, 1989; Crook, 1991; Rose, 1991; Rosenau, 1992; Seidman and Wagner, 1992; Alexander, 1992, pp. 338-361; Seidman, 1994; 1998; Luntley, 1995; Alcoff, 1996). Philosophy's contribution, in their mouths, remains wedded to its capacity for negativity and reconstruction, for humanism and existentialism, for hope and despair, for pessimism and affirmation, for commitment and reservation, for community yet pluralism, for identity yet difference, for passion and reason, for liberty and republicanism, and for a balanced life, based upon *Contingency, Irony and Solidarity* (Rorty, 1989). For Europeans, the long tradition of idealism, especially the Hegelian version of historical and dialectical unfolding remains a source of great potential (Plant, 1997, p. 375; Gibbins, 1997, pp. 491-497). But coherentism and Putnam's version of internalism still appeal as non-foundational accounts of truth generation (Putnam, 1981).

In both practice and philosophy, an ethics and politics without absolutes, in the hands of anti-foundationalists, turns out to veer towards tolerance and away from dogma, towards pluralism and away from sovereignty, towards the recognition and respect for difference as against identity, towards an accommodation of invention within tradition, towards civil and social rather than universal natural or human rights, towards cosmopolitanism as against nationalism or communitarianism. In each case the force of the argument stems from the refusal to ground judgements on absolute and universal beliefs. All veer towards what is now called 'coherentism' or the argument that truth claims can only be justified by reference to other claims within a system: the more one belief coheres with others widely held, the more it is considered justified (Sellars, 1973; Leher,

1974; Harman, 1975; BonJour, 1985; Delanty, 1976). If this argument is compelling, then, according to Toulmin, we must usher out the received philosophy of the past and invite entry into a new intellectual cosmopolis, with plural schemes of justification.

MacIntyre, Rorty and Walzer on the response to politics without foundational justification

Three thinkers can be taken, briefly, to illustrate the anti-foundationalist position in regard to politics and law. Alasdair MacIntyre, Richard Rorty and Michael Walzer will be examined to see how they consider we should justify political and ethical constructs. I will make further reference to those who struggle with the implications of what acceptance of their position entails, namely William Connolly, Iris Young and Ulrich Beck. MacIntyre's brilliant case against the foundations of modernity is paradoxical. Having argued that the roots of modernity will not hold up the edifices of the Enlightenment, namely, reason, science and progress, he seeks solace in one major tradition, the Christian tradition. As McMylor argues, MacIntyre always sought solace in restoring the relationship between 'the sacred and the secular' (McMylor, 1994, pp. 3-5). While he understood the acids that had eaten away at culture and morality in modernity in his earlier works, namely *Marxism, Existentialism, and Subjectivism,* it was the abandonment of longer traditions of, and institutions for, the good life that vexed him. Modernity had resorted to a series of foundational myths to re-ground itself, namely utility, rights, consent, reason, and some non-foundational myths based upon changing emotions, subjectivity, commitment (Gutting, 1999, pp. 70-75). Aristotelianism, Christianity, Idealism and Romanticism were positions that allowed valid schemas of justification, because they were grounded in community not individuals, grounded in forms of life and not rational principles or procedures. MacIntyre, like Oakeshott, considers rationalism, both the theory and the practice to be the cause of the fate of modernity, and both consider rebuilding practices that support communities as key to the solution (McMylor, 1994, pp. 169-173). Virtues, MacIntyre argues, are relative to practices, and practices are a form of communal activity. Virtues, and other moral qualities, are to be judged by the conformity of acts to socially ascribed norms implicit in social practices. Being virtuous is to morality like being competent is to doing your job or playing jazz piano (Luntley, 1995, pp. 209-216). Making sure you are doing the right job, pursuing the good life, is the remaining big task. The good life is found, in turn, within the traditional practices to which we belong and are immersed, liberalism being one. Reason is the capacity we have to explore the inner resources of a tradition or negotiate the varying reasons implicit in conflicting traditions.

Richard Rorty proposes solutions in more pragmatic fashions, appealing to the resources of literature and narratives as well as philosophy and existing practices. Narratives, or the stories we tell each other, are the glue of being in the world. Social Criticism is vital for exposing false foundations and their resulting edifice, but without true foundations the philosopher can offer only narrative, conversation and pragmatism. Narrative is story, fiction that is shared by a community which bonds or cleaves its members. Political narratives, such as the story of the American Revolution, the Constitution and Founding Fathers, do act as substitutes for foundation. Dangerous as narratives may be, it becomes vital to subject the narrative to deconstruction, to multiple reading and re-readings, allowing many audiences access to the sacred text. But above all narrative is a feature of conversation. Rorty quotes Oakeshott's famous essay on 'The Voice of Poetry in the Conversation of Mankind', in testimony to the belief that truth and right are, and should be seen as the products of conversation, dialogue, and discourse (Rorty, 1980, pp. 264, 389-394; Oakeshott, 1961). Rorty advocates a 'conversation of the West' as the best source of truth and right for the future. Giving reasons in conversations is, in fact, the only source of reliable justification (Gutting, 1999, p. 25). In conversations, the outcomes are never prejudged or predetermined by what has gone before. Conversations are governed by rules but these are formative not constitutive, they are contingent not fixed as structuralists believe.

But conversations, he had learned from Oakeshott and Wittgenstein, always take place within practices, goings-on or forms of life that give them context, purpose and meaning. To both thinkers, practice was central to politics, and philosophy's job was to elaborate, explore and defend voices where necessary. Rorty, like Oakeshott, Dallmyer and Connolly, was keen that politics and philosophy explore the language and intimations of past and existing public practices with a view to their potential to maintain and develop public institutions and solidarity (Rorty, 1993, pp. 58-61). Rorty advocates building upon ethnic and cultural identities, as well as other traditions, using them as 'a ladder which we eventually hope to throw away' (Rorty, 1991, p. 58). His ideal is pragmatic, 'My ideal world is one in which there is enough equality in wealth and power so that people are more or less free to continue or change cultural traditions as it suits them' (ibid., p. 89). He is not a cosmopolitan, whom he sees as elitists, like Lyotard and Beck, nor a multi-culturalist like Connolly, Young and Walzer, rather a pluralist ethnocentrist, who wishes to encourage a variety of communities to co-exist in shared spaces, help and linked by pragmatic institutions and common languages (Rorty, 1991, pp. 211-222; Beck, 2002, pp. 36-37; Hall, 1994, pp. 174-183). He claims neutrality as between ideals, prophesies and even political arrangements, relying for judgement on a historical comparison of what works (Rorty, 1993, p. 53; Balsleu, 1991, pp. 58, 89). What works in the west are republicanism, liberalism, toleration and democracy. While he differs little from the American liberal tradition in these allegiances, he differs massively in his argument, resting his allegiance upon pragmatism, and 'liberal ironism', in his 'non rationalist and non-universalist way'; (Rorty, 1989, pp. 44, 73-95; Gutting, 1999, pp. 58-67). The individual is best keeping allegiances ironical when commitment is so often given upon fragile foundations, the best defence is pragmatic liberalism. The nearest we can get to solidarity with others comes from pragmatic concerns and 'sympathy' (Rorty, 1993; Geras, 1995, pp. 89-103). In the end there are no good grounds for anything, except good arguments, and philosophy has no monopoly on these. Poetry, literature, indeed any conversational narrative, can have equal, if not more secure purchase on truth and right (Clark, 1990, pp. 171-183; McGuinness, 1997).

Michael Walzer's route to anti-foundationalism suggests his political response. Pluralism is the recognition of the fact that societies have multiple conflicting social components, and the value that each has a right to practice and enhance its form of life. Moral orders already exist, enshrined in plural communities and bodies, they do not need foundational legitimation, justification nor construction. The job of the politician and the theorist is to act as a sympathetic 'interpreter', and a 'connected' social critic of each group and its needs. Interpretation of community and identity, is a capacity required to both theorise justice and engender constructive practice in a pluralistic order (Walzer, 1995). Like MacIntyre and Connolly, Walzer emphathises getting inside implicit, embedded pre-understandings, as a prelude to deeper theoretical explorations (McMylor, 1994, p. 172). Engaged social criticism is about elaborating the potential to remove problems and develop answers to issues within, and between, social groups, an argument similar to Oakeshott's exploration of 'intimations' within traditional practices. Distributive justice, likewise cannot be deduced from *a priori* principles, but must be a reflexive response to existing practices. We are shown how an anti-foundationalist can do moral philosophy, as we are with Michael Luntley (Luntley, 1995, pp. 207-224). Duty and rights, Walzer sees, as relational not abstract, derived from, and entailed within, the roles and positions within the relationships we have in the communities to which we belong (Walzer, 1970a; 1970b). Justice, for citizens, can only be an arrangement that recognises and 'make sense of all the pieces of their social life' recognising differences in roles, relationships and membership, the spheres of justice (Walzer, 1984; Miller and Walzer, 1995). Walzer's solutions to the lack of universal foundations then is to a kind of pragmatic pluralist egalitarianism, providing all communities with the resources they need to flourish (equality) by themselves and alongside competitor groups, and yet allowing them the right to deploy them as best suites themselves. The 'autonomy of spheres will make for a greater sharing of social goods than will any other conceivable arrangement', by allowing both 'mutual respect' and 'a shared self respect' within 'complex equality' (McMylor, 1994, p. 321).

For my own part the most fruitful way out of the minefields bounded by such foundations as nationalism and community on one side, and individualism, and liberal market politics on the other, is cosmopolitanism (Held, 1995; Gibbins, 1999; Beck, 1999; 2002; Featherstone, 2002; Turner, 2002). Resisting the communitarianism of MacIntyre, the republican conservatism inherent in Rorty, and building upon the pragmatic pluralist egalitarianism of Walzer, it offers to transcend even the transnational and transcultural solution, that Walzer found hard to envisage (1984, pp. 29-30; Rorty, 1998; 1991, pp. 211-222). Cosmopolitanism attempts to transcend the parochial and the national in a manner imagined and argued by Kant and Hegel, by envisaging the individualised autonomous self inhabiting an experiential world where there is 'a pluralisation of borders', allowing citizens of the global space to permutate and share identities, and build new 'we's' across time and space (Beck, 2002, pp. 17-22, 29-36). This form of 'internalised globalisation' would allow the construction of ' a historically new quality and form of social differentiation', ... 'a new way of doing business and working, a new kind of identity and politics as well as a new kind of everyday space-time experience and of human sociablility emerging' (ibid., pp. 29-30). Like Beck, but for different reasons, I concur with the *Cosmopolitan Manifesto*, that asks us to 'unite to create an effective cosmopolitan world politics', with new questions being asked, new political subjects, parties and new institutions finding answers and solutions to issues of global duty, duty, rights and justice as well as production, consumption and trade (ibid., pp. 41-42; Gibbins and Reimer, 1999; Turner, 2002, pp. 45-63).

Other contending political positions that stem from positions close to anti-foundationalism include the poststructuralism of Foucault and Irigary, for whom discourse alone allows development; exploration of reflexivity, working back from the preconditions of discourse or language to what is entailed in a practice; and philosophy as narrative. Habermas, while not essentially anti-foundationalist seeks solutions in the freedom to communicate and exchange ideas and in enhancing communicative competences. Dallymyr seeks solutions in memberships of plural bodies above and below the state; Bernstein advocates, 'an engaged fallibilistic pluralism' in which we take the contestability of all rules and procedures seriously and commit ourselves to 'a community of inquirers and interpreters', similar to Connolly's 'agonistic democracy'; Hirst (1994), Pettit (1997) and others seek solutions within the republican traditions of direct democracy; Parekh and Kymlika explore multi-culturalism; Judith Squires and Jeffrey Weeks seek 'invented moralities' and 'principled positions' established in identify politics; Gibbins and Reimer prescribe 'new politics' a pluralistic politics of self-expression, as responses to a shallower world with no firm foundations. We advocate the establishment of reflexive values – those that all members of any society would need to flourish – and the development of civic rules and practices. Oakeshott supported the re-invention of the civic tradition, and Bryan Turner argues for a new citizenship to be forged around the virtues that enhance a cosmopolitan order, re-enactment of which will build trust. Stephen Crook assesses numerous other strategies in his critique of *Modernist Radicalism*, summarised in the final chapter on 'Post-foundational Radicalism', that puts its faith on relationship building in practice and relationalism in theory (Crook, 1991, pp. 192-219). But all this begs the question, is the case against foundationalism well argued?

Unpacking and Questioning the Questions of Foundations

For my purposes eight questions have been identified and distinguished (Table 1) which directly relate to the overall question of foundationalism as stated by Toulmin. Within the scope of an introductory chapter it is only possible to unpack these questions and issues lightly, hazard some tentative suggestions on matters for consideration, and offer some proffered, but tentative answers. These can be compared usefully with the six affirmative propositions of anti-foundationalism that Goldman attributes to the postmodernist:

1) There are no such things as transcendental truths
2) Knowledge, reality and truth are the products of language
3) If there were any transcendental or objective truths, they would be inaccessible and unknowable by human beings
4) There are no privileged epistemic positions, and no certain foundations for beliefs
5) Appeals to truth are merely instruments for domination or repression
6) Truth cannot be attained because all putatively truth-orientated practices are corrupted and biased by the politics of self-serving interests.
   (Goldman, 1999, p. 10).

I will travel lightly with Table 1, but with a confidence that the reader can find the elaborated discussions in the numerous texts cited. Only questions 1 to 3 will attract detailed analysis.

Are there any foundations to knowledge and to truth claims, that are indubitable, permanent and authoritative? Are there any knock-down arguments for justifying beliefs?

Western philosophy and science have debated these questions for over two millennia with ever less conviction that an assertive answer can be confidently given. Anti-foundationalists answer always in the negative: there are no truth criteria that are independent of the structure of the claims being made, whether that structure be based upon reason, experience, ideas, matter or revelation. The traditional debates can be found in numerous philosophical textbooks and are not evidenced independently here (Chisholm, 1989). However we can point to what most students of philosophy soon learn, which becomes the engine of their vocation, that there are no secure, indubitable and agreed foundations or grounds for knowledge for philosophers in the west. Rather there are a plurality of apparently incommensurable answers to a plurality of divergent and distinct questions of knowledge and truth, about which conversation and arguments persist. But the worse still for foundationalists are the arguments of Wittgensteinians and the post-analytic writings of Richard Rorty and

Richard Bernstein, for whom words, and hence statements, and propositions, have no essential meaning, disallowing all knock-down justifications or proofs (Conway, 1989). Foundationalists generally need to see thinking and language as 'mirrors of nature', or at least as having the capacity to mirror the external world, but language, philosophy and semiotics have proved the analogy false. Languages, far from being passive mirrors, actively construct meaning and reality in a myriad of ways and in a myriad of forms. Essentialism, so essential to foundationalist rhetoric, may now have to be conceived, as Quentin Skinner puts it, as a 'myth', hence the anti-essentialism closely related to anti-foundationalism (Skinner, 1969; Melkonian, 1999, pp. 27-30).

Two other confident arguments against foundationalism can be kept in mind – relativism and ethnocentrism. The first argues that all truth claims are relative to something inside the proposition (the language used, social beliefs implicit or practices presumed) and cannot be tested only by reference to claims outside of the proposition; there are no independent criteria for judging truth. The second is the claim that local cultural or ethnic beliefs and values underpin and are embedded in every knowledge and truth claim. Both, if true, are fatal to arguments for foundationalism.

Are there any reliable foundations to ground western moral claims to right?

How do we know how to act if the aim is to do the right, the good or the just? Can we appeal to any grounds or foundational standards, rules, principle or procedures? Are there any foundations to private ethics and political morality? Anti-foundationalist ethical theorists, such as Charles Taylor, Walzer, Rorty and MacIntyre and others, answer these questions in the negative, denying that western philosophy, culture and practice have any secure foundations short of traditions, pragmatism or expediency (Timmons, 1999; Levisohn, 1993). Plant (1991, p. 323) concludes that, 'We have no clear idea how conceptions of the good can be rationally grounded and have no clear view about how empirical aspects of an account of human nature would support a theory of human flourishing'. This issue has been made more, rather than less critical, since the end of the Cold War. With the decline of state-sponsored ideology the space for cultural, religious and ethnic rivalries has grown (Ali, 2002). The foundationalists, in this context, are the fundamentalists, those who consider that the depth of their convictions provides justification for their political actions. The catalogue of fundamentalisms reads like a *who's who* of infamy, if we judge right by the criteria of tolerance, letting people be what they want to be. Fundamentalist foundationalism is the most profound threat to western ways of living and forms of life since the demise of totalitarian systems, and its foundations are never absolute, nor universal, nor indubitable (Beck, 2002, pp. 37-42). No foundational belief by a Zionist or Muslim; no Catholic or Protestant, no Basque or Catalan, no French or Canadian nationalist is immune to anti-foundational deconstruction.

While wider and further debate is needed to sustain my non-foundationalist argument, we can make the provisional conclusion that, despite the range of ingenious discoveries of the foundations of morality in western philosophy, these are all open to, and succumb to, a myriad of persuasive attacks and denunciations. The case for permanent and indubitable foundations to western morality are not well made, and not widely shared or practised, in the west. We need to look for the answers in efforts to re-invent ethics and morality in the non-foundational fashions shown by Rawls, MacIntyre, Walzer, Connolly, Young, Gibbins and Reimer. Without absolutes and with a myriad of conflicting and incommensurable demands, the strategy for maximising the best outcomes for all is reflexive. What ethical principles can we invent that allow all groups to realize their ideals and maximise their autonomy? The answer is set out in my 'Principles for a Postmodern Civil Society' (Gibbins and Reimer, 1999, pp. 155-160).

Are there any permanent foundations or justificatory grounds upon which to establish academic disciplines, such as political science and theory?

The history of philosophy and ideas is littered with attempts to found, ground and justify disciplinary knowledge. Foundationalists believe that a few legitimating principles, either have or will be discovered, that will allow adjudication between knowledge claims. Revelation has been tried and found wanting, as the debates over Gallilean and Papal cosmologies indicate. But the most potent and sustained foundationalist argument has rested on the claim that science alone can provide the grounds for testing knowledge claims. Positivism, from Bacon's *New Atlantis*, through the Enlightenment, the sociologies of St. Simon Comte, Mill, Marx and Durkheim, to logical positivism, focused on grounding knowledge in method, rather than substantial content. Science, it was hoped, had a unified meta-method that when discovered would allow application to non-scientific disciplines with valid and beneficial results. The first hope has proved elusive; the sciences have proved to be a loose, and often conflictual family, that share neither methods nor tests of validity.

Application of positivism to the arts and social sciences has also met stubborn opposition. Postmodern philosophers of history and social sciences, have accepted the postmodern hypothesis that not only was science multi-paradigmed, lacking meta-theoretical overarching coherence, but that the very metaphors of *discovery* and *explanation* were inappropriate when applied to the human and social, where *interpreting* and *understanding* were more appropriate (May and Williams, 1996; Crotty, 1998). Even the notion of divergent *sui generis* methods for each discipline posited by Oakeshott and Collingwood, have proved over-ambitious, each discipline now being regarded as itself populated by many divergent methods and theories for testing knowledge claims. Today, the metaphor of *discovery,* which implies there being something fixed to discover, is giving way to metaphors of *exploration* and *construction* (Gibbins, 2001; 2002). The very term 'justification' can be shown to have several, not one, valid meanings and usages (Goldman, 1988, pp. 51-53).

Richard Rorty, in various works but especially *Philosophy and the Mirror of Nature*, is responsible for the popularity that anti-foundationalism has obtained since 1980 (Rorty, 1979). His argument, as Goldman observes, is that 'there are no privileged positions, and no certain foundations for beliefs. All claims are judged by conventions or language games which have no deeper groundings. There are no neutral grounds for settling disagreements' (Goldman, 1988, pp. 26-27). Rorty's attack on Descartes' famous justificatory doctrine, he calls *infallibilist foundationalism,* is widely accepted as valid. We just cannot abstract, then privilege internal subjective mental states from all other factors in experience. Rorty himself has traversed a spectacularly wide terrain from the Greeks to today, from the Americas to the east, from philosophy to literature, from epistemology through linguistics, to ethics, politics and aesthetics, and back. It is his anti-foundational style of argument, wide in application, not the decisive blow to Cartesian fundamentals, that is the basis for his fame and relevance today (Rorty, 1967; 1977; 1979; 1982; 1989; 1991a; 1991b). His argument is summed up as follows: 'since truth is a property of sentences, since sentences are dependent for their existence on vocabularies, and since vocabularies are made by human beings, so are truths' (Rorty, 1979, p. 21). The anti-foundationalist arguments of

Wittgenstein, that all justifications are themselves only justified by conventional rules of the particular language game being played, are hard to argue down, despite Goldman's countering claim that justifications are grounded on 'appeals to truth conduciveness' or their likelihood to produce truths (Goldman, 1988, p. 29). The now traditional claim that anti-foundationalists conflate justification with interpretation is also deployed by Goldman. Goldman does not provide any good arguments here to challenge Barnes and Bloor's conclusion about the sociology of knowledge, that, 'there are no context free or super-cultural norms of rationality' (Barnes and Bloor, 1982, p. 27). Rorty and Bernstein, in addition, join many others, in denying the possibility of objectivity, to any form of judgement or practice (Bernstein, 1984; Rorty, 1991).

Key Issues Around which Debates must Hinge, such as Supervenience, Relativism and Ethnocentricity

What are the foundations of foundationalism? Are they fixed, firm and permanent?

Foundation as a term has several distinct meanings. It is one of a family of metaphors that are used to signify space solidity and stability, some other family members being structures, territory, property, boundaries, borders, areas, rooms, doors, buttress, estate, home, centre, periphery, square, domain, travel, speed, height, width, order, disorder. The most used is related to buildings and architecture and refers to the substructure upon which the superstructure is erected. Structuralism, as a theory, is a metaphorical sister to foundationalism, and suffers many of its logical defects. Alternative metaphors and imagery operate in the territory of time, to support or encourage change, e.g. revolution, progress, dynamics, post (Gunnell, 1987). In philosophy and politics the metaphor suggests that there are substructures underpinning all knowledge and activity, something to which changes are related. These underlying foundations are supposed to be observable and can be tested to establish whether they can support knowledge claims and the legitimation of activities above. Why should this metaphor, and any analogy of knowledge with architecture, be accepted? There are no good reasons for this, and indeed it is precisely the issue of the promiscuity and unreliability of metaphor, words and representation, that set Rorty on his more general anti-foundational mission (Melkonian, 1999, pp. 22-25).

Following Donald Davidson and Wittgenstein, Rorty argues that metaphors are polemical tools whose power lies in their capacity in particular historical usage, not in their universal formal capacity to tap underlying foundations for meaning. Metaphors work via rhetoric not metaphysics. Poetry, which plays with imagery and the meaning of words, is closer to understanding human activity than philosophy. We can see that with the two most persistent metaphors in politics: the first, space, justifying continuity; and the second, time, justifying change.

Metaphors, as in all imagery, are parasitical, in the sense that they require a host referant, going on with its own vocabulary and practices, without which they cannot work. Unless we know about shipbuilding and sailing we cannot know the metaphorical meaning of 'the ship of state', or the Platonic allegory of the 'navigator', or Robert Filmer's 'trimmer'. Often, the form of life which gave the original metaphor power to refocus understanding and actions, dies or changes leaving the metaphor 'dead', mystifying or a ghostly presence. The power of verbal imagery lies in likening something not known to what is known about: i.e. I don't understand the Christian world until I am told it is part of God's 'kingdom', and He is the 'creator'; or the role of the new leader of the Holy Roman Church is that of a 'father', and we subjects are his 'children'. The claimed similarities in the relationship are often absurd, but the imagery may remain powerful. But when the referant becomes irrelevant, the metaphor gradually ceases to work. If knowledge, morality and politics were ever like buildings, they are not today. If foundationalists persist with the metaphor, we should remind them that there are new and revolutionary building technologies, consumer requirements and designs that are replacing those imperial and panopticonal structures built for modernity; and that the perviousness of borders is today reflected in a new literature of re-setting boundaries. Literary criticism should be a central part of political science, because in politics imagery is the most widely used and effective polemical and rhetorical device. We may consider that the ghostly presence of foundations in our representational language should no longer attract serious usage.

If the imagery is poor the logical arguments for anti-foundationalism are better. The debate is focused on supervenience. Supervenience, coined by Donald Davidson in 1970, describes the situation in which one property or quality depends upon some other property or quality. So one claim can only be justified with a supervening (intermediary) premise, property or principle. Originally used to explain the interdependence of mental and physical properties, it has 'drifted' to cover moral properties, and with me, to the interdependence of political and legal qualities and properties (on 'drift' in the meaning of words see Grote, 1872; 1874). One kind of property, e.g. right, justice, or truth, is present if another kind of property, e.g. honest motives, rule of law, or evidence, is present. Either the appeal is to something inside the language game, the internal context (hence relativism), or to something outside the game, the external context (objectivism). To avoid circularity of justificatory arguments, it is normal strategy to appeal to an external belief that is itself held to be true, e.g. the categorical imperative, equity, proof. For this to work we have to have the external facts established as true and the belief (an evaluation, a normative proposition) that this belief legitimates or justifies the former one. The supervenience strategy suggests, that all higher-level beliefs can be reduced to low-level beliefs so long as the supervening evaluative principles hold good (Hare, 1953; Blackburn, 1973; Davidson, 1980; Kim, 1993; Loewer, 1994; Sarellos, 1995; Alexander, 1997; Drai, 1999).

Now, this strategy supports the anti-foundationalist argument for several reasons. If we are asked to justify a claim, say that a policy is worth implementing, we may justify this according to some qualities or factors that supervene between the policy and its value, namely, it was effective, that it was ethical and economical, that it has no unforeseen consequences. Now most justifications apply to another item in the internal context, such as a lawyer appealing to precedent (relativist). If the appeal is to something external (objective), forensic evidence, then we invite arguments that the evidence is irrelevant, inadmissible or invalid. Now all of these qualities and factors appealed to are themselves open to challenge as to whether they are relevant, appropriate, valid, timely and efficient. All of these criteria are themselves imprecise, many faceted and contestable in terms of meaning, operation and application. In political science research, for instance, what we take as indicators of (say) support for a policy, are debatable, as are how we measure these, and how we shape the questions that will tap the measures. In short, supervenience points out that in all justification unreliability enters at many supervening levels. This argument can be applied to political and legal argument with devastating effect to foundationalist presumptions and arguments.

In addition supervenience suffers from the logical defects that all forms or reductionism face (Sarellos, 1995; Alexander, 1997; Drai, 1999).

Complex wholes cannot be understood by the device of reducing them to their component parts as it is the system of relationships and interdependence between them that characterises the whole. 'A whole is greater than its parts', and on these grounds Aristotle and Durkheim are right to defend holism as against individualism, and holism against reductionism. Supervenience also invites vicious regress as well as circularity. There must always be another supervening quality or property – so we get a version of Zeno's paradox. But for philosophers the argument has hinged on the issue of whether there are any 'immediately given or apprehended' privileged foundations to rest on, or, whether in justification, all claims are just mediated by other claims in a circular and self-justifying manner, in the form of, 's' holds 'b' because he holds 'bi', and he holds 'bi' because he holds 'bii', and so on relentlessly. The foundationalist wants a knock-down 'b' that is immediately apprehended as universally and absolutely true – it has to be 'irreflexive'. Anti-foundationalists deny there is either a 'meta-justification' of justifications or any privileged grounds for particular ones (Chisholm, 1982; Blackburn, 1973; Davidson, 1980; BonJour, 1985; Kim, 1993; Platigna, 1993; Loewer, 1994; Ward, 2001). For coherentists this is not a problem, it rather describes the situation. George Moore had identified the problem in *Principia Ethica* (1901). If the there is to be yellowness or goodness or beauty there has to be a quality of it to judge by. This must have universal form and applicability. He hoped, as did all analytic philosophers, to locate such immediately apprehended, intrinsic and simple properties (Moore, 1922). Post-analytic philosophers, and especially his colleague Wittgenstein, considered the enterprise fatally flawed and impossible. All words have multiple uses, most of which are valid in some linguistic and social contexts but not in others. There is no hope of locating the intrinsic meaning or quality of yellowness or goodness because they have none. Yellow is a signifier with no necessary and absolute connection to what it signifies. That there may be no such things as the 'given' in 'immediate-apprehension' completes the anti-foundationalist attack (Grote, 1865; 1901; Russell, 1901; Ross, 1970; Fales, 1996; BonJour, 2000). We may however consider some form of 'modest' or 'weak foundationalism' that concedes more to coherentism (Goldman, 1988). To my mind, the debate may be best summed up by arguing that there are no 'final guarantees' in justificatory argument, but the alternative is not eternal insecurity. We may be able to construct limited lifetime guarantees that give better, rather than no, or worse, guarantees or truth and right. It is this I want to argue for now. Before this we could explore usefully other major themes implicit in this debate, especially representation, relativism and ethnocentrism, but the debate would take us to the same conclusion.

Anti-Foundationalism and the Fate of the West: Chaos or Cosmopolis?

> For Lyotard, the epistemological mark of our post-modernity is the loss of authoritative underpinning conceptual structures to serve as the 'foundation' of rational knowledge, such as Descartes looked for in Euclid (Toulmin, 1990, p. 172).

Stephen Toulmin, in *Cosmopolis: The Hidden Agenda of Modernity*, has charted a journey many thinkers, like myself, have taken in the past four decades, from confidence in the 'received view' and practices of modernity; through 'doubt' and discomfort that modernity had lost its momentum, towards a new 'horizon of expectation', in which we search for new ways of thinking and living which do not require modernist, or any, perspective with fixed foundations (ibid., pp. 1-4). Toulmin does not argue in detail the historiography or sociology of this change after the seventeenth century, but his outline can be fleshed out with more contemporary insights. Toulmin identifies a connection between intellectual crisis and accelerated attempts to ground foundations. Conversely anti-foundationalism has run its course at the time that western values and practices have colonised the world via globalisation. My proposition here is that there is a synchronicity between the decline of intellectual foundationalism, fragmentation of the political and social foundations of modernity, the nation state and the class system, and globalisation. Reaching their zenith in the late nineteenth century, foundationalism, the state and modernity began a decline in the twentieth, which has led to the new situation called variously postmodernity, late modernity, and the second modernity. Politics needs now to operate without foundations, indeed they inhibit revision. They act to limit us too much, and become excuses for repression, conservatism, nationalism and fundamentalism. We need a language of time, the 'post' discourse as an antidote to the language of permanence and space. At the minimum we might join Cerny in talking of 'the new architecture of politics (Cerny, 1997).

We need now to rewrite the narrative of this period to focus on three great shifts: the exhaustion of nation state rivalry in the two World Wars and the Cold War; the imbrication of social life, and especially the restructuring of classes and cultures; and the decline of the Newtonian-Cartesian world picture. The dream of foundations for civilised order has ended on battlefields; in workplaces, homes, aesthetic and intellectual sites amongst intellectuals at a similar time, and not by chance. Toulmin identifies a last effort to rebuild modernity on rational principles in the 1920s and 1930s with the Vienna Circle; the Cambridge philosophies of Russell (Science), Moore (Analysis) and the early Wittgenstein of the *Tractatus*, while Stalinism on one side and Keynes, Beveridge and the Marshall Plan on the other, sought to solidify a new world order. But all three failed to have longevity.

Intellectually several currents have eroded our foundations. The late Wittgenstein of the *Philosophical Investigations*, exposed the myths of essentialism in language and meaning; Einsteinian physics revealed the relativity of space and time and others discovered the inner chaos of the atom; we then realized new metaphors for knowledge, the idea and practice of knowledge as a fragile web. Politically both post-structuralism and anti-foundationalism have examined and reinforced the erosion of the nation state from inside and out, and identified the resulting requirement to build transnational and global arrangements to reconcile conflicts of all sorts (Bull, 1977; Brown, 1988; Giddens, 1998; Cerny, 1997; Gibbins and Reimer, 1999, pp. 19-36, 115-134). The key features of the new order we identify as unpredictability, disorganised capitalism, the growth of consumer society and life style pluralisation, the development of mass media society, socialisation replaced by media-isation, and globalisation, in which global/local relations and inner experiences displace the national, and the restructuring of inequality around exclusion.

Politics without foundations cannot be discussed in the same ways as it was with foundations. The mantras of ambivalence, ambiguity, dissonance, re-alignments, imbrication, and bricolage must litter any accounts (Connolly, 1987). Futures, will be plural, 'an eclectic mixing of old and new elements in a variety of distinct local and global forms' (Gibbins and Reimer, 1999, p. 140; Macridis and Plummer, 2002, chapter 25). Foundationalism was always closely associated with the 'pursuit of certainty' and 'perfection', and anti-foundationalism is closely associated with the recognition that certainty in human life is a dangerous dream. The erosion of old boundaries will allow re-setting of some, crossing of others, and transcultural lives for many (Mair, 1987). The binary of public and private property, national and international are being undermined every day by technological processes, travel and business organisations. The development of transcultural behaviour and transnational bodies will solidify relationships, and international co-operation should foster institutions for global justice, law and authority. The hope and horizon of expectation for a pluralistic new politics, expressing the dynamics of new cultures and identities, inhabiting new space and time frameworks, coincides with efforts to establish a new global economic and international order, and intellectual efforts after intellectual cosmopolis.

Three institutions and practices are emerging as resources, both in theory and practice, to shape the new political order: *global governance*; *civil society and cosmopolitanism*. The first, predated by experiences of past empires, Chinese, Roman, Holy Roman, British and Austro-Hungarian, carries the hopes, nurtured by Kant and Hegel, that global processes may achieve what global institutions have failed to achieve, governance without government (Beck; Giddens; Held; Rhodes, 1996; Rosenau and Czempiel, 1992). Civil society within its republican traditions, from Locke, to Montesquieu, Hegel and Oakeshott, offer the institutional arrangements best equipped to bridge the gaps between public and private, us and them, we and others, in an age without foundations but in need of rules (Keane, 1988; Pettit, 1999; Oakeshott, 1975; Hall, 1995; Giddens, 1994; 1998).

Cosmopolitanism, with a tradition going back to the Greeks and Romans, offers us a self-management system for handling a world of polis and cosmos (nature), order and chaos, cultural pluralism and conflict (Toulmin, 1990, pp. 67-70; Jones, 1999; Held, 1995; Held and Archibugi, 1995; Hill, 2000; Beck, 2002; Turner, 2002). Pragmatism suggests that the worst strategy is to attempt to shore up old or invent new mythical foundations, as represented in various kinds of fundamentalism and nationalisms. The best strategy is to conserve what works, to argue and make piecemeal changes, judged as appropriate by their capacity to work – to reconcile, nurture and accommodate diverse groups and cultures. Fundamentalisms, like ideologies, deal with the existential experience of present uncertainty, with a mythical escatology of historical and teleological purpose.

Conclusion

What started with a roar has ended in a whisper, anti-foundationalism has not had the profound effect on political thinking that was expected by its proponents. Far from being revolutionary or radical it has sided most effectively with liberalism and conservatism in their most American versions, which is the case made by its critics (Gander, 1999; Geras, 1995; Hall, 1994; Crook, 1991; Melkonian, 1995; Fraser, 1990). What I have attempted here is to draw out the more radical implications of our realization of the frailties of the foundations upon which western modernism is built. Not all of my quoted sources are signed up anti-foundationalists in the Rorty mould, but all have subscribed to the critique of the foundationalist icons of western liberal democracy, universal rights, representative government, individualism, and capitalism. What I hope to have shown is that western societies can continue to evolve, in new and exciting ways, once the ideology of foundations, borders and boundaries is dropped. What the post-analytic movement has revealed is how much we have been under the sway of false idols, and how much more freedom and opportunity we can now have for invention, imagination and construction. We now need to see epistemology, like ethics and aesthetics, as normative and evaluative enterprises. Postmodernist political theorists have explored the potential of what anti-foundationalism made possible, but failed to explore, to good effect.

But one bonus from the foundationalist controversy has been the rediscovery of tradition, and often forgotten traditions, as resources. This is not the first intellectual or epoch to experience fundamental change and restructuring brought about by the challenge to our foundations. Sheldon Wolin, Eric Voegelin, J. Gunnell and J. G. A. Pocock have guided us on how we can understand such events in history, by looking at the way motifs and metaphors of space, mathematics, foundation, borders, are resorted to, when stability and order are eroded. Motifs and metaphors of time are the antithetical resource, stressing pre-, re- and post-change and development, history and utopia. But we also have traditions that are premised upon time and change, which can be harnessed for theory and practice. It is these we need to re-invoke in the effort to re-invent. At the beginning of the twenty-first century we would be advised in the west to release our attachment to foundations; eschew fundamentals and fundamentalism with all our powers. We should affirm and harness the multitude of political traditions in our past and present, local and global, using pragmatics – 'what works to maintain continuity and allow change' – as the criteria of selection. Justification should be derived from the internal context of the practice, or form of life under consideration, and should be sought neither from transcendental, nor absolute, nor universal foundations.

References

Alcoff, L. M. (1996), *Real Knowing: New Versions of Coherence Theory*, Cornell University Press, Ithaca NY.

Alexander, P. G. (1997), *The Self, Supervenience and Identity*, Ashgate, Aldershot.

Ali, T. (2002), *The Clash of Foundationalisms: Crusades, Jihads and Modernity*, Verso, London.

Bauman, Z. (1987), *Legislators and Interpreters: on Modernity, Postmodernity and Intellectuals*, Polity, Cambridge.

Bauman, Z. (1991), *Modernity and Ambivalence*, Polity, Cambridge.

Bauman, Z. (1992), *Intimations of Postmodernity*, Routledge, London.

Bauman, Z. (1997), *Postmodernity and its Discontents*, Polity, Cambridge.

Baynes, K. et al. (eds) (1986), *After Philosophy: End or Transformation?*, MIT Press, Cambridge MA.

Beck, U. (1992), *Risk Society. Towards a New Modernity*, Sage, London.

Beck, U. (1996), *The Reinvention of Politics*, Polity, Cambridge.

Beck, U. (1997), *Democracy*, Polity, Cambridge.

Beck, U. (1998), 'The Cosmopolitan Manifesto', *New Statesman*, 20, pp. 28-30.

Beck, U. (2002), 'The Cosmopolitan Society and Its Enemies', *Theory, Culture and Society*, 19 (1-2), pp. 17-44.

Bernstein, R. (1976), *The Restructuring of Social and Political Theory*, University of Pennsylvania Press, Philadelphia.

Bernstein, R. (1984), *Beyond Objectivism and Relativism*, Blackwell, Oxford.

Bernstein, R. (1985), *Philosophical Profiles: Essays in a Pragmatic Mode*, Cambridge University Press, Cambridge.

Bernstein, R. (1991), *The New Constellation: The Ethical - Political Horizons of Modernity/Postmodernity*, Polity, Cambridge.

Blackburn, S. (1973), 'Supervenience Re-visited', in *Essays in Quasi-realism*, Oxford University Press, New York.

BonJour, L. (1985), *The Structure of Empirical Knowledge*, Harvard University Press, Cambridge MA.

BonJour, L. (2000), 'Review of Fales, E. "A Defence of the Given"', *Nous*, XXXIV, (3), p. 468.

Bradley, F. H. (1876), *Ethical Studies*, Oxford University Press, Oxford.

Brown, S. (1988), *New Forces, Old Forces and the Future of World Politics*, Scott, Foresman and Company, Glenview.

Bull, H. and Watson, A. (eds) (1984), *The Expansion of the World Order*, Clarendon, Oxford.

Cerny, P. (1990), *The Changing Architecture of Politics*, Sage, London.

Chisholm, R. C. (1982), *The Foundations of Knowing*, Minneapolis University Press, Minneapolis.

Chisholm, R. C. (1989), *The Theory of Knowledge*, 3rd ed., Prentice Hall, Englewood Cliffs NJ.

Connolly, W. (1984), *The Terms of Political Discourse*, Martin Robertson, Oxford.

Connolly, W. (ed.) (1984), *Legitimacy and the State*, Blackwell, Oxford.

Connolly, W. (1994), *Politics and Ambiguity*, University of Wisconsin Press, Madison.

Connolly, W. (1991), *Identity/Difference: Democratic Negotiations of Political Paradox*, Cornell University Press, Ithaca NY.

Conway, D. (1989), *Wittgenstein on Foundations*, Highland–Humanities, Atlanta.

Crook, S. (1991), *Modernist Radicalism and its Aftermath*, Routledge, London.

Crook, S. et al. (1992), *Postmodernization: Change in Advanced Society*, Sage, London.

Crotty, M. (1998), *The Foundations of Social Research*, Sage, London.

Cuttrofello, A. (1998), 'Speculative Imagination and the Problem of Legitimation: on David Inram's "Reason, History and Politics"', *Social Epistemology*, 12 (2), pp. 117-126.

Davidson, D. (1980), 'Moral Events', *Essays on Actions and Events*, Oxford University Press, New York.

Dagger, R. (1997), *Civic Virtues*, Oxford University Press, Oxford.

Dallmayr, F. R. (1984), *Polis and Practice: Exercises in Contemporary Political Theory*, MIT Press, Cambridge MA.

J. van Deth and Scarbrough, E. (eds) (1995), *The Impact of Values*, Oxford University Press, Oxford.

Drai, D. (1999), *Supervenience and Realism*, Ashgate, Aldershot.

Featherstone, M. and Lash, S. (eds) (2002), *Recognition and Difference: Politics, Identity and Multiculture*, Sage, London.

Fraser, N. (1990), 'Solidarity or Singularity: Richard Rorty between Romanticism and Technocracy', in A. Malachowski (ed.) (1990), *Reading Rorty*, Blackwell, Oxford.

Fuller, S. (1999), *The Governance of Science: Ideology and the Future of the Open Society*, Open University Press, Milton Keynes.

Gander, E. H. (1999), *The Last Conceptual Revolution: A Critique of Richard Rorty's Political Philosophy*, State University of New York Press, New York.

Geras, N. (1995), *Solidarity in the Conversation of Mankind: The Ungroundable Liberalism of Richard Rorty*, Verso, London.

Gibbins, J. (1989), *John Grote, Cambridge University and the Development of Victorian Ideas*, doctoral thesis, University of Newcastle upon Tyne.

Gibbins, J. (ed.) (1989), *Contemporary Political Culture: Politics in a Postmodern Age*, Sage, London.

Gibbins, J. (1990), 'The New State and the Impact of Values', unpublished paper, *European Science Foundation*.

Gibbins, J. (1992), 'Liberalism, Nationalism and Idealism' in R. Bellamy (ed.) 'Nationalism', *History of European Ideas*, 15, pp. 491-497.

Gibbins, J. (1995a), 'Lifestyles', unpublished paper, *European Science Foundation*.

Gibbins, J. (1998a), 'Postmodernism, poststructuralism and social policy', in J. Carter (ed.) *Postmodernism and the Fragmentation of Welfare*, Routledge, London, pp. 31-48.

Gibbins, J. (1998b), 'Sexuality and the Law: The Body as Politics', in T. Carver and V. Mottier (eds) *The Politics of Sexuality*, Routledge, London.

Gibbins, J. (1998c), 'John Grote and Modern Cambridge Philosophy', *Philosophy*, 73, pp. 453-477.

Gibbins, J. and Reimer, B. (1995), 'Postmodernism' in J. van Deth and E. Scarbrough (eds), *The Impact of Values*, Oxford University Press, Oxford, pp. 301-331.

Gibbins, J. and Reimer, B. (1999), *The Politics of Postmodernity: An Introduction to Contemporary Politics and Culture*, Sage, London.

Giddens, A. (1991), *Modernity and Self-Identity, Self and Society in the Late Modern Age*, Polity, Cambridge.

Giddens, A. (1992), *The Transformation of Intimacy, Sexuality, Love and Eroticism in Modern Society*, Polity, Cambridge.

Giddens, A. (1994), *Beyond Left and Right: The Future of Radical Politics*, Polity, Cambridge.

Giddens, A. (1998), *The Third Way: The Renewal of Social Democracy*, Polity, Cambridge.

Goldman, A. J. (1988), 'Strong and Weak Justification', *Philosophical Perspectives*, 2 *Epistemology*

Goldman, A. J. (1999), *Knowledge in a Social World*, Clarendon, Oxford.

Grote, J. (1865), *Exploratio Philosophica*, Part I, Deighton and Bell, Cambridge.

Grote, J. (1872a), 'Papers on Glossology', *Journal of Philology*, 4, pp. 55-66.

Grote, J. (1872b), 'Papers on Glossology', *Journal of Philology*, 4, pp. 157-181.

Grote, J. (1874), 'Papers on Glossology', *Journal of Philology*, 5, pp. 153-182.

Grote, J. (1876), *Treatise on the Moral Ideals*, Cambridge University Press, Cambridge.

Grote, J. (1900), *Exploratio Philosophica*, Part II, Cambridge University Press, Cambridge.

Gunnell, J. (1986), *Between Philosophy and Politics, The Alienation of Political Theory*, University of Massachusetts Press, Amherst.

Gunnell, J. (1987), *Political Philosophy and Time: Plato and the Origins of Political Vision*, University of Chicago Press, London.

Gutting, G. (1999), *Pragmatic Liberalism and the Critique of Modernity*, Cambridge University Press, Cambridge.

Hall, D. L. (1994), *Richard Rorty: Prophet and Poet of the New Pragmatism*, State University of New York Press, New York.

Hare, R. M. (1952), *The Language of Morals*, Oxford University Press, Oxford.

Harris, D. (1987), Justifying *Welfare: The New Right versus the Old Left*, Blackwell, Oxford.

Held, D. and Archibugi, D. (eds) (1995a), *Cosmopolitan Democracy: An Agenda*, Polity, Cambridge.

Held, D. (1995b), *Democracy and the Global Order*, Polity, Cambridge.

Hertzog, P. (1985), *Without Foundations: Justification in Political Theory*, Cornell University Press, Ithaca NY.

Hill, J. (2000), *Becoming Cosmopolitan*, Rowman and Littlefield, Lanham, Maryland.

Hirst, P. (1994), *Associative Democracy*, Cambridge University Press, Cambridge.

Hollis, M. and Lukes, S. (eds) (1982), *Rationality and Relativism*, Oxford University Press, Oxford.

Ingram, D. (1995), *Reason, History and Politics: The Communitarian Grounds of Legitimation of the Modern Age*, State University of New York Press, Albany NY.

Jones, C. (1999), *Global Justice: Defending Cosmopolitanism*, Oxford University Press, Oxford.

Kaase, M. and Newton, K. (1995), *Beliefs in Government*, Oxford University Press, Oxford.

Keane, J. (1988), *Democracy and Civil Society*, Verso, London.

Kim, J. (1993), *Supervenience and Mind*, Cambridge University Press, Cambridge.

Kuhn, T. (1970), *The Structure of Scientific Revolutions*, 2nd edition, University of Chicago Press, Chicago and London.

Kymlicka, W. (1995), *Multicultural Citizenship*, Clarendon, Oxford.

Lash, S. and Urry, J. (1987), *The End of Organised Capitalism*, Polity, Cambridge.

Letwin, S. (1965), *The Pursuit of Certainty*, Cambridge, Cambridge University Press.

Levisohn, J. A. (1993), 'On Rorty's Ethical Anti-foundationalism', *Harvard Review of Law*, 3, (1), pp. 48-58.

Loewer, B. (ed.) (1994), *New Essays on Supervenience*, Cambridge University Press, Cambridge.

Luntley, M. (1995), *Reason, Truth and Self: The Postmodern Recondition*, Routledge, London.

Lynch, M. (1998), 'Coherence, Truth and Knowledge', *Social Epistemology*, 12, (33), pp. 217-225.

Lyotard, J. F. (1984), *The Postmodern Condition: A Report on Knowledge*, Manchester University Press, Manchester.

MacIntyre, A. (1981), *After Virtue: A Study in Moral Theory*, Duckworth, London.

Maier, Charles S. (ed.) (1987), *Changing Boundaries of the Political. Essays on the Evolving Balance Between the State and Society, Public and Private in Europe*, Cambridge University Press, Cambridge.

Maine, H. (1862), *Ancient Law*, Dent, London.

Malachowski, A. (ed.) (1990), *Reading Rorty*, Blackwell, Oxford.

May, T. and Williams, M. (1996), *Introduction to the Philosophy of Social Research*, UCL Press, London.

McGuinness, B. (1993), *Anti-foundationalism and Justification in Political Philosophy*, doctoral thesis, University of Newcastle upon Tyne.

McGuinness, B. (1997), 'Rorty Literary Narratives and Political Philosophy', *History of the Human Sciences*, 10, pp. 29-44.

McMylor, P. (1994), *Alasdair MacIntyre: Critic of Modernity*, Routledge, London.

Melkonian, M. (1999), *Richard Rorty's Politics: Liberalism at the End of the American Century*, Humanity Books, New York.

Miller, D. and Walzer, M. (eds) (1995), *Pluralism, Justice and Equality*, Oxford University Press, Oxford.

Mills, C. W. (1956), *The Power Elite,* Oxford University Press, London.

Moore, G. E. (1903), *Principia Ethica*, Cambridge University Press, Cambridge.

Oakeshott, M. (1933), *Experience and its Modes*, Cambridge University Press, Cambridge.

Oakeshott, M. (1961), *Rationalism and Politics*, Methuen, London.

Oakeshott, M. (1975), *On Human Conduct*, Clarendon, Oxford.

Pelleker, J. F. (2000), 'A Problem for Goldman on Rationality', *Social Epistemology*, 14, (4), pp. 231-245.

Pettit, R. (1997), *Republicanism: A Theory of Freedom and Government*, Clarendon, Oxford.

Plant, R. (1991), *Modern Political Thought*, Blackwell, Oxford.

Plantingna, A. (1990), 'Justification in the Twentieth Century', *Philosophy and Phenomenological Research*, 50, supplement.

Pocock, J. G. A. (1972), *Politics, Language and Time,* Methuen, London.

Prichard, H. A. (1968), *Moral Obligation and Duty and Interest. Essays and Lectures*, Oxford University Press, London.

Putnam, H. (1981), *Reason, Truth and History*, Cambridge University Press, Cambridge.

Rajchman, J. and West, C. (1985), *Post-Analytic Philosophy*, Columbia University Press, New York.

Rennger, N. (1995), *Political Theory, Modernity and Postmodernity*, Blackwell, Oxford.

Rorty, R. (1979), *Philosophy and the Mirror of Nature*, Blackwell, Oxford.

Rorty, R. (1989), *Contingency, Irony and Solidarity*, Cambridge University Press, Cambridge.

Rorty, R. (1991), *Cultural Otherness: Correspondence with Richard Rorty*, Indian Institute of Advanced Studies, Shimlar.

Rorty, R. (1991a), *Objectivity, Relativism and Truth*, Cambridge University Press, Cambridge.

Rorty, R. (1993), 'Human Rights, Rationality and Sentimentality', in S. Shutes and S. Hurley (eds), *On Human Rights: The Oxford Amnesty Lectures*, Basic Books, Boston, pp. 111-134.

Rorty, R. (1998), *Achieving our Country: Leftist Thought in Twentieth Century America*, Harvard University Press, Cambridge MA.

Rhodes, R. A. W. (1996), 'The New Governance: Governing without Government', *Political Studies*, 44, pp. 652-667.

Rosenau, J. and Czempiel, E. O. (1992), *Governance without Government: Order and Change in World Politics*, Cambridge University Press, Cambridge.

Ross, J. J. (1970), *The Appeal to the Given*, Allen and Unwin, London.

Ryle, G. (1963), *The Concept of Mind*, Penguin, Harmondsworth.

Sandel, M. J. (1982), *Liberalism and the Limits of Justice*, Cambridge University Press, Cambridge.

Savellos, E. E. (1995), *New Essays in Supervenience*, Ashgate, Aldershot.

Simons, J. (2001), 'Politics and Truth: Immanence, Practice and Constellations', *Social Epistemology*, 15 (1), pp. 43-58.

Skinner, Q. (1969) 'Meaning and Understanding in the History of Ideas', *History and Theory*, VIII, pp. 3-53.

Skinner, Q. (1985), *The Return of Grand Theory in the Human Sciences*, Cambridge University Press, Cambridge.

Skinner, Q., Rorty, R., and Schneewind, J. B. (eds) (1984), *Philosophy in History*, Cambridge University Press, Cambridge.

Squires, J. (ed.) (1993), *Principled Positions: Postmodernism and the Rediscovery of Values*, Lawrence and Wishart, London.

Taylor, C. (1989), *Sources of the Self: The Making of the Modern Identity*, Harvard University Press, Cambridge MA.

Timmons, M. (1999), *Morality without Foundations: A Defence of Moral Contextualism*, Oxford University Press, New York.

Toulmin, S. (1990), *Cosmopolis: The Hidden Agenda of Modernity*, Chicago University Press, Chicago.

Turner, B. (2002), 'Cosmopolitan Virtue, Globalisation and Patriotism', *Theory, Culture and Society*, 19 (1-2), pp. 45-63.

Voegelin, E. (2000), *Plato, Volume I, Order in History*, Missouri University Press, London.

Voegelin, E. (2000), *Plato and Aristotle, Volume II, Order in History*, Missouri University Press, London.

Walzer, M. (1970a), 'The Obligation to Disobey', in I. Kent (ed.), *Revolution and the Rule of Law*, Prentice Hall, Englewood Cliffs NJ.

Walzer, M. (1970b), *Obligation: Essays in Disobedience, War and Citizenship*, Harvard University Press, Cambridge MA.

Walzer, M. (1983), *On Toleration*, Yale University Press, London.

Walzer, M. (1984), *Spheres of Justice: A Defence of Pluralism and Democracy*, Martin Robertson, Oxford.

Walzer, M. (1985), *Interpretation and Social Criticism*, Harvard University Press, Cambridge MA.

Weeks, J. (ed.) (1994), *The Lesser Evil and the Greater Good: The Theory and Politics of Diversity*, Rivers Oram Press, London.

Weeks, J. (1995), *Invented Moralities: Sexual Values in an Age of Uncertainty*, Polity, Cambridge.

West, C. (1989), *The American Evasion of Philosophy: A Genealogy of Pragmatism*, Macmillan, Basingstoke.

Winch, P. (1958), *The Idea of a Social Science and its Relation to Philosophy*, Routledge and Kegan Paul, London.

Wittgenstein, L. (1922), *Tractatus Logico-philosophicus*, Routledge and Kegan Paul, London.

Wittgenstein, L. (1953), *Philosophical Investigations*, edited by G. E. M. Anscombe, R. Rees, and G. H. von Wright, Blackwell, London.

Wittgenstein, L. (1957), *On Certainty*, Blackwell, Oxford.

Wolin, S. (1961), *Politics and Vision: Continuity and Innovation in Western Political Thought*, Allen and Unwin, London.

Wolin, S. (1989), *The Presence of the Past*, Johns Hopkins University Press, Baltimore.

Yeatman, A. (1994), *Postmodern Revisionings of the Political*, Routledge, London.

Young, I. M. (1990), *Justice and the Politics of Difference*, Princeton University Press. Oxford and Princeton N.J.

3 Capitalism in the Raw (or, how the death of socialism made anti-capitalists of us all)

JOHN CARTER

Introduction

Recent decades have seen what were nagging doubts grow into an established orthodoxy. That orthodoxy, expressed in its starkest terms, claims to see the end of the socialist project and ultimate victory of free markets and commodification. The West has won and capitalism reigns unchecked. As such, progressives should either do nothing and learn to love the market or, at best, explore Third Ways, partnerships and other forms of amelioration.

This chapter looks backwards and forwards. It firstly considers how the above hypothesis developed and was ultimately made flesh in the UK in the form of New Labour. In particular it will suggest that academic frameworks and theories – particularly the 'post' literatures – interacted with domestic and international events to create the present government and its approach. The Third Way then can be seen as academia's evil golem, sent out to undermine the left and accommodate socialists to the marketplace. In the second part of what is ultimately a polemical contribution I will consider an ironic consequence of both the changes in capitalism and attendant academic theories. The fall of the Berlin Wall and seeming victory of commercially driven diversity and flexibility might have indeed destroyed Labourist politics and old-style hierarchical revolutionary movements. This however was a process of creative destruction which has both produced the first signs of a more dynamic progressive movement and, importantly, cleared a space for it on the left. As such, the all-pervasiveness of lifestyle capitalism, with its social and environmental costs, seems to have catalysed a generation. Moreover, today's campaigners confront capitalism in its broadest manifestation – locally and globally. These directly anti-capitalist activists are also less likely to have their energies dissipated into traditional labour movement or Trotskyist politics. The very forces that have brought us the triumphant free market then have emptied the battlefield, opening the way for a more radical, dynamic and possibly even effective left movement.

I will begin with an account of how both events and theories got us to where we are now, and conjured up New Labour. Then we look at just how much our current government embodies and promotes the dash towards a flexible and globalised free market economy. Finally, the chapter will draw some more hopeful conclusions about the current anti-capitalist movement (ACM) and its mode of engagement with the enemy.

Drawing a Line Under the Past: the Posts

Over the last thirty years or so academia has developed a number of ways of saying that the world of classical twentieth-century modernity is dead. Noting, naming and theorising new epochs is not a new phenomenon and is pretty integral to the way that political scientists, sociologists and other theorists establish their names. There has though been a heavy emphasis on 'postness' of late and with it a contribution to the new millennia's zeitgeist. Equally whilst these frameworks are not ineluctably 'right wing' or defeatist, there is much in them that at the very least fellow-travels with the Third Way. In fact I would go further, to suggest that this academic work sits at the centre of what has become a new globalised and commodified orthodoxy. As these ideas are well known they will be considered here in outline only.

Postfordism and the desperately flexible worker

Along with its twins the post-industrial and information society theses, postfordism offers an epochal account, largely centred on the workplace, productive life and the economy. Over the last quarter century, so the argument goes, these have become so different that a death needs to be announced – that of Fordism.

Fordism reigned from perhaps the 1930s through to the 1970s, in the guise of the mechanised factory, assembly line and mass-produced goods/markets. Work was directly regulated by supervisors and the high division of labour and repetitive nature of tasks created alienation and apathy. This in turn formed the basis for much of the left's strategy – a class-based politics located in the workplace and premised on the common interests of all employees. In one guise this produced the social democratic axis between trade unions and reformist left parties and in another fuelled revolutionary movements. The latter (Trotskyist or Leninist) saw their role as vanguarding workers beyond the immediate economistic struggles of the workplace into more 'conscious' actions against the state itself.

Fordist mass production, so that narrative goes, internationally ran out of steam in the 1970s. As a labour process it reached its limits and was eclipsed amid the oil crises, political upheavals and raised consumer expectations of that period. Since then we have seen an emerging consensus – the postfordist thesis – comprised of insights from a disparate mix of Marxist academics, business schools and management gurus. To them flexibility is the new workplace norm, facilitated by new information technologies and driven by the needs and opportunities of the increasingly globalised marketplace.

A key aspect of the postfordist thesis is the notion of *flexible specialisation*. This suggests that firms have abandoned the idea of performing all tasks in house and, with that, the need for a permanently large workforce. Instead they subcontract functions out to other companies, including ancillary work such as catering and cleaning but also more central operational tasks. With this firms become more fleet of foot and flexibly specialised, able to concentrate on that which they do best. That itself may no longer be the actual physical production of goods and commodities. The rapid decline of manufacturing and rise of the service sector is one of the developments noted by postfordist (and post-industrial) theorists. However a more fundamental shift may be taking place, where the central task for companies is to respond to and create niche markets, promoting lifestyle marketing to the very forefront of corporate life.

In this vision the economy as a whole becomes less a series of lumbering corporate giants and more a dynamic array of smaller and downsized units living on their wits in a competitive but weightless environment. Bureaucracy as an organisational form is no more and postfordism is said to be characterised by flatter hierarchies and a shift from the rule book to the entrepreneur.

A close cousin of the flexible specialisation thesis is to be found in the notion of the *flexible firm* and its belief that companies are increasingly splitting their workforce into a core and periphery. Core workers are those with permanent or long-term contracts and thus a degree of security (with consequently higher wages and access to training and promotion). The periphery however is comprised of a growing army of part-timers and those on temporary or rolling contracts. This group, often women and members of ethnic minorities, have few of the trappings of a career and are disciplined by the peripheral nature of their contract. Increasingly this precarious and anxious form of employment has spread beyond ancillary workers and now affects those working on central functions such as IT staff. As a way of maintaining a workforce this of course has many advantages for capitalists, building in as it does an easy mechanism to vary staffing levels in times of boom and bust. It also creates a sizeable group of people whose eyes will be on their next contract rather than a trade union membership card. Needless to say, this was a model favoured by Conservative administrations and employers' organisations as they battled against red tape and for the 'right to manage'.

Postfordism as a labour process needed of course to be brought into being. In part this has come about as certain ways of producing and working diffuse osmotically through the international economy, with a little help from governments, management gurus, the International Monetary Fund (IMF) and others. However, for change to actually come about there is still a need for agency or, more simply, people to actually fight the battles. This is to note the crucial role played by *managers* – the well-paid shock troops of the new workplace flexibility. In this way academics on both left and right have examined similar phenomena – the former in sorrow, the latter as cause for celebration. For Clarke and others (Clarke and Newman, 1997; Clarke, Gewirtz and McLauglin, 2000) the recent valorisation of mangers and political commitment to managerialism as an ideology needs to be unpicked and its near-contradictory strands noted. On the one hand a 'new managerialism' can be detected, comprised of TQM, appraisal systems, customer centredness and other ways of shaping the very souls of workers. In this way firms commit staff to the goals of the organisation via self-monitoring rather than old-style hierarchical supervision. However traditional Taylorism[1] is far from dead and may have been given a new lease of life with the new information technologies. Staff in call centres for example find that, literally, their every word can be monitored by supervisors (along with the duration of toilet breaks and every moment away from the machine). The technology is also able to supply the exact phrase that they should use at each stage of their interaction with the customer, adding a transatlantic ersatz humanity to their work.

Postmodernism: we're all consumers now

Academia's even more ambitious theorisation of newness comes of course in the shape of postmodernism. This too denotes a new epoch, described in predominantly cultural, aesthetic and political terms. Although a slippery and wide-ranging narrative the central elements of this view can be summarised: we have now seen (or at least are currently seeing) the demise of twentieth-century modernity with its grand narratives; truth claims; belief in science and progress; socialism; planning and stable social formations. It comes to an end as a failed vision and defeated political project.

Intellectually and philosophically postmodernism derives much from French philosophy and poststructuralism. As such, all that is solid melts into air – the nation state, social class, religion and ideology. In place of *reality* we now have a world of surfaces, simulations, images and media representations. Everything becomes playful, ambivalent and contingent. With this the notion of a left politics based on social class, the workplace or 'scientific socialism' becomes pointless. People's identities are multifaceted and shifting, something to be recreated and redefined over time rather than objective or immutable. Accordingly, if there is to be a radical politics at all it can only be in the loose coalitions and shifting alliances of the new social movements. Anyway, there is little to be gained by seeking power within a nation state. Power is diffuse and amorphous, as much a property of the image as the state.

A version of the postmodern is at the very heart of today's consumer capitalism. The self-referential and the ironic are the lifeblood of the marketing, advertising and branding industries, rejoicing as they do in the shallowness of things. Their task is to transform images into lucrative lifestyles and commodities. Whether this lifestyle is universally available though is something about which a passing note of caution is required. Outside of the affluent West it is difficult to portray day-to-day life as a playful pursuit of branded designer icons (for all but the elites in those societies). Similarly, life in North Korea or under the Taliban hardly resembled the ludic exploration of difference and diversity imagined by the postmodernists. We should also remember that the poor in the West are similarly excluded from capitalism's banquet (whilst still encouraged to dream its dreams). As such consumption may have assumed a greater centrality in people's lives, but as always, cultural trends play out differently in diverse social and geographical settings.

This development of postmodern consumerism went, chronologically, hand in hand with the victory of the New Right across the Western world in the 1980s (and continues under the Third Way banner). This is far from coincidental of course and the two projects may share common assumptions about human nature. Equally, low levels of personal taxation, de-regulation and privatisation have furthered the spread of the commodity form.

Having presented postfordist and postmodern analysis as implicitly part-responsible for the sins of New Labour, it is important momentarily to temper that conclusion. For these frameworks contain within them much that describes both the recent past and the nature of contemporary society. As with any theoretical account, when concrete situations are examined counterfactuals can be produced and the templates cannot fit all situations. Nevertheless the posts offer important accounts of major socio-economic and cultural trends and have, rightly, been influential. Also, we should again note that radical strands exist within these theories such as the neo-Marxist postfordist Regulationist School.[2] Similarly the postmodern emphasis on diversity and difference has informed both the content and form of recent radical politics, particularly the women's movement.

My purpose in this chapter however is not to engage with or dispute these ideas in themselves, but to simply observe the way they have influenced and shaped what is seen to be *possible* for the left. For three decades of theorising and commentary have certainly created an orthodoxy, a commonly held set of assumptions about what governments of the centre left can do. Acceptance of globalisation, the need for some degree of inequality and, most of all, the primacy of the market inevitably limits choices and makes some variant of the Third Way the only game in town. New Labour however seem to have made virtue out of necessity, playing a zealous role in the promotion of a flexible future.

From Ivory Tower to Millbank

All of this academic writing had to find its way into New Labour's political psyche and strategic assumptions. As such we need to consider how this happened and the nature of the transmission mechanisms. One starting point is Eric Hobsbawm's influential article, *The Forward March of Labour Halted* (1981). Originally delivered as the Marx Memorial Lecture of 1978, this noted the long-term decline of the Labour vote from 1951 (trends which continued of course throughout the 1980s). Hobsbawm also pointed to the disappearance of the manual working class and growth of sectionalism amongst the working population. The 'proletariat' therefore was both smaller and no longer homogeneous – something which upset the calculations of both the reformist and revolutionary lefts. In other words, they could no longer be 'deployed' as a bloc – to either vote or insurrect. The industrial militancy visible in the late 1970s was for Hobsbawm economistic – a use of collective action in pursuit of economic (rather than political) ends. As such, it was more likely to lead to a political backlash rather than left advance (to some extent a prescient reading of the 1979 General Election).

In the 1980s a key instrument for promoting the flexible future message and moving Labour from its statist assumptions was *Marxism Today*, the monthly journal of the British Communist Party (by then predominantly Euro-communist) (Finlayson, 1999). For *Marxism Today* writers the ongoing victory of the Conservatives in the guise of Thatcherism was of the utmost importance. Rather than a mere swing of the electoral pendulum it represented a decisive shift in values amongst the working class and the population as a whole. In this way the right had taken advantage of cultural and socio-economic change to forge a new political consensus around the nation, entrepreneurship and the free market. As a result Labour could not return to power by simply re-jigging their Keynesian economics and public ownership policies. What had gone were the common bonds and sense of collective identity on which the welfare state had been built and the trade unions operated. In their place *Marxism Today* saw a new individualism and consumerism spreading to all sectors of society with consequent opposition to high taxation and forms of common social security.

In addition to this political and cultural analysis *Marxism Today*'s contributors sought to propagate the postfordist message of the changed workplace, flexible production and niche marketing (in, for example, their *Manifesto for New Times*, 1988). The products of this new economy were in turn presented as drivers of the rampant consumerism and lifestyle marketing that emerged in the late 1980s boom.

In these debates ways forward for socialists might include support for co-operatives, small-scale enterprises, local authority initiatives and such – alongside some degree of state action. However there was little sense of getting beyond capitalism and whatever future was envisaged included a functioning free market. In the pages of *Marxism Today* this message was delivered by a mixture of academics, cultural commentators and Labour politicians themselves. For the latter the need for new thinking was reinforced by each of the Party's four election defeats from 1979 and by events elsewhere. Foremost of these was the crumbling and ultimate death of the eastern bloc of Stalinist regimes, governments that exemplified the worst of top-down state 'socialism'. From this the ultimate victory of capitalism was proclaimed loudly and the process that produced New Labour moved on apace.

After *Marxism Today* ceased publication many of its contributors and proponents of new thinking moved into the Think Tank industry (Demos, Institute for Public Policy Research, etc.). In due course their influence on the birth of New Labour became yet more direct as key individuals became special advisers to Shadow Cabinet members and, ultimately, Ministers. Today a number of these brave advocates of New Times have found comfortable berths in their own consultancies or the PR industry.

The final piece of the jigsaw that takes us directly to New Labour in office came in the shape of *The Third Way*, produced by Tony Blair's favourite academic and dinner guest Professor Anthony Giddens (1998). This work and associated hype provided the first Labour Administration with something they could at least claim as intellectual coherence. For the themes and even specific phrases of *The Third Way* had a major influence on the government and its policies – despite the negative reaction the work received elsewhere (for example Callinicos, 1999).

As with the theoretical frameworks discussed earlier, Giddens too emphasised the momentous changes seen since the 1970s. For him these included technological advance, globalisation, the decline of tradition and traditional communities and the appearance of new types of risk. These shifts and most of all the increased pace of change, made impossible the old state-run social democratic project. Giddens' grand aim was no less than to revitalise social democracy for the new age, but in doing so transform it into something 'beyond left and right'. For whilst *The Third Way* rejects the consequences of the rampant free markets of the Thatcher/Reagan years Giddens also made his feelings unambiguously clear about the traditional left: 'Socialism and communism have passed away, yet they remain to haunt us' (1998, p. 1). This then is a centre-left project, that is quite able to encompass Bill Clinton's period in office (ibid., p. 25) and one that will be most definitely built within capitalism and working with the market mechanism. In a risky world, social cohesion is Giddens' goal, but, rejecting the methods of the past, 'social cohesion can't be guaranteed by the top-down action of the state' (ibid., p. 37). Cohesion itself is explicitly not old-style equality: 'The new politics defines equality as inclusion and inequality as exclusion' (ibid., p. 102). 'Exclusion itself is not about gradations of inequality, but about mechanisms that act to detach people from the social mainstream' (ibid., p. 104).

Adding further encouragement to New Labour, *The Third Way* also called for a new mixed economy made of a 'synergy between the public and private sectors, utilising the dynamism of markets, but with the public interest in mind'. At the heart of this were to be 'responsible risk takers' (ibid., p. 100).

New Labour in Office: the Word made Flesh

It is not difficult to show the imprint of all of this theorising on the post-1997 Blair Governments and that the Party has made a conscious break with its own past. It might seem like left-wing churlishness to simply brand them 'as bad as the Tories' though there is a real sense in which Labour has picked up the reins as they slipped from John Major's cold dead hand. As such the restructuring of British capitalism and, in particular, the public sector, continues at even greater speed and in broadly the same direction. However, Labour have done much to make this project their own with an avalanche of new policies, legislation and initiatives. My purpose here is not to explore the precise differences between Labour and Conservative attempts to build an enterprise culture, rather it is to show that Labour *are* seeking that goal – and that the academic ideas outlined earlier are integral to that effort. Lack of space disallows a systematic account of Labour's time in office and so instead I will take the more peevish route of quoting their own words.

Stephen Byers is far from shy that Labour is building a free market future, driven by business heroes. For example, in a speech to the London Business School he spoke of 'shifting British culture onto a more enterprising and less risk-averse track' (quoted in Wilson, 2000, p. 153). Similarly, promoting the Party's approach to competition, 'the new policy is about skills, innovation and enterprise. Above all it is about competition to create dynamic innovative firms' (DTI, 2000). This somewhat slavish attitude to the enterprise culture is pretty common amongst Ministers.

Labour's attitude to flexible labour markets and globalisation can be demonstrated at different levels. These include the desire they show to opt out of every Brussels directive offering a measure of protection for employees and the pro-liberalisation role played in the World Trade Organisation (WTO). Similarly their willingness to deal with the anti-globalisation message by branding its advocates as troublemakers and even terrorists speaks volumes. Again though we should take it from the horse's mouth. Blair himself this time, speaking to *Forbes* magazine, said that 'I have made it quite clear we will retain a flexible labour market here'. Moreover, 'it is important to push forward measures of liberalisation within Europe...[and]...at an international level we push ahead on the WTO' (quoted on Socialist Alliance Website, 2001).

The passing of the torch from Conservative to New Labour has done little to dampen governmental attachment to managerialism. A number of writers point out that the present administration clearly sees managers as central to its attempts to transform the public sector. Cutler and Waine (2000) for example agree that the managerialism of the 1980s and 1990s remains under Labour, but suggest that the Party has made the concept its own with a slight shift in emphasis. In particular, they note an increased use of performance measurement in the welfare services, over and above that used by the Conservatives. Also, Labour have modified public sector quasi-markets – particularly in the fields of health and education. This has largely been through the adoption of public-private 'partnerships', as opposed to a pure competition model.

Newman (2000) similarly highlights the issue of managerialism as the key to Labour's welfare and public sector policies. For her the present administration has taken the concept and transformed it into the discourse of *modernisation*. This is a key term used by the Prime Minister and others in government when justifying change, a word that instantly brands opponents of change as self-interested dinosaurs wedded to restrictive practices. ·It instantly and intentionally conjures up a division between forward-looking entrepreneurs, risk takers and their governmental advocates on the one hand, and on the other inefficient, backward looking trade unionists and the plain indolent. This is probably just the way Tony Blair does see the world or, as he said in his speech to the 1999 Party Conference, 'the forces of conservatism are still strong in the public sector'. Indeed he confided to the British Venture Capitalists Association that he 'bore the scars' of struggles with public sector workers 'on his back' (quoted in Taylor-Gooby, 2000, pp. 331-2). For Newman, as for Cutler and Waine, what is distinctive about *modernisation* are the partnerships that have been created to bring the private sector into the running of public services.

A flavour of the modernising mindset can be found in the White Paper, *Modernising Government*, with its commitment to 'joined-up government' and deregulation. It also illustrates the New Labour fetish with IT with a commitment that all dealings with government should be available on-line by 2008. The White Paper reveals the other face of modernisation, a desire to denigrate the past. As such,

> we live in an age where all of the old dogmas that haunted governments in the past have been swept away. We now know that better government is about much more than whether public spending should go up or down, or whether organisations should be nationalised or privatised' (Cabinet Office, 1999).

Or, as Tony Blair put it, 'we need to break decisively with the tradition of monolithic, centrally driven public services. We need to mobilise the small battalions and give them freedom to innovate and change. I want local managers and professionals to be entrepreneurs' (quoted in *The Guardian*, 21 May 2002).

Labour's Giddensian re-definition of inequality as exclusion is equally evident, in policies such as the New Deal. At its heart lies the Calvinist assumption that the poor are excluded because they do not work and that pretty much all of the currently unemployed can be bullied or restarted into employment. The nature and security of that work is irrelevant as is the growing gap between the lowest and highest paid (notwithstanding the Minimum Wage of £4.10 per hour). Inclusion involves work, so work they must. Labour will most assuredly not raise income tax to secure equality, that of course being one of the 'old dogmas'. In defining inequality as exclusion the Government locates it as a technical/organisational failure rather than a structural consequence of free markets. This shift is central to the work of the Social Exclusion Unit whose remit is to 'help improve government action to reduce social exclusion by providing joined-up solutions to joined-up problems' (Cabinet Office, 2000). The Unit itself operates as a 'partnership', bringing together individuals from the public, commercial and voluntary sectors to think new thoughts (in areas like rough sleepers, truancy and teenage pregnancy). This work is about leadership, innovation and collaboration – not the creation of a more equal society. The inequality under New Labour has of course widened.

All of this portrays Labour as a party actively building a postfordist flexible economy that rejoices in the commodity form. With its media obsessions, stage army of advisers and image fixations this is also a party of surfaces and postmodern shallowness. As Naomi Klein (2000, p. 70) has observed, Blair's attempt to rebrand the nation as Cool Britannica came only after he had rebranded his party itself.

More Capitalism = More Anti-Capitalism

Thus far then we have beheld the erection of a big tent. Under its canvas sit academics, gurus, business leaders and the political parties, all proclaiming capitalism's new age. In these circumstances it is not surprising that much of the old left – be it in the Labour Party, Communist Party or other revolutionary outfit – seems to have assumed the role of political Flat Earth Society. As their varied strategies assumed a degree of old-style class solidarity and elite-driven political progress, history appears to have overtaken them. Though far from ever a revolutionary force, the decline of the once mighty British Trades Union Congress (TUC) is somehow poignant. From its government making and breaking days in the 1970s the TUC itself has chosen to move with the (new) times. To quote their website,

> these are changing times. We live in an age when high quality goods and services are demanded outside of normal working or opening hours. Competitiveness, flexibility and quality services are key concepts in the organisation of work today (TUC, 2001).

Most pathetically of all the TUC has responded by establishing its own *Partnership Institute* to 'create a sea change in British workplaces by establishing partnership as the modern and successful approach to industrial relations' (TUC, 2001). They also offer to hire out 'consultants' to employers and other unions.

As noted above, this is, however, a process of creative destruction, a forest fire wiping away old ways of thinking and encouraging new growth. Before examining these new shoots we need to again visit social theories, ideas that are influencing the emerging ACM. The first of these was originally published over thirty years ago, Guy Debord's *The Society of the Spectacle*. In this far from accessible work Debord sought to abolish a distinction between art and life by abolishing the former as a separate category or activity. His argument was that life itself should be creative, meaningful and elegant. However, for our purposes, the book can be seen as a kind of anarchist postmodern analysis of Western culture. Everywhere reality was being replaced by images – what Debord called the 'Spectacle'. The Spectacle was 'capital accumulated to the point where it becomes image' (1994, p. 24). This amounted to a totalitarian control of the conditions of existence by the powerful through diverse means and forms of representation. In this way 'the world of the commodity [rules] over all living experience' (ibid., p. 26) and 'all that was once directly lived has become mere representation' (ibid., p. 12).

Whilst a 'difficult' work this was no detached or ironic observation and Debord's purpose in revealing the Spectacle was to oppose it. He and the Situationists were active in the Paris events of 1968 and proposed a kind of guerrilla war against capitalism including vandalism, sloganising, disruption of cultural events and university occupations. The intention was to create 'situations' that revealed the nature of the spectacle and its hold over daily life, and in doing so subvert it (Vague, 1997).

Despite its influence on punk (via Malcolm McLaren) and on the campaign of the Angry Brigade and other 'terrorist' groups in the 1970s, Situationism did not survive organisationally (the Situationist International was disbanded in 1972 and Debord himself committed suicide in 1995). Equally his actively anti-capitalist account of the Spectacle has been overtaken by varieties of postmodern thinking that veer between the detached and the positively celebratory. However, as Philip Baker noted, reviewing a recent biography of Debord, 'the Situationist's style and tactics have remained a blueprint for dissent, notably in recent anti-globalisation protests' (*The Guardian*, August 25, 2001). Moreover, an updated account of the Spectacle sits at the very heart of today's ACM – Naomi Klein's *No Logo*. Though utterly different to Debord's work stylistically (less theoretical but drastically more readable), *No Logo* lays bare the process by which capitalism uses forms of representation to shape desire and reinvent itself. As such Klein's work also can be seen as an examination of a postmodern phenomena, but which like Debord's uses its observations to fuel opposition.

Klein's starting point is the 1980s when many large firms decided to promote brands rather than products per se. This was perhaps part of the flexible specialisation phenomenon, a way of making companies less unwieldy and burdened by making 'things'. On the back of a liberalisation in international trade they were able to buy cheap Third World manufactured goods – cheap that is because of the appalling wages paid and lack of workers rights in the Far East and elsewhere. In this way the economies of developing countries were tied into exploitative forms of globalisation and flexible production – as the low maintenance but essential outposts of multinational operations. As such, globalisation should be seen as an uneven process, one that produces different effects in rich and poor nations and regions. Consequently, as Vale illustrates in a later contribution to this volume, a more interdependent world has become a drastically more unequal one.

For Klein (2000, p. 4) 'what these companies produced primarily were not things but images of their brands. Their real work lay not in manufacturing but marketing'. Western multinationals such as Nike and Gap were in the process of transmuting inert goods into vital lifestyle icons. This was to become a multi-billion dollar industry centred on the generation of glossy surfaces and images, hardly at all connected to the physical properties and qualities of the product itself. This process then was about the promotion of brands and logos, ephemeral and 'weightless' but crucial to the success of a particular company. For Klein these devices have become so central to our consumer society that 'logos, by the force of ubiquity, have become the closest we have to an international language' (ibid., p. xx).

In this analysis much of capitalism's battle should be regarded as a battle between brands in which companies find new ways of spreading brand identities into every area of daily life. As well as traditional advertising and marketing this now includes web strategies, the promotion of cultural events and sponsorship of TV programmes/channels and even schools – an insidious worming into the collective consciousness. Celebrity has become a central weapon in this war as lifestyle and image are attached to particular brands and firms. As such our postmodern fascination for the rich and famous is channelled and deployed by the multinationals to create yearnings and consumer imperatives. However the marketing strategies that produce that yearning, in tune with the times as they are, always remains edgy, ironic and self-referential. As Klein argues, everything is presented in inverted commas.

In building and marketing their brands the multinationals are nothing if not shameless. They are quite willing to use symbols from the very movement that now opposes them, linking their products to images of 'urban warriors' and hip young anti-corporate dudes. Guy Debord called this 'recuperation', a process of incorporating that which is threatening to it into the Spectacle itself.

Not content with stealing from the ACM, the capitalists have also appropriated imagery from the new social movements and equality campaigns of the 1980s and 1990s. Advertising campaigns have adopted a kind of diversity approach, what Klein (ibid., p. 117) calls a 'candy coated multiculturalism', in which different sexualities, lifestyles and ethnicities are used to impart cool to commodities. This also has the advantage of giving the ads themselves a resonance in different communities and geographical locations. Paradoxically, they are using 'diversity' to create mass global markets for branded products.

As well as these important individual insights, works like *No Logo* have two specific messages for the ACM. Firstly, Klein's text focuses attention onto the multinational corporations themselves – their actual ways of working and ability to shape both markets and human desires. It also emphasises their growing power in an era when the nation state is apparently in decline and 51 of the world's top 100 'economies' are multinationals and only 49 are countries (ibid., p. 340). As such, their victory – the omnipresence of the commodity form and its brands – acts as a kind of political provocation to protesters. In this way a kind of logic is building up: there is now no unbranded space in which to live and dream beyond the influence of capitalism. In that case we might as well forge a new space – which by definition can only be outside of or beyond capitalism. By that logic everyone who is alienated by junk mail, MTV, Posh'n'Becks, the Swoosh or the Golden Arches is only a few steps from becoming an anti-capitalist.

A second consequence of the trends noted by Klein is that the current movement cannot but be internationalist. The brands and the cultural forms that they generate may have reached their zenith in the affluent nations of North America, the EEC and the Pacific Rim. However activists cannot avoid linking these forms of consumption to the places where the actual goods are produced and the workers exploited in ways that have been rare for more than a century here. This binding of First and Third World struggles might traditionally be understood as opposition to economic imperialism. However, much more importantly it has brought Western activists into direct contact with the struggles of Third World trade unionists and campaigners – something that rarely happened in the past despite the left's repeated professions of internationalism. The multinationals and branders now loom large, as an unmissable target for all of these militants, be they in Manila or Manchester.

More provincially, the UK has seen important shifts in the composition of its left and radical forces over the last decade or so. After the celebrated Anti-Poll Tax struggles and riots of the late 1980s the movement became more sporadic for much of the 1990s. These years saw seemingly disparate actions and flashpoints around environmental issues, particularly direct action against the construction of new roads. At places like Twyford Down in England campaigners showed their utter alienation from both the public inquiry game and notion of directing their protest through Parliament. Instead they confronted the destruction of the environment in the most direct way possible – physically. There was also a brief coalescence around opposition to the Criminal Justice Act 1994 and other pieces of legislation that sought to criminalise raves and other forms of unregulated entertainment and protest (McKay, 1998). This saw a temporary alliance between established campaigning groups and areas of youth culture (though dance music too has long since been 'recuperated' and branded).

Only at the very end of the 1990s however could a true ACM be said to exist in this country. That in turn was linked to the onset of regular large-scale international protest against various bodies promoting free markets and trade liberalisation. These included the anti-WTO 'Battle of Seattle' in 1999 where around 70,000 protesters confronted the police, disrupted the conference and attacked some of the economic symbols of globalisation. Protests have continued at subsequent international capitalist gatherings (for example 20,000 marched against the IMF/World Bank in September 2000 in Prague). The Genoa meeting of the G8 heads of government in July 2001 produced an estimated 300,000 demonstrators, despite attempts by the Italian state to close the city (all figures taken from Birchman and Charlton, 2001, pp. 340-1). Infamously, Berlusconi's government launched a series of violent attacks on the protesters, particularly at the Genoa Social Forum, culminating in the death of a protester. As well as this rolling programme of demonstrations that seek to harry and challenge the globalisers, May Day has also become established as an international day of action against the new economic order. In the UK this has become a major national focus for anti-capitalist forces, a day out, protest and carnival all rolled into one (for a recent history of the evolution and organisation of May Day see Do or Die, 2000).

As well as these set-piece, high-profile gatherings the last decade has seen the establishment and growth of a panoply of broadly anti-capitalist groupings. A tiny selection of these would include Reclaim the Streets; Globalise Resistance; Peoples Global Action; Earth First!; the Wombles and a range of campaigns around world development and debt, GM foods and other issues. To this we should add organisations involved in research such as Corporatewatch and a number of alternative media such as

SchNews and *Indymedia*, providing both an electronic and print infrastructure for the movement. In other words there is a lot going on – defined in terms of both numbers and breadth of issues covered. And rather than a series of individual protest groups this should be seen as a fluid but effective network of (usually) co-operative organisations. The internet is of course at the heart of this co-operation with its immediacy, mutual links and cheap publicity. Other new technologies such as relatively inexpensive video cameras also have a role to play in the movement and the dissemination of ideas.

With all of this diversity is there any sense in which common goals for the movement can be specified? First there is absolutely no energy wasted on seeking the election of left administrations at either the local or national level. The ACM either ignores or actively opposes these Parliamentary structures in and of themselves. Even the concept of 'the state' is less prominent than in the discourses and campaigns of the old left. The ACM will certainly attack individual governments and their policies and in Britain does so. However the real focus is on the guardians of the new economic order, the IMF, World Bank and WTO. It is also of course on high profile corporations such as McDonalds, Nike, Nestlé and Monsanto – as symbols of the new order and for what they actually do. Moreover these multinationals are seen to be utterly beyond redemption. Campaigners are not seeking to establish ethical business or codes of practice – they are fighting their right to exist.

Whilst recognising that the ACM contains a range of styles and beliefs, a recent edition of SchNews laid out five common principles:

1) A determination to resist capitalism practically – using various forms of direct action
2) Taking a lead from movements of the South – seeking inspiration from groups such as the Zapatistas in Mexico
3) Building practical alliances with others such as greens, socialists, strikers and anti-racists
4) Showing a healthy disrespect for legality
5) Breaking with 'official' movements and parties that hold our struggles back (such as the Labour Party and TUC in this country).

(SchNews, September 2001).

It is worth pausing here to draw parallels with the radical environmental movement. For green campaigners too have used loose, non-hierarchical networks and organisations and maintain both a local and global focus. Similarly both movements use imaginative tactics and forms of direct action in their protest (maybe even sharing a common dress code). A linked point is that both sets of campaigners are, in the language of political science, 'outsider groups'. That is they lack any point of contact with governments and the state, or the personal and social links that business and more conservative campaigners have with decision makers. This non-involvement with (and indeed active opposition to) traditional state structures is both a hallmark and strength of the anti-capitalist and radical environmental movements.

It is perhaps misleading to speak of comparisons *between* the two movements. Instead environmental groups should be regarded as *components of* the ACM. Organisations like Earth First! and Reclaim the Streets for example have been major players in the development of a domestic anti-capitalist mobilisation. Similarly, as measured through website links and the groups taking stalls at bookfairs and the like there is a high profile for environmental issues within the ACM. As a result it is best to see these as overlapping movements with shared visions, enemies and forms of struggle. Moreover the ACM has broken with the old Marxist left's goal of a future industrial society whose bounties would be under democratic control. Today's anti-capitalist vision is (at least implicitly) one of a sustainable green future built outside the assumptions of the growth paradigm.

As well as noting the influence of radical environmentalists on the ACM, we should also recognise the reverse. Wall (2001) argues that a number of Green Parties became domesticated in the 1990s and even sidetracked into ruling coalitions, with a consequent acceptance of globalisation and neo-liberalism. However with the birth of the ACM

> environmentalists have been drawn into a heterogeneous patchwork of anti-capitalists and the discourse of radical green politics has mutated in a number of ways. While challenging the growth illusion, greens have increasingly seen the roots of ecological devastation as fuelled by specific economic forces and have increasingly been prepared to take to the streets in pursuit of another way (ibid., p. 152).

There is though one point on which at least part of the environmental movement diverges from the ACM. Many greens hope for a future based on communal living and the generation of local infrastructures and priority setting. Others though, including some radicals, look to the state for forms of regulation to combat the ecological excesses of productivism and capitalism. They may also see a need for protectionism as a way of reducing international trade and building up local and regional economies. This desire for a regulatory and interventionist state sits uneasily with an ACM whose centre of gravity is increasingly around a no-state anarchist position.

If all of this gets us some way to understanding what the ACM is we still need to think about the extent to which all of this assorted campaigning hangs together as an actual *movement*. There are perhaps three reasons for describing the current protests that way:

1) Quite simply the willingness of groups to work together and co-operate – be it at the local level, on May Day or through website links. There is in this a lack of exclusivity and permeability in which people participate with the like-minded rather than join something with rules and tight internal structures. So whilst organisation clearly exists in the ACM it is never an end in itself.

2) Across the ACM there is a sense of alienation from capitalism rampant, a feeling of hostility to the Spectacle and its reach into everyday life. This alienation is perhaps best understood as an emergent moral critique. For now that the old Leninist language and account of capitalism has faded, protesters on the left have been freed to describe things as they are. With this the ACM is able to discuss the exploitation of workers in the Far East or environmental degradation in straightforward human terms – a kind of post-religious and pretty much post-Marxist morality.

3) A third sense in which we now may have an actual movement can be seen in essentially negative terms. There simply are no other radical routes to take at the moment. As there is no point in battling for a left victory in the Labour Party so is there little to be gained from becoming a Trotskyist foot soldier. In this way a gap has opened up and anti-capitalism becomes pretty much the only show in town.

It is important to recognise how different to traditional Trotskyist/Leninist groupings the current ACM is. Not only lacking the hierarchy and formality of these organisations, today's protesters are not faced with near biblical texts and ideological positions from which they must not waver. Also avoided is the Trotskyist step-programme logic, where workers and others are initiated into 'immediate struggles' and then only after a due period of political education allowed into the inner sanctum of revolutionary politics. In the ACM there are open meetings and no secrets, everyone joins as an equal and can participate as much or as little as they want. Instead of becoming an Socialist Workers Party (SWP) paper seller someone involved in Reclaim the Streets might be involved in organising street parties and road closures. As such, humour, imagination and carnival are the weapons of the new movement – a hedonistic propaganda of the deed. In short, the appearance of the ACM marks an anarchist turn amongst UK (and international) radicals. This is an anarchism that not only opposes the power of the multinationals, but is against all manifestations of hierarchy – personal, organisational and political. In applying these principles to their own structures, anarchist anti-capitalists follow the prefigurative principle: by refusing to set up leadership positions and central committees there is an assumption that all participants have an equal voice. Joint or collective actions only take place after a degree of consent has been achieved – a consent given by autonomous individuals. These ways of working are prefigurative in the sense that the struggle for a future society is conducted in accordance with the principles on which participants want it to be built. This can be contrasted with the Trotskyist belief that a free and equal society can only be achieved through disciplined 'leadership'. For the ACM then, as David Graeber (2001) has recently argued, ideology and organisation are intertwined and mutually reinforcing of each other.

Having painted a picture of a vibrant movement there are however a number of potential problems facing the ACM. The first of these is a growing fear that Trotskyists in the form of the SWP are playing their traditional role, using the passion and energy of anti-capitalist protests to get recruits for their own cause. As always their aim is to provide 'leadership' and ultimately divert activists into the party. This is not the first time this has happened and, as Leeds Earth First! put it in their *Vampire Alert*, 'The SWP has a long history of seizing on every new "issue" or movement and recruiting who they can and then moving onto the next big thing' (Leeds Earth First!, 2001; see also SchNews, September 2001, which reveals the SWP's attitude towards the ACM). This effort is being carried out through Globalise Resistance, an effective front organisation with its own paid organiser (an SWP member). The concern here is not that potential activists will simply be mopped up by a 'rival' but that the movement could lose its vitality and commitment to direct action under Trotskyist leadership. Currently the SWP are not only arguing that activists should avoid direct action and illegality but that overtures should be made to the left of the Labour Party. In effect, that the anti-capitalist movement should stop opposing capitalism.

A second concern relates to whether the ACM had a bad war. For after 11 September many activists and groups threw themselves into opposition to the US/UK attacks on Afghanistan. In this they condemned the hypocrisy of the West in attacking a country already devastated by American-backed militias and made predictions as to the consequences. These might include open warfare between the Christian and Islamic worlds and open ethnic conflict within countries like Britain. At the time of writing (Spring 2002) there has been greatly increased conflict over Kashmir and the Palestinian uprising has intensified, but there are few signs of a wider conflagration. With the Taliban ejected from Afghanistan, Bush and Blair are able to suggest that their war aims have been met, even claiming a renewed (sanctimonious) moral purpose. In these events the left has predictably been sidelined and wrong-footed. As *The Guardian* put it the ACM may have a robust economic analysis 'but has neglected to draw up a foreign policy' (January 17, 2002). How and with what speed the ACM is able to regain the momentum it possessed prior to 11 September remains to be seen.

A final and concluding set of questions remain as to the future of the ACM. For even if its politics and body language stays predominantly libertarian, issues over structure cannot long be avoided. Is it enough that the movement has a sense of common purpose and identity (around the notion of anti-capitalism)? Alternatively, does the lack of a co-ordinating body run the risk of dissipating energies and enthusiasm? There is perhaps a trade-off here, in that some kind of national body might improve the organisational capacity of the movement, creating more focused and possibly effective forms of protest. However such a co-ordinating body, even if run as a decentralised federation, would pose its own risks. Not least of these would be the kind of factional infighting and power plays that typify nation-wide political movements. Moreover the very vitality and inventiveness that has epitomised the ACM thus far could be lost in what might become a more professional but ultimately less open and vibrant campaign.

Questions may also ultimately need to be asked as to the emphasis so far put upon large-scale demonstrations (particularly those against the WTO, G8 and IMF). That these actions lead to mass confrontations with the police and see direct attacks on McDonald's is not itself a concern for most protesters (nor should it be). Indeed such events provide a feeling of collective power and show that it is possible to reclaim public spaces from capitalism. However for things to move forward and the movement to put down deep roots in communities there may be a need for more balancing, positive action. This may be starting to happen in the shape of squats that grow into community centres, the establishment of food co-operatives and the like. There may though be a need for a greater demonstration of alternative ways of living and working, alternatives that in turn develop a grass-roots anti-capitalism in practice.

Whether the ACM will sustain itself over time is of course an open question. However it is fairly safe to assume that traditional forms of political representation in the UK and elsewhere have been undermined and are losing popular support. The 2002 UK General Election saw only 59 per cent of the people willing to undertake the essentially passive act of voting, with turnout for local government polls in freefall. In these circumstances experiments designed to make voting youth friendly (by mobile phone and e-mail) smack of desperation. Similarly the idea that the trade unions and Labour Party will resume the franchise they held as guardians of working class industrial and political interests is far-fetched. Moreover the very social fragmentation that the postmodernists point to has recreated the landscape of radical politics. For in a world where opinions and interests are only tenuously attached to class position the future of the new social movements seems assured. People will continue to come together in temporary alliances around shared visions, as well as for purposes of self-protection. Whether these alliances gravitate towards an anti-capitalist position remains to be seen. However the spectacle of the free market rampant and unchallenged, as it has been since the demise of the Soviet Empire, has in a very brief period done much to create a movement. The continuation of that system – globally exploitative consumer capitalism – is likely to fuel that opposition for the foreseeable future.

Notes

[1]   A system of 'scientific management' based on the ideas of F. W. Taylor. In this approach, work processes are studied and broken down into individual tasks and optimum methods established. This in turn is accompanied by close and detailed supervision of employees who find that their workplace autonomy is accordingly reduced.

[2]   An approach to studying the development of capitalism over time and the different forms it takes. This is considered at the level of the *accumulation regime*, which relates

to the way that work is organised in factories and other settings to secure profitability (or 'accumulation'). This study of the workplace is complemented by analyses of the *mode of regulation* – the way that social practices and organisational forms also assist the continued existence of capialism and exploitation.

References

Birchman, E. and Charlton, J. (eds) (2001), *Anti-Capitalism: A Guide to the Movement*, 2nd edn., Bookmarks Publications, London.

Cabinet Office (1999), *Modernising Government*, available at http://www.cabinet-office.gov.uk/moderngov/1999/whitepaper. (Accessed 16 October 2001.)

Cabinet Office (2000), *Social Exclusion Unit: What's it all About?*, available at http://www.cabinet-office.gov.uk/seu/index/faqs.html. (Accessed 2 October 2001.)

Callinicos, A. (1999), 'Social Theory Put to the Test of Politics: Pierre Bordieu and Anthony Giddens', *New Left Review*, 236, pp. 77-102.

Clarke, J., Gewirtz, S. and McLaughlin, E. (eds) (2000), *New Managerialism New Welfare?* Sage, London.

Clarke, J. and Newman, J. (1997), *The Managerial State*, Sage, London.

Cutler, T. and Waine, B. (2000), 'Managerialism Reformed? New Labour and Public Sector Management', *Social Policy and Administration*, 34 (3), pp. 318-32.

Debord, G. (1994), *The Society of the Spectacle*, Zone Books, New York.

Do or Die (2000), *May Day*, Do or Die, 9, available at http://www.eco-action.org/dod/no9/may_day.htm. (Accessed 23 June 2000.)

DTI (2000), Speech by Stephen Byers to the Social Market Foundation, available at http://www.dti.gov.uk/index.htm. (Accessed 3 April 2001.)

Finlayson, A. (1999), 'Third Way Theory', *Political Quarterly*, 70 (3), pp. 271-9.

Giddens, A. (1998), *The Third Way: the Renewal of Social Democracy*, Polity, Cambridge.

Graeber, D. (2002), 'The New Anarchists', *New Left Review*, 13, pp. 61-73.

Guardian, (2001), *Blair Pledges Break from Monolithic Public Services*, 21 May.

Guardian, (2001), *Culture Vulture*, 21 August.

Guardian, (2002), *Did the Left Lose the War?*, 17 January.

Hobsbawm, E. (1981), 'The Forward March of Labour Halted?', in Hobswam, E. et al. (eds), *The Forward March of Labour Halted?*, Verso/Marxism Today, London, pp. 1-19.

Klein, N. (2000), *No Logo*, Flamingo, London.

Leeds Earth First! (2001), *Vampire Alert*, available at http://www.leedset.org.uk/swp. htm. (Accessed 25 January 2002.)

'Manifesto for New Times', supplement to *Marxism Today*, October 1988.

McKay, G. (ed.) (1998), *DiY Culture: Party and Protest in Nineties Britain*, Verso, London.

Newman, N. (2000), 'Beyond the New Public Management? Modernising Public Services', in Clarke, J., Gewirtz, S. and McLaughlin, E. (eds), *New Managerialism New Welfare?* Sage, London, pp. 45-61.

SchNews (2001), *Monopolise Resistance? How Globalise Resistance would Hijack Revolt*, September, available at http://schnews.org.uk/mr.htm. (Accessed 2 December 2001.)

Socialist Alliance (2001), *New Labour's Programme for a Second Term*, available at http://www.Socialistalliance.net/policies. (Accessed 7 February 2002.)

Taylor-Gooby, P. (2000), 'Blair's Scars', *Critical Social Policy*, 20 (3), pp. 331-48.

TUC (2001), *Changing Times Campaign*, available at http://www.tuc.org.uk/changingtimes. (Accessed 19 March 2002.)

Vague, T. (1997), *Anarchy in the UK: The Angry Brigade*, AK Press, London.

Wall, D. (2001), 'Green Anti-Capitalism', *Environmental Politics*, 10, (3), pp. 151-54.

Wilson, G. (2000), 'Business, State and Community: "Responsible Risk Takers", New Labour and the Governance of Corporate Business', *Journal of Law and Society*, 27 (1), pp. 151-77.

4 Technologies, Surveillance and Totalitarianism

DAVE MORLAND

Introduction

Totalitarianism is a difficult concept. To begin with there is little agreement about what it is or what it means, and when it is employed it is often done so in a pejorative, uninformed manner. It is also a concept that now seems obsolete, a word from a bygone era. Like fascism, totalitarianism may appear to be from an age of ideologies that have had their time. With the collapse of the Berlin Wall and the demise of the Cold War political commentators rarely mention the 't' word. Occasionally, it is brought out of retirement to assault unpalatable political regimes that are deemed to be a menace to the so-called free world. But just as the fears of an Orwellian *1984* nightmare have gradually diminished then so the term totalitarian has receded from current usage.

The purpose of this chapter is to argue that it is time to resurrect the term totalitarianism. The reason for this is that contemporary society is on the verge of degenerating into a mode of socio-cultural totalitarianism. This is not the political totalitarianism that constitutes the particular model of tyrannical government discussed by people like Friedrich and Brezinski (1966). Rather, this is a different paradigm, more akin to that offered by Marcuse, but born out of a long process of technological and scientific developments, as evidenced by Mumford. Today, that potential is disseminated by contemporary information and communication technologies (ICTs), which form the nucleus of a new surveillance assemblage. It is in this sense that ICTs facilitate a convergence of the social, the cultural and the economic that establishes a new totality, a rhizomatic network of digital nodes and interconnections that constantly monitor and deterritorialise the individual into a series of digital dopplegangers. In the process, the individual's dominion of privacy is obliterated by an omniscient, omnipotent system that leaves her or him not only depoliticised and voiceless, but helpless in face of a dominant techno-scientific myth. Fuelled by this myth and nurtured by capital, this rationale or technique is in danger of begetting a new form of totalitarian society.

It is not the intention of this chapter to assert that the UK or any other West European society is de facto a totalitarian society. Certainly, the days of a crude and brutal political totalitarianism have long vanished across Western Europe; although this is not to say that claims for the existence of totalitarian states could not be made with reference to other parts of the globe. Rather, the aim of this chapter is to suggest that the term totalitarianism can be meaningfully employed in a new direction. Shedding the crude political apparatus of a one-party state, a secret, terroristic police force and control over the mass media that, among other things, indelibly marked certain political regimes as totalitarian, does not mean that the term no longer has any use or relevance. One of the most important benchmarks of a totalitarian state, for example, has always been the disintegration of the barrier between the public and the private. What liberal political philosophers have labelled the sovereignty of the individual, that supposedly inviolable sphere of privacy and self-concerning action which the state has no right to interfere with or encroach upon, is viciously trampled upon by totalitarian regimes. This essay will demonstrate how society in the twenty-first century is perilously close to penetrating that sphere again, and is steadily eroding our defences against this invasion of our private lives.

One of the key factors in this assault is the rise of a dominant techno-scientific myth. This is not a recent event, for as history reveals this myth has inhabited human culture, with periodic reversals such as the medieval era, since the dawn of civilisation. To locate the origins of this myth and techno-scientific rationale this chapter will begin by drawing on the writings of Lewis Mumford, an erudite and prodigious historian of technology. It will then consider other contemporary commentators on technology, before utilising post-structuralist thought to illustrate the impending danger of a new socio-cultural totalitarianism.

Lewis Mumford: the Narrative of Technics

One of Lewis Mumford's most enduring contributions to social and cultural theory is his insistence that the machine is an integral part of our culture. In his works on the development of technology within society (notably *Technics and Civilisation* and *The Myth of the Machine*), Mumford furnishes an analytical template that reveals the motors of technological innovation and social evolution. To comprehend the nature of the machine, for Mumford, is equivalent to a revelation of the true nature of society and humankind. His concept of the megamachine, for example, illustrates how changes in technics are propelled forward by deep-rooted philosophical approaches and scientific methods. Hence, while capitalism may be adept at taking advantage of and moulding these approaches and methods to its own ends, it is itself an indirect outcome of these deeper and fundamental forces. The development of the machine is emblematic of the inextricable relationship between technics and civilisation, a relationship that is 'the result of human choices and aptitudes and strivings, deliberate as well as unconscious' (Mumford, 1934, p. 6).

The machine is not to be confused with machines, which may be identified as specific things such as the printing press. Rather the machine represents 'the entire technological complex' that incorporates knowledge, skills, tools, instruments, apparatus and machines (ibid., p. 12). And technics is the broader category that envelops the relations between humankind, our environment and the machine across human history. In *Technics and Civilisation*, Mumford charts a course through history that unearths the interrelationship between the machine and civilisation, and analyses the connection between technology and culture through three overlapping phases: the eotechnic; the paleotechnic; and the neotechnic. Broadly speaking, the eotechnic era was characterised by a water-and-wood complex. The paleotechnic phase was marked by a coal-and-iron complex, whilst the neotechnic period bore the impression of an electricity-and-alloy complex.[1]

Throughout human history the machine has been both an instrument of liberation and repression (ibid., p. 283). Whilst reflecting Proudhon's insistence that liberty and authority are two uncomfortable historical bedfellows that 'persist, always in opposition to each other' (Proudhon, 1979, p. 7), Mumford's notion of an enduring tension within technics constitutes the bedrock of his position. The machine has forever 'presented two aspects: one negative, coercive, and too often destructive; the other positive, life-promoting, constructive' (Mumford, 1967, p. 191). The classic announcement of his thesis was published in *Authoritarian and Democratic Technics*. Quintessentially, his argument

> is that from late neolithic times in the Near East, right down to our own day, two technologies have recurrently existed side by side: one authoritarian, the other democratic, the first system-centred, immensely powerful, but

inherently unstable, the other man-centred, relatively weak, but resourceful and durable (Mumford, 1964a, p. 2).

This Manichean conflict is reflected in both Mumford's material critique of the social relations of production within society (of which capitalism is included but not definitive), and the idealist philosophy of history that serves as the ontological basis of his entire analysis of technics, culture and politics. Mumford stresses, however, that there is no necessary connection between capitalism and technics (1934, p. 27). To begin with, democratic technics existed well in advance of authoritarian technics, which emerged 'around the fourth millennium B.C.' (Mumford, 1964a, p. 3). In terms of its overall genesis, 'technics was related to the whole nature of man, and that nature played a part in every aspect of industry: thus technics, at the beginning, was broadly life-centred, not work-centred or power-centred' (Mumford, 1967, p. 9). With the rise of authoritarian technics, as mediated through the megamachine that was responsible for the construction of the great pyramids, humans 'were reduced to their bare mechanical elements and rigidly standardised for the performance of their limited tasks' (ibid., p. 191). Humans were again subject to the same degradation of their nature under capitalism, the era that gave birth to the next megamachine, as the machine was employed 'not to further social welfare, but to increase profit: mechanical instruments were used for the aggrandizement' of the bourgeoisie, just as they were utilised for the benefit of the pharaohs (Mumford, 1934, p. 27; and 1967, p. 205).

To understand the ontological basis for the abiding conflict between democratic and authoritarian technics it is necessary to examine Mumford's analysis of the megamachine. In his later two-volume work, *The Myth of the Machine*, Mumford devotes the first part of this project to what may be termed a speculative philosophical anthropology. Central to this anthropology is Mumford's rejection of Marx's notion of man *qua Homo faber*. According to Mumford there has been an overemphasis on humans as tool-making beings (Mumford, 1967, p. 5). For Mumford, humans are proprietors of culture and consciousness. Symbols rather than tools facilitated humankind's evolution from a 'purely animal state' (ibid., p. 24). For 'man is pre-eminently a mind-making, self-mastering, and self-designing animal' (ibid., p. 9). If there is an irreducible essence that defines what it is to be human it is our capacity for self-transformation, for self-transcendence (ibid., pp. 10, 30 and 43-44). Humans fashioned meaning, symbols and signs before they manufactured tools, and it is within this cultural arena that humanity's ability for self-transcendence is most significant.

Mumford is clear that the origin of the machine is located in the domain of our consciousness. The machine and the megamachine by definition are products of the human mind (Mumford, 1964b, p. 430). It is in this sense that Zuckerman argues that Mumford's anatomy of the complex of the megamachine is 'an account of man's advancing abdication of his mind' (1990, p. 371). Mumford's commitment to Hegelian idealism informs his perception of a perpetual conflict between democratic and authoritarian technics. Nonetheless, Mumford offers an implicitly Marxian moral critique of the megamachine.

Like all megamachine complexes the aim of the project is to exert 'control over both human communities and the natural environment' (Miller, 1990, p. 153). The birth of the megamachine coincides with the rise of civilisation in ancient Egypt. To be more precise, the megamachine emerged from the womb of 'a radically new type of social organisation: a product of myth, magic, religion, and the nascent science of astronomy' (Mumford, 1967, p. 11). And within this new order the power and authority of the organisers of the megamachine were marshalled to effect a monstrous 'regimentation of human components' in which 'once-autonomous human activities' (ibid., p. 12) were crushed under the ominous weight of mass culture and mass control. Mumford's moral denunciation of the outcomes of the new megatechnics is unmistakeable. Subordinated by the megamachine, the individual 'will become a passive purposeless, machine-conditioned animal whose proper functions...will either be fed into the machine or strictly limited and controlled for the benefit of de-personalised, collective organisations' (ibid., p. 3). Within the environs of the megamachine the individual is analogous to a vestigial instrument, 'reduced to a standardised servo-mechanism: a left-over part from a more organic world' (Mumford, 1964b, p. 430).

Although the above quote refers to the latest manifestation of the megamachine the place of the individual here illuminates the structure and dynamics of the megamachine itself. The first megamachine, which embodied the new Egyptian social order and organisation that constructed the great pyramids, was composed entirely of human parts. But the megamachine could only function so long as 'the religious exaltation, the magical abracadabra and the royal commands that put it together were accepted as beyond human challenge by all members of society' (Mumford, 1967, p. 190). Seemingly, the megamachine is grounded in a monarchical-theological-magical matrix. That the megamachine depends upon organised but secret knowledge held by some form of priesthood is incontestable. In addition, the megamachine demands a hierarchical command structure to implement its orders. For this purpose a bureaucracy is indispensable (ibid., pp. 199-200). The final component in this tripartite life-giving framework is myth. Myth is crucial to the support of the megamachine, as it 'could not be permanently held together without being sustained by a profound magico-religious faith in the system itself' (Mumford, 1967, p. 229).

The myth of the machine is an almost universal belief in technological progress, in the development of science and the expansion of power. These things are held to be good. As an integral part of human culture, technology, science and our power over nature have long assumed a quasi-moral probity. It is not that they are good in an absolute sense. Rather, they are good because they embody a new rationality, an instrumental rationality that promotes above all else the efficient functioning of the technological complex. If translated into a political context the megamachine becomes analogous to the political totalitarian state. Within this form of rule, the state is supported by an official ideology and various other apparatus, such as a state-controlled mass media and a secret police. The purpose of these state apparatus is to facilitate the objectives of the regime, just as the aims of technology and science are to support the megamachine. Of course it would be erroneous to read back a twentieth-century concept into the social organisation of the fourth century B.C. in Egypt, but the megamachine of the military-industrial complex of the 1960s bears visible totalitarian traits. (Mumford, 1964b, p. 264) The totalitarian ethos of absolute commitment to the higher organism, the megamachine, signals a portentous development for Mumford (ibid., p. 286).

> Our contemporaries are already so conditioned to accept technological 'progress' as absolute and irresistible, however painful, ugly, mentally cramping, or physiologically damaging its results, that they accept the latest technical offering, whether a supersonic plane or a 'learning cell', with smiling consent, particularly if the equipment is accompanied by a 'scientific' explanation and seems technologically an 'advanced' type.

Whether it be the pharaohs of ancient Egypt or the new technocratic elite the megamachine exerts an almost unassailable authority that stems from the system itself. In *Authoritarian and Democratic Technics*, Mumford (1964a, pp. 5-6) informs us how, in this new systems-centred collective, this Pentagon of power, there is no visible presence who issues commands: unlike Job's God, the new deities cannot be confronted, still less defied. Under the pretext of saving labour, the ultimate end of this technics is to displace life, or rather, to transfer the attributes of life to the machine and the mechanical collective, allowing only so much of the organism to remain as may be controlled and manipulated.

Within the megatechnic environment individuals have been subject to a persuasive and pervasive new religion, a scientific religion that is grounded in and coincides with the rise of the mechanical philosophy. As Marx maintains, the megamachine of the military-industrial complex that occupies Mumford's thoughts during *Myth of the Machine*, is the 'latest socio-political and economic expressions of this mechanistic philosophy' (1990, p. 172). The foundations for the later labour machine of capitalism were cemented into the Egyptian megamachine, and the megamachine of the military-industrial complex represents the culmination of four centuries of philosophical and scientific evolution after the interlude that was the medieval age.

As expounded by the likes of Copernicus, Kepler, Galileo, Bacon and Newton, a 'new scientific philosophy took over' that accelerated the development of machines (Mumford, 1964b, p. 65). Moreover, as 'mechanical power increased and as scientific theory itself, through further experimental verification, became more adequate, the new method enlarged its domain' (ibid.). The new science gradually replaced the explicatory authority of the Christian church and its traditional priesthood. In the wake of scientific discovery there emerged a new priestly caste, whom as proprietors of scientific knowledge were to form the basis of an emerging technocratic elite. The most critical turning point arrived in the neotechnic phase of history. Two hugely important events occurred during this period. First, the new scientific method was extended from the domains of mathematics and the physical sciences to living organisms and human society. The second major incident witnessed the direct application of this increasingly authoritative and self-validating knowledge to technics and social and economic life (Mumford, 1934, pp. 215-17).

One consequence of this expansion of the scientific method was that the method and its knowledge base assumed quasi-religious significance. Technological innovations became inexorably intoxicating. During the eighteenth and nineteenth centuries technological developments were synonymous with social progress, an attitude of mind that charted a 'virtually unchallenged' course through this era (Hadjilambrinos, 1998, p. 182). A second and associated consequence was the return to the mechanisation of the individual after the craft guilds of medieval times.[2] As Mumford had claimed during his discussion of the original megamachine, individuals were centrally co-ordinated and controlled with each 'behaving as a mechanical component of the mechanised whole' (Mumford, 1967, p. 196).

Herein lies the hallmark of the megamachine, in which individuals are 'reduced to their bare mechanical elements and rigidly standardised for the performance of their limited tasks' (ibid., p. 191). The malignant core of megatechnics with its new scientific method results in a 'system that deliberately eliminates the whole human personality, ignores the historic process, overplays the role of the abstract intelligence, and makes control over physical nature, ultimately control over man himself, the chief purpose of existence' (Mumford, 1964a, p. 6). For anyone who has personal experience of working in a production or assembly-line factory context, the feelings of anonymity and dehumanisation that occur remain a vivid memory long after that employment may have ceased (at least they did for this author).

Logos: Scientific-Techno Rationality

In his *The Technological Society* (1964), Jacques Ellul offers an analysis of the development of technology that although different from Mumford also supports and reinforces Mumford's depiction of a dominant scientific-technological rationality. Ellul's analysis hinges on his concept of technique. Technique is neither reducible to the machine nor technology. It is 'the totality of methods rationally arrived at and having absolute efficiency (for a given stage of development) in every field of human activity' (Ellul, 1964, p. xxv). For Ellul, technique embraces rationality, efficiency and procedure, and whilst technique preceded science it developed and extended itself considerably in science's wake.

Ellul identifies three subdivisions of technique. Economic technique is concerned with the organisation of labour and economic planning. The technique of organisation is associated with commerce, industry, states, administration, the police and warfare. Finally, human technique envelops disciplines such as genetics and propaganda. What is of interest here is Ellul's argument that in the course of its own development technique has become autonomous. It absorbs the human individual and now 'elicits and conditions social, political and economic change' (ibid., p. 133).

In a similar manner to Mumford's conception of the mechanical philosophy and scientific method that powers the megamachine, Ellul's notion of technique has become so dominant and so pervasive that it obliterates what is individual and personal. Indeed, 'technique causes the state to become totalitarian, to absorb the citizens' life completely. (ibid., p. 284) Assuming the form of a mass instrument, technique engenders totalitarianism by its mode of action. In its capacity to transform everything it comes into contact with, technique

> aspires to take over the individual, that is, to transform the qualitative into the quantitative. It knows only two possible solutions: the transformation or the annihilation of the qualitative. It is precisely by way of the former that technique is totalitarian, and when the state becomes technical, it too becomes totalitarian, it has no alternative (ibid., p. 287).

It is worth reinforcing the distinction between technique or logos and individual technologies or machines at this juncture. What both Mumford and Ellul are pointing to is the existence of a framework, a techno-scientific rationale that defines what is valid in terms of procedure, efficiency and control. Consequently, particular examples of machines or technologies, like the central processing unit (CPU) of a computer, are embraced to the extent that they facilitate technique or logos. ICTs, for instance, are not in themselves totalitarian, but insofar as they add leverage to Ellul's concept of technique they add to the totalitarian capacity of technique. It would be erroneous to argue that the prospect of a socio-cultural totalitarianism has suddenly emerged with the advent of the computer. Rather, the analysis of Mumford and Ellul highlights the long history of technique as an authoritarian, centralising and controlling force within human societies.

The concerns of Mumford and Ellul have echoed in the more recent writings of scholars such as Giddens, and Robins and Webster. In his *The Nation State and Violence*, Anthony Giddens (1985, p. 7) argues that if social systems are to reproduce themselves successfully they must make effective use of resources.

> Two types of resource can be distinguished – the allocative and the authoritative. By the first of these I refer to dominion over material facilities, including material goods and the natural forces that may be

harnessed in their production. The second concerns the means of domination over the activities of human beings themselves.

The development of these resources is critical to the state. Without this 'heightened administrative power' the state could neither organise itself internally nor act convincingly on the world stage (ibid., p. 256). At the same time this concentration of allocative and authoritative resources within the state amounts to a building of power that is inherently dangerous. One reason for the potential danger is that central to the establishment of effective administrative power are strategies of surveillance, either in the form of direct supervision of individuals' activities or, more significantly, as 'the accumulation of 'coded information', which can be used to administer the activities of individuals about whom it is gathered' (ibid., p. 14).

The potential danger that Giddens identifies here is nothing less than that of totalitarianism. This potential for totalitarianism becomes endemic when

> the state can successfully penetrate the day-to-day activities of most of its subject population. This, in turn, presumes a high level of surveillance, based upon...the coding of information about and the supervision of significant segments of the population (ibid., pp. 302-303).

Robins and Webster acknowledge Giddens' argument and suggest that authoritative control is now 'subsumed within the machinery of allocative control: power expresses itself through the discipline of calculative and rational social management and administration' (1999, p. 94). Similarly to Giddens, they also identify the potential of totalitarianism and locate the source of that potential in information management.

> What we have is an ever more extensive information apparatus – propaganda, censorship, advertising, public relations, surveillance, etc. – through which opinion management has become not only authoritarian, but also routine and normative. Our argument is that the totalitarian aspect of this process is to be found in its increasingly systematic (totalising), integrated and 'scientific' ambitions and tendencies....The logic of information control and management is, rather, an integral and systemic aspect of the modern nation state (ibid., pp. 144-145).

Giddens and Robins and Webster concur, then, that the state, insofar as it encapsulates mechanisms of allocative control, is at risk of becoming totalitarian. The process of administrative control exerted by the state engenders a mode of planning and administration that decodes the flows and patterns of power and control. Taylor's principles of scientific management are one example, then, of the way in which ICTs are integral to the increasingly 'extensive, efficient and systematic colonisation of social knowledge' (ibid., p. 125).

Surveillance and Totalitarianism

Unsurprisingly, not all academic analysts are persuaded that contemporary states are on the verge of degenerating into totalitarianism. In his recent text, *Surveillance Society*, David Lyon argues that surveillance societies are not totalitarian by nature. That surveillance societies exist and are visible is no longer in question. But they are 'not surveillance states' and do not amount to 'situations of totalitarian control' (Lyon, 2001, pp. 35 and 38). Rather, for Lyon, surveillance is about power and social orchestration (ibid., p. 125). The distinction between surveillance society and surveillance state in Lyon is vitally important, and is reflective of classical accounts of political totalitarianism.[3] Understood from a political perspective, the maintenance of civil society is that which keeps totalitarianism at bay. Once that distinction is broken down and the state obliterates civil society then totalitarianism becomes rampant. To the degree that Lyon's account is commensurate with a political understanding of totalitarianism it offers a valid argument. Lyon's text also provides an extremely useful analysis of the various strands of surveillance theory. He identifies four theoretical threads. The first is that of the nation-state that 'focuses on the political imperatives that require surveillance' (ibid., p. 109). This is the strand to which he assigns Giddens. The second thread, bureaucracy, is akin to the first. Weber is the key theorist here, and surveillance is cited as a product of rationalisation. The third strand, which Lyon seems to value most highly, is the technologic. Jacques Ellul's notion of technique is acknowledged as pivotal here. The final theoretical school of thought within surveillance theory is that of political economy. Under the auspices of this thread, surveillance is regarded as the 'strategic means for the reproduction of one class and its interests over another' (ibid., p. 112). The work of Robins and Webster is considered central here.

Whilst Lyon offers an informative taxonomy of surveillance theory, his own claim that surveillance societies do not equate with a type of surveillance state rather misses the point. Traditional political interpretations of totalitarianism are no longer adequate in facilitating an appropriate understanding of and insight into contemporary socio-cultural totalitarianism. Inextricably associated with moral pronunciations against the Hitler and Stalin regimes of the past, political totalitarianism's core feature is the breakdown of the distinction between public and private, between the state and civil society. In the process of the invasion and obliteration of private life, the state established for itself the objective of total control, exerted in part and perpetuated by one orthodox political doctrine. That the state might not achieve total control is incidental. The important point is that it attempts to do so.

How well, then, does Mumford's concept of the megamachine fit into this totalitarian model? To the extent that Mumford's arguments about the development of the megamachine resonate with overtones of social Taylorism, then they fit well. It was the beginning of the twentieth century that gave birth to a new recurrence of the scientific method that led to our obsession with efficiency. As described by Robins and Webster, the scientific management principles of F. W. Taylor entail 'expert direction by engineers, factory planning, time and motion study, standardisation, and the intensive division of labour' (1999, p. 96). The key objective of Taylorism is efficiency, which is nurtured by way of co-ordination and control of the manufacturing process under the watchful eye of trained experts. Both workers and machines are treated as cogs in a larger machine. Planning is the prerequisite of efficiency under the Taylor system, and both together amount to effective control of the workforce. Accordingly, 'efficiency translates into domination and the engineering of people becomes subsumed within the engineering of things' (ibid.). Similarly, the mechanisms of control which include planning, information, knowledge and skills are rapidly appropriated by the managerial classes, and herein may be found the origins of the Information Revolution (ibid., pp. 96-7).

Obviously, Taylorism is not dependent upon ICTs or other forms of technology, but insofar as ICTs aid the rational and scientific management of Taylorism they are put to effective use. For Robins and Webster (ibid., p. 109) it is clear that this

> exploitation of information resources and technologies has expressed itself, politically and culturally, through the dual tendency towards social planning and management, on the one hand, and surveillance and control on the other. In historical terms, this can be seen as the apotheosis of Lewis

Mumford's megamachine: technology now increasingly fulfils what previously depended upon bureaucratic organisation and structure.

The inherent monitoring and data-gathering capacities of ICTs has displaced many functions that were previously undertaken by more cumbersome bureaucratic organisations. In plain language, the scientific management principles of Taylorism that were previously applied to manual labour are now increasingly applied to intellectual labour as the efficiency of the CPU leaves the organic human brain stumbling in its wake. The instrumental rationality that is at the heart of the original scientific method and which underscores its return in Taylorism is now unerringly extended to the role of the technocrats themselves. In the shifting climate of technological innovation the knowledge base that legitimates technocratic rule is rapidly reconfiguring itself in favour of computer programmers and software engineers.

It is worth recalling here that despite an attempt to exert total control over its populace, totalitarian regimes (and potentially totalitarian regimes) cannot hope to achieve this completely. Vestiges of resistance always remained in these regimes, even in the face of extensive apparatus of control and surveillance. Similarly, today, whilst ICTs may be extensively employed in the surveillance industries there are some that utilise the code and infrastructure of ICTs to provide alternatives and engage in resistance (for example, crackers (formerly known as hackers) and the development of Linux).

Mumford's megamachine is symbolic of speed, power and control. Indeed, the very principle of total control is endemic to both Mumford's notion of the megamachine and Ellul's idea of technique. The new megamachine has tapped into Taylorism's information flows to find its own sustenance. ICTs are emblematic of speed, technique, efficiency, control and power. They resonate with the mechanical philosophy and scientific-technological rationality that Mumford identifies as integral to the megamachine. ICTs are representative of control over nature and control over humanity. For Robins and Webster, Taylorism is the lifeblood of this new megamachine. But the success of the megamachine is also dependent upon its myth.

The function of the myth of the megamachine was to support the system, if only because the megamachine was representative of efficiency and introduced a more rational method than was previously available (Mumford, 1967, pp. 193 and 208). But as the new millennium awakens, the focal point of the myth is to be found in the new ICTs. The new technologies bolster the scientific method by virtue of their innate capacities. As symbols of speed, scientific calculation and efficiency they are judiciously positioned to become the next incarnation of the megamachine. And those with the new secret knowledge, the authors of the programming code, are set to become the new priesthood of this machine.

But the above arguments fare less well in addressing the other components of political totalitarianism. Nowhere in Mumford, Giddens, or Robins and Webster will the reader discover a credible explanation about the dominance of one orthodox political doctrine. The reason for that is that nowhere do they endeavour to present such an argument. On occasion Robins and Webster proffer persuasive arguments about the foreclosure of serious and open political debate in the realms of cyberspace, but this is never intended as a serious claim that digital totalitarianism lurks in the corners of chat rooms. Similarly, there is no serious argument here to suggest that surveillance is solely an activity performed by the state. To be sure the state and its agencies engage in surveillance, but they are not alone in this exercise. Recognition of this wider culture of surveillance demands not a political model of totalitarianism, but a socio-cultural account of totalitarianism. Only by reconceptualising the nature of totalitarianism can we begin to appreciate how ICTs mediate the potential for totalitarianism.

Of course, such models have long been in existence. Herbert Marcuse's *One Dimensional Man* delivers a message that overlaps significantly with the arguments of Mumford and Ellul. For Marcuse, society is dominated by a scientific-technological rationality that he terms 'Logos'. This is not a neutral drive toward efficiency, if only because that quest subsumes the desire to control and dominate.

> In the medium of technology, culture, politics, and the economy merge into an omnipresent system which swallows up or repulses all alternatives. The productivity and growth potential of the system stabilize the society and contain technical progress within the framework of domination. Technological rationality has become political rationality (Marcuse, 1991, p. 14).

Logos becomes totalitarian precisely because it 'obliterates the opposition between the private and public existence, between individual and social needs' (ibid., p. 13). And this techno-scientific rationality is so dominant that it no longer makes sense, to Marcuse, to speak of one class dominating the rest (Tormey, 1995, pp. 110-111).

Whilst such conclusions would not sit well with analysts like Halcli and Webster (2000), who argue that there remains a firm class basis underpinning the economic disparities of the information age, Marcuse does provide an important stepping stone to an alternative analysis. This analysis is required in order to provide both a convincing rebuttal of Lyon's judgement that surveillance societies fall short of the surveillance state and therefore cannot be categorised as totalitarian, and to overcome the limitations of previous arguments in addressing some of the dimensions of political totalitarianism. By switching the focus of totalitarianism from the political to the socio-cultural the archetypal feature of totalitarianism, the obliteration of the private, is refocused and decoded into a more meaningful concept. Although not completely remote from its political cousin the socio-cultural model mirrors more closely that nature and dynamics of contemporary society.

Surveillance as Decoded Flows: Socio-Cultural Totalitarianism

A useful starting point for this analysis can be found in post-structuralist thought. Post-structuralism is closely associated with the writings of Foucault and Derrida. Put simply, it is a rejection of explanations (as found in Marx for example) that the human condition can be explained by reference to underlying structures, such as economics, that are subject to objective analysis outside the discourse that constructs these structures. Structuralists contend that the individual is moulded by external structures (eg, political, economic, sociological, linguistic) that are beyond his or her control. Perhaps the most famous figure associated with post-structuralist thought is Michel Foucault.

> He agreed that language and society were shaped by rule-governed systems, but he disagreed with the structuralists on two counts. Firstly, he did not think that there were definite underlying structures that could explain the human condition and secondly he thought that it was impossible to step outside of discourse and survey the situation objectively (Jones, no date).

Of particular value to the analysis of this paper is the work of Deleuze and Guattari, described by one commentator as the 'world's first systematic theorists of technological fascism' (Kroker, 1992, p. 109). In works such as *A Thousand Plateaus*, they introduce the concept of multiplicity into phenomena we often think of as discrete, as structured, as stable. Hence they contend (Deleuze and Guattari, 1988, p. 254) that

> each individual is an infinite multiplicity, and the whole of Nature is a multiplicity of perfectly individuated multiplicities. The plane of consistency of Nature is like an immense Abstract Machine, abstract yet real and individual; its pieces are the various assemblages and individuals, each of which groups together an infinity of particles entering into an infinity of more or less interconnected relations.

The concept of multiplicity is symbolised through the rhizome. With no centre or visible beginning or end a rhizome spreads itself horizontally and makes innumerable connections with other rhizomes and within itself. As Deleuze and Guattari point out, bulbs and tubers are rhizomes as are rats and couchgrass. What is important here is that 'any point of a rhizome can be connected to anything other, and must be' (ibid., p. 7). Extending the analysis, Deleuze and Guattari (ibid., p. 8) employ the image of a wasp pollinating an orchid.

> The orchid deterritorializes by forming an image, a tracing of a wasp; but the wasp reterritorializes on that image. The wasp is nevertheless deterritorialized, becoming a piece in the orchid's reproductive apparatus. But it reterritorializes the orchid by transporting its pollen. Wasp and orchid, as heterogeneous elements, form a rhizome.

In becoming-wasp and becoming-orchid, the orchid and the wasp, respectively, facilitate the deterritorialization of one and the reterritorialization of the other. In doing so the rhizome or multiplicity grows and spreads.

Deleuze and Guattari also subject the state to this analysis of multiplicity. Here a conception of the state emerges that signifies its multiple forms and modes of action. Their distinctive approach to the state emerges in their philosophical distinction between deterritorialisation and reterritorialisation. In *What is Philosophy?*, they argue (1994, pp. 67-68) that we 'need to see how everyone, at every age, in the smallest things as in the greatest challenges, seeks a territory, tolerates or carries out deterritorialisations, and is reterritorialised on almost anything – memory, fetish or dream.'

This process of deterritorialisation and reterritorialisation permeates the state and the city (ibid., p. 86). For Deleuze and Guattari, the primordial despotic state that accompanies Marx's Asiatic mode of production is the original abstraction that is realised in concrete existence in different settings. Now, however, the state is 'subordinated to a field of forces whose flows it co-ordinates and whose autonomous relations of domination and subordination it expresses' (ibid., p. 221). Today, then, the state is formed out of the decoded flows it invents for money and property; it is formed out of the dominating classes; it cowers behind the things it signifies, and 'is itself produced inside the field of decoded flows' (ibid.).

Within the narrative of decoded flows the state becomes a set of operations, a rhizomatic network, a form of becoming. And the 'surveillant assemblage' is part of the state form (Haggerty and Ericson, 2000, pp. 606-608). Surveillance, then, should be considered not as solely the exercise of state power. Rather, surveillance is a potentiality associated with multiple intersections of various digital media across the network of decoded flows. These interconnections arise for diverse reasons and there is no one centre of power. Consequently, there is no fixed target to identify as culpable or responsible; that is the nature of the assemblage.

The multiplication of the individual is no more apparent than in the decoding of the human body. For Deleuze and Guattari, the body is deterritorialised and reterritorialised in a series of data flows. As Haggerty and Ericson observe (ibid., pp. 612-613), surveillance begins

> with the creation of a space of comparison and the introduction of breaks in the flows that emanate from, or circulate within, the human body. For example, drug testing striates flows of chemicals, photography captures flows of reflected lightwaves, and lie detectors align and compare assorted flows of respiration, pulse and electricity.

Surveillance is about the creation of multiple digital models of individuals that reside on databases of law enforcement agencies, welfare agencies, financial institutions, marketing corporations, travel companies, insurance conglomerates, telecommunication groups and many others. This multiplication of the individual unleashes a series of digital dopplegangers that haunt the unsuspecting individual's every move as a spectre lurking in the shadows of cyberspace.

This multiplication of the individual is reflective of the strategies of control and domination that are inherent within the logic of the techno-scientific rationale that Mumford, Ellul and Marcuse have identified. Manifested as a desire for power and control that inhabits the marketing strategies of trans-national corporations and the ethos of governance, this technique is perilously close to becoming totalitarianism. The multiplication of the individual also mediates an invasion of private life by this surveillance assemblage. Privacy is now overwhelmed by the flows and force of the surveillance society. As Haggerty and Ericson (2000, p. 616) put it, privacy has become 'less a line in the sand beyond which transgression is not permitted, than a shifting space of negotiation where privacy is traded for products, better services or special deals.' This clearly reveals that privacy has been commodified under the development of capital, but there is more to it than that. Privacy is often traded in economic transactions, and to some degree individuals must either agree or acquiesce to that exchange of commodities. Indeed, as Martin (1993, p. 117) highlights, there may be much 'public support for surveillance', especially when it is directed at reducing crime or welfare fraud. But Martin errs in his insistence that to focus on privacy amounts to a defence of liberal individualism and a preoccupation with the individual as subject (ibid., pp. 115-116). Privacy is vitally important here, precisely because it is pivotal in maintaining barriers against totalitarianism. Martin's conclusion, that 'Orwell's *1984* is much more totalitarian' than the so-called liberal-democratic societies of today, is predicated on the assumption that whilst 'surveillance is deeply embedded in today's social institutions' the majority of it is undertaken 'with the very best of intentions' (ibid., p. 126).

The fundamental problem with this argument is that it misconceives the totality of surveillance. To be sure, surveillance is carried out by social, political and economic institutions, but it is driven inexorably forward by the logic of control and domination that is the motor force of the techno-scientific rationale that saturates every fold of our social, political, economic and cultural fabric. A telling example of this is the huge increase in surveillance technologies used by law enforcement agencies. The operation of CCTV cameras and Gatso speed cameras is indicative of the way in which those technologies enable improvements in efficiency and control. Accordingly, they are employed at an accelerating rate across many parts of the UK. Similarly, whilst the introduction of the Regulation of Investigatory Powers Act (2000) was introduced on the premise of cracking down on serious crime, its ultimate driver was the increased efficiency to be had by electronic monitoring (the black boxes on ISP servers) of e-mails and other forms of electronic communication.

Surveillance is not coincidental, it is systemic. It occurs at multiple levels, is often intrusive, unwanted and invisible. Without even realising it, individuals are decoded and reterritorialised into economic, political, and social flows. Their digital dopplegangers populate hundreds if not thousands of different databases. The invasion of privacy, then, occurs not only at the political level, but at the social, economic and cultural levels. As Paul Virilio has commented, totalitarian societies 'colonize their own people' (Armitage, 1999, p. 50). And here the role of contemporary technologies is pivotal. Technology 'colonizes the world, through globalitarianism...but it also colonizes bodies, their attitudes and behaviours' (ibid., p. 51). It is for this reason that understanding totalitarianism as solely political is no longer apposite. As Haggerty and Ericson (2000, p. 619) note, 'the surveillant assemblage marks the progressive "disappearance" of disappearance'. Socio-cultural totalitarianism both emanates from the logos of the techno-scientific rationale that aims at total control and domination, and extends its tentacles from every interconnection and node of the digital rhizome that constitutes today's society.

Socio-cultural totalitarianism is not the product of some hideous twentieth century political regime that is bent on the destruction of certain segments of the population. It is much too rational to be associated with the irrational and destructive actions of a tyrant. Likewise, it is not the product of technologies themselves, nor the product of a particular mode of production. It is, rather, the outcome of a technique that in the guise of Mumford's labour machine first made its appearance thousands of years ago. That technique was fortified by the collapse of superstition and faith and the deification of science. Today, socio-cultural totalitarianism is mediated by contemporary technologies that are emblematic of that technique. It is the domination of the system-centred, authoritarian technology, identified by Mumford, that seeks to control not only the physical world but all of its human inhabitants. To be sure, there is resistance and long may it continue; but this is a potentially totalitarian framework of control. It is omniscient and omnipotent by virtue of its digital multiplication of the individual and its obliteration of the individual's sphere of privacy. To the degree that totalitarianism is about total control, in the realms of the social and the cultural the individual has nowhere left to hide. As Hannah Arendt (1967, p. xxvii) once commented, in a totalitarian society 'coexistence is not possible.'

Notes

[1]   Mumford's categorisation of human history into distinct if interpenetrating phases owes much to the work of Patrick Geddes, who invented the terms paleotechnic and neotechnic (Williams, 1990: 51; Wilmott, 1995).

[2]   Where the megamachine had been explicitly absent was in the materialisation of the megamachine *qua* labour machine. In other words, the structure and ethos of the megamachine, the standardisation, the co-ordination and the command structure have been an enduring feature of human cultures in the form of the army, i.e., the megamachine *qua* military machine.

[3]   The classic account of totalitarianism is provided by Friedrich and Brezinski (1966).

References

Arendt, H. (1967), *The Origins of Totalitarianism*, Allen and Unwin, London.

Armitage, J. (1999), 'From Modernism to Hypermodernism and Beyond: An Interview with Paul Virilio', *Theory, Culture and Society*, 16 (5-6), pp. 25-55.

Burrows, B. (1996), 'Mumford's the word', *Futures*, 28 (5), pp. 506-08.

Casillo, R. (1992), 'Lewis Mumford and the Organicist Concept in Social Thought', *Journal of the History of Ideas*, pp. 91-116.

Davis, Allen F. (1993), 'Lewis Mumford: Man of Letters and Urban Historian', *Journal of Urban History*, 19 (4), pp. 123-31.

Deleuze, G. and Guattari, F. (1984), *Anti-Oedipus: Capitalism and Schizophrenia*, Athlone Press, London.

Deleuze, G. and Guattari, F. (1988), *A Thousand Plateaus: Capitalism and Schizophrenia*, Athlone Press, London.

Ellul, J. (1964), *The Technological Society*, Vintage Books, New York.

Feenberg, A. (1996), 'Marcuse or Habermas: Two Critiques of Technology', *Inquiry*, 39 (1), pp. 45-70.

Friedrich, B. J. and Brezinski, Z. (1966), *Totalitarian Dictatorship and Autocracy*, Praeger, New York.

Geoghegan, V. (1981), *Reason and Eros: The Social Theory of Herbert Marcuse*, Pluto Press, London.

Giddens, A. (1985), *The Nation State and Violence*, Polity Press, Cambridge.

Golding, P. (2000), 'Forthcoming Features: Information and Communications Technologies and the Sociology of the Future, *Sociology*, 34 (1), pp. 165-84.

Hadjilambrinos, C. (1998), 'Technological Regimes: an Analytical Framework for the Evaluation of Technological Systems', *Technology in Society*, 20 (2), pp. 179-94.

Haggerty, K. D. and Ericson, R. V. (2000), *'The Surveillant Assemblage'*, British Journal of Sociology, 51 (4), pp. 605-622.

Halcli, A. and Webster, F. (2000), *'Inequality and Mobilization in* The Information Age*'*, European Journal of Social Theory, 3 (1), pp. 67-81.

Hillis, K. (1996), 'A Geography of the Eye: The Technologies of Virtual Reality', in R. Shields (ed.), *Cultures of Internet: Virtual Spaces, Real Histories, Living Bodies*, Sage, London.

Hughes, Thomas P. and Hughes, Agatha C. (eds.) (1990), *Lewis Mumford: Public Intellectual*, Oxford University Press, Oxford.

Jones, R. (no date), 'Post Structuralism', available at http://www.philosopher.org.uk/index.htm . (Accessed 03 April, 2003.)

Jordan, T. (2001), 'Language and libertarianism: the politics of cyberculture and the culture of cyberpolitics', *The Sociological Review*, 49 (1), pp. 1-17.

Kellner, D. (1984), *Herbert Marcuse and the Crisis of Marxism*, University of California Press, Berkeley.

Kroker, A. (1992), *The Possessed Individual: Technology and Postmodernity*, Macmillan, London.

Lyon, D. (2001), *Surveillance Society: Monitoring Everyday Life*, Open University Press, Buckingham.

Marcuse, H. (1991), *One-Dimensional Man: Studies in the Ideology of Advanced Industrial Society*, Routledge, London.

Martin, B. (1993), 'Antisurveillance', *Anarchist Studies*, 1 (2), pp. 111-129.

Marx, L. (1990), 'Lewis Mumford: Prophet of Organicism', in Thomas P. Hughes and Agatha C. Hughes (eds.), *Lewis Mumford: Public Intellectual*, Oxford: Oxford University Press.

Miller, Donald L. (ed.) (1986), *The Lewis Mumford Reader*, Pantheon, New York.

Miller, Donald L. (1989), *Lewis Mumford: A Life*, Weidenfield and Nicolson, New York.

Miller, Donald L. (1990), 'The Myth of the Machine: I. Technics and Human Development', in Thomas P. Hughes and Agatha C. Hughes (eds.), *Lewis Mumford: Public Intellectual*, Oxford University Press, Oxford.

Mumford, L. (1934), *Technics and Civilization*, Routledge, London.

Mumford, L. (1964a), 'Authoritarian and Democratic Technics', *Technology and Culture*, V (1), pp. 1-8.

Mumford, L. (1964b), *The Myth of the Machine II. The Pentagon of Power*, Secker and Warburg, London.

Mumford, L. (1967) *The Myth of the Machine I. Technics and Human Development*, Secker and Warburg, London.

Proudhon, P-J. (1979), *The Principle of Federation*, University of Toronto Press, Toronto.

Robins, K. and Webster, F. (1987), 'Dangers of Information Technology and Responsibilities of Education', in R. Finnegan, G. Salaman and K. Thompson (eds.), *Information Technology: Social Issues. A Reader*, Hodder and Stoughton, Sevenoaks.

Robins, K. and Webster, F. (1999), *Times of the Technoculture: From the Information Society to the Virtual Life*, Routledge, London.

Schwarztmantel, J. (1994), *The State in Contemporary Society: An Introduction*, Harvester/Wheatsheaf, London.

Segal, Howard P. (1990), 'Mumford's Alternatives to the Megamachine: Critical Utopianism, Regionalism, and Decentralisation', in Thomas P. Hughes and Agatha C. Hughes (eds.), *Lewis Mumford: Public Intellectual*, Oxford University Press, Oxford.

Tormey, S. (1995), *Making Sense of Tyranny: Interpretations of Totalitarianism*, Manchester University Press, Manchester.

Williams, R. (1990), 'Lewis Mumford as a Historian of Technology in *Technics and Civilization*', in Thomas P. Hughes and Agatha C. Hughes (eds.), *Lewis Mumford: Public Intellectual*, Oxford University Press, Oxford.

Wilmott, P. (1995), 'Guru in search of a disciple', *The Times Higher Education Supplement* (17/11/1995), p. 29.
Zuckerman, M. (1990), 'Faith, Hope, Not Much Charity: The Optimistic Epistemology of Lewis Mumford', in Thomas P. Hughes and Agatha C. Hughes (eds.), *Lewis Mumford: Public Intellectual*, Oxford University Press, Oxford.

PART II
UK ISSUES

5 New Labour, the Third Way and Ideological Politics

ANDREW SHEPHERD

The Decline of Ideological Politics

The 'world system' characterised by mass manufacturing, mass consumption, state organisation of social and economic maintenance, and underscored by Keynesian fiscal and welfare policies, had sustained growth and comparative prosperity throughout the post-war years (Burrows and Loader, 1994, pp. 1-2; Jessop, 1994, pp. 14-15; Allen, 1992, pp. 186-188; Penna and O'Brien, 1996, pp. 46-47; Gamble, 1994, p. 17). The social democratic consensus was effectively maintained by the economic consensus of this Fordist system. Significant changes occurred however in the late 1960s and early 1970s, with governments finding it more difficult to manage economies. The social democratic hegemony began to break down, forcing new policy agendas upon governments. While this was not new the problem was one of size, 'it was bigger' (Gamble, 1994, pp. 14-15). Political cohesion was increasingly unattainable. The world system and social democratic consensus had reached critical mass (Coxall and Robins, 1998, p. 27). Crisis package initiatives were used throughout the 1970s in attempts to combat the socio-economic problems and win back consent, corporatism, social contracts and wage restraints (Gamble, 1994, pp. 14 and 31; Fielding, 1997a, p. 92-100; Tomlinson, 1997, p. 12; Coxall and Robins, 1998, p. 27). Such methods brought down successive Labour and Conservative governments in the UK: Heath, 1973-4 miners' strike; Callaghan, 1978-79 public sector strikes (Fielding, 1997a, p. 106; Coxall and Robins, 1998, p. 27). As Gamble (1994, p. 15) noted, 'Waiting for the storm to pass was no longer enough. The world outside was never going to be the same again.' This had long-term repercussions for the social democratic consensus, increasingly seen to be un-viable (Gamble, 1994, pp. 22-23). A post-Fordist society was emerging.

What About the Workers?

The global changes had a significant impact on the two-party structure, 'class' alignment and ideological politics. Theorists from the 1960s onwards debated what the consequences would be for the socio-political system. Changes in voting behaviour were a phenomenon before global recession and such embourgeoisement and affluent worker theories have been postulated (Abrams, Rose and Hinden, 1960; Goldthorpe et al., 1968; Butler and Stokes, 1974; Bell, 1974; Braverman, 1974; Heath et al., 1991). Braverman (1974) argued, however, that changes in the labour processes had resulted in work becoming more 'proletarianized' (1974, p. 291). Skills became less important. 'Routinization' of work was extensive, more alienation and de-skilling was the result (Braverman, 1974). The post-industrialist Bell (1974) contended that the labour process was less proletarianised, with workers becoming more skilled. Workers also inculcated a middle-class perspective. 'Class' consciousness was declining, workers were becoming more individualist, and less inclined towards collective class struggles (Bell, 1974, pp. 123-164 and 358-367). In Braverman's (1974) view proletarianisation would cause greater disaffection and resistance. Socio-economic change was influencing class perceptions (Moran, 1989, pp. 64-68). Crucially, Labour drew support from the working class during the 1950s and 1960s. Class was the catalyst in electoral behaviour (Sanders, 1997, p. 53) and it was to become, 'a source of many of its electoral troubles in the 1970s and 80s' (Moran, 1989, pp. 65-66). Running the economy was more important to voters (Butler and Stokes, 1974, pp. 193-208; Moran, 1989, pp. 68-69). This was the new electorate.

Out of this political maelstrom emerged anti-consensual ideas on the future of the socio-economic structure (Gamble, 1994, pp. 22-25; Coxall and Robins, 1998, p. 28). Monetarist economists argued the old consensus politics was the root cause of the problems (Kolberg and Esping-Anderson, 1992, p. 10). With economic decline and ineffective policies by both Labour and Tory administrations, there was fertile ground for New Right thinking, with its demands for the disengagement of the state from socio-economic policy and the assertion of market freedom (O'Gorman, 1986, pp. 54-55; Robins and Savage, 1990; Moran, 1989, pp. 100 and 188-192; Clark, Cochrane and Smart, 1987, p. 134). The free market would be less bureaucratic, comparatively inexpensive and would be free from constraint by government, professionals and trades unions (O'Gorman, 1986, p. 53;

George and Wilding, 1992, pp. 27-28; Coxall and Robins, 1998, pp. 31 and 73). As Johnson (1990, p. 4) analysed, 'When Mrs. Thatcher came to power she was already convinced of the correctness of the New Right's ideas and set about attempting to translate them into policies'. It was the 'strategic sense' of its objectives and its pragmatism on achieving them, rather than detailed policy plans, that distinguished it as very different from its predecessors (Gamble, 1994, p. 6). It understood the need to 'establish a claim to political, moral and intellectual leadership', and from this the synthesising of that 'popular mandate' with the 'realities of managing the state machine' (Gamble, 1994, p. 8). From 1979 onwards their ideological imperatives became increasingly divisive and exploited the socio-economic decline.

The Development of the Third Way

By the 1980s it was inevitable that changes were needed in the Labour Party's ideology. To reverse socio-economic breakdown and be electable, a new hegemonic project was necessary (Hall, 1988). The process of rethinking began after the 1983 general election defeat (Shaw, 1994, p. 41). Labour gained 28% of the vote and only 38% of blue-collar votes (Sanders, 1997, p. 48; Moran, 1998, p. 72). Labour was 'a pathetic unelectable shambles' (Gould, 1999, p. 142). In the Fabian lecture, *The Future of Socialism* (1985), Kinnock outlined the 'third way' of 'democratic socialism'; a philosophy 'distinct' from the ultra-Left and the 'atavistic and timid' premise of social democracy (1985, p. 1). He stressed the 'electoral reality' of the necessity to broaden Labour's appeal. Awareness of social changes, mobility and affluence, necessitated a re-emphasis of the 'ethical' characteristics of Labour's socialist heritage and re-assertion of democratic socialism as 'modern values' not the 'ghost' of the past (ibid., pp. 3 and 5; Shaw, 1994, p. 41; Gould, 1999, pp. 20-22). The compromises of the later 1987 manifesto *Britain Will Win* (Labour Party, 1987) reflected the 1983-7 'tentative and piecemeal' changes. Labour was neither a state socialist nor a social democratic party (Jones, 1996, pp. 119-120).

Change was certain after the 1987 defeat, with the launch of a policy review to widen appeal by abandoning seemingly unpopular policies (Shaw, 1994, p. 81; Peele, 1990, pp. 79-80). In 1989, *Meet the Challenge, Make the Change* was published, which set out the revised policies and strategy that a future Labour government would pursue. Stressing individual freedom, democratic society and an 'enabling state' (Labour Party, 1989, pp. 5 and 8) it did abandon public ownership. The document endorsed (if qualified) the market economy (Labour Party, 1989, pp. 5 and 8; Jones, 1996, pp. 123-124; Shaw, 1994, pp. 85-87 and 92). The economic role of government was 'to help the market work properly where it can, will and should – and to replace it where it can't or shouldn't' (Labour Party, 1989, p. 6). Kinnock (1994, p. 545) later acknowledged, however, there was no 'central theme'. To some Kinnock transformed Labour from a state socialist party to a European social democratic variant (Jones, 1996, p. 129; Peele, 1990, pp. 78-79; Marquand, 1991, p. 201; Gamble, 1990, pp. 357-358). These reforms did not connect with the electorate in the 1992 election (Jones, 1996, p. 130; Pelling and Reid, 1996, p. 185). Labour was 'still not trusted' (Gould, 1999, pp. 158-159). Labour had tried to re-invent itself and counter Thatcherism. What emerged was civil war within its ranks, a fatal division as far as the electorate were concerned.

The commitment to modernisation of Labour's policies was maintained by John Smith from July 1992 (Fielding, 1997a, p. 143). Smith's social democratic stance was born of his Christian socialist beliefs (Wilkinson, 1999, p. 45). Jones (1996, p. 132) noted of this, 'the distinctive feature of this ethical socialism were a belief in community and the interdependence of individual freedom and collective action'. Smith had intended to publish a personal statement of democratic socialist values, as a supplement to, rather than replacement of, Clause IV (Jones, 1996, p. 133; Shaw, 1994, p. 224; Rentoul, 1995, pp. 413-414). However, in 1993, Jack Straw argued for a full revision in *Policy and Ideology* (1993, p. 2), to recast the Party's objectives and ensure they related to 'the realities of life in the 20th and early 21st century'. This was necessary he argued as Labour's ideological vision had 'failed to keep pace not only with prosaic changes to Labour policy, but with more fundamental changes in Britain and in the world as a whole' (ibid., p. 4). The Clause had become a totem and its revision was vital in the 1990s for Labour to revitalise its 'appeal to the electorate as the governing party which takes Britain into the 21st century' (ibid., p. 28). Smith, hoping to have his value statement adopted by Conference, continued with his long-term strategy of party unity, 'one man, one vote' reform and the preparation of policies, notably the influential Commission on Social Justice Report (Jones, 1996, p. 134; Shaw, 1994, p. 224; Commission on Social Justice, 1993a, 1993b and 1994). Smith's era is interesting and does represent a period of more realistic and organised resistance to the Tories. On 12 May 1994, however, John Smith died.

The Mission

After July 1994, Tony Blair wanted faster modernisation (Gould, 1999, pp. 181-182). The reason for the defeat was already understood by Blair. The Party had failed to adapt fully enough to socio-economic changes; its programme, organisation and mentality belonged to a bygone age (Shaw, 1996). Complete modernisation was the key (Gould, 1999, pp. 218 and 231). In an article 'Forging a New Agenda', Blair (1991, p. 32) argued the challenge was 'to re-establish the agenda for public action without the failings of collectivism'. The idea was to replace ideas of state socialism with ethical socialism and its emphasis on 'the need of society to act together to achieve what the individual cannot do alone', and the 'use of the power of society to protect and advance the individual' (Blair, 1991, p. 32). Such socialist principles implied 'the notion of a clearly identified community, embodying the public interest or public good, standing up on behalf of individuals, against the vested interests that hold them back' (Blair, 1991, p. 32).

This had implications for economic policy, the theoretical debates on economic organisation were dead or relegated to means, not ends. A new economics of public interest was proposed, of partnerships to achieve public interest objectives (ibid., p. 33). In *Socialism* (1994), Blair argued that people and society are willing to listen to the values of the Left, of social justice, cohesion, equality of opportunity and community, due to the insecurity and limitations of Thatcherism. Reasserting the true purpose of socialism, Blair (1994, p. 4) stated, 'The basis of such socialism lies in its view that individuals are socially interdependent human beings... . It is, if you will, social-ism'. Further, it contains an ethical and subjective judgement that individuals owe a duty to one another and to a broader society – the Left view of citizenship (ibid.).

Socialism, defined in this way, rather than 'narrow timebound class or sectional interests' or 'economic prescriptions', allows socialism (and the Party) to be 'liberated', 'learning from history rather than being chained to it' (ibid.). It was argued that the old Left has no answers to today's socio-economic problems, and the Right 'either ignores them or, in the case of bad management practice, endorses it' (ibid., p. 5). Labour had the chance to 'capture the ground and language of opportunity', via policies based on its 'traditional principles', but 'applying them in a different way for the modern world...released from false ideological constraints' (ibid.).

Within this broad policy agenda in economic terms, while addressing the weakness of industry, enhancing opportunities in education and training, partnership at work and reducing unemployment, government would act to 'promote the public good' (Blair, 1994, pp. 5-6). In social terms, this would involve reducing crime, improving quality of life, a new constitution, open government and a modernised welfare state to eliminate poverty. By re-establishing its core identity Labour could, 'win the battle of ideas' (ibid., p. 6). This being achieved, a radical 'coalition of support' which 'transcends' old electoral divisions can decide the future of the country through the 'power and energy of our ideas and our vision for the country' (ibid., p. 7). This theme continued. In Blair's leadership acceptance speech, he asserted it was not just a programme, 'It is a mission of national renewal, a mission of hope, change and opportunity.' (Blair, 21 July 1994). He talked of rebuilding the, 'bonds of common purpose', of 'a community of people' and the task of national renewal being to 'provide opportunity and security in this world of change'. This Left-of-centre agenda 'breaks new ground, that does not put one set of dogmas in place of another, that offers the genuine hope of a new politics to take us into a new millennium'. Socialism, Blair asserted, is not about a 'fixed economic theory defined for one time but a set of values and principles definable for all time' (ibid.).

What is again clear here is an understanding of socio-political conditions and the necessity to be broad-based to win over the indifferent and hostile or suspicious former Labour, but now Tory, voters. The emphasis on social justice and the need to re-invent society was a direct attack on the individualism (Gould, 1999, pp237-238). In mid-1994 Blair had consulted Brown and Mandelson on his wish to rewrite Clause IV (Gould, 1999, p. 215), as private poll findings had shown a 'fear of the unknown...regarding Labour' (cited in Sopel, 1995, p. 139). It was crucial for the modernisers to change Labour and convince voters 'that it had ceased being "Old" and was now "New Labour"' (Shaw, 1996, p. 198; Gould, 1999, pp. 219-220). At the 1994 Party Conference, Blair unleashed his proposal on Clause IV; Labour required 'a modern constitution that says what we are in terms the public cannot misunderstand and the Tories cannot misrepresent' (Blair, 4 October 1994). 'Parties that do not change die, and this party is a living movement not an historical monument' (ibid.). A new ethos, put in march-or-die terms. The old clause did not reflect Labour's 'values or our total view of the economy' (Blair, 'Socialist Values in the Modern World' speech, Sedgefield, 28 January 1995).

The new Clause IV was published in March 1995, its main emphasis being on community, social justice and economic aims. Part 1 of the Clause stated:

> It believes that by the strength of our common endeavour we achieve more than we achieve alone,…for all of us a community in which power, wealth and opportunity are in the hands of the many not the few, where the rights we enjoy reflect the duties we owe' (Labour Party, 1995a).

Part 2 redefined Labour's economic aims: a competitive market operating in the public interest; and a partnership between private and public ownership. The new clause (at a special conference, 29 April 1995) was secured by 65% of votes (90% constituency votes and 54.6% Union votes; notably, most Unions did not ballot their members) (Gould, 1999, p. 230; Jones, 1996, pp. 144-146). This was a seminal event. It marked symbolically the 'ideological transition from traditional socialism to social democracy' (Jones, 1996, p. 147). Blair and the modernisers could now push ahead with their vision of a 'New Britain'.

The Central Ideas of the Third Way

With the new ideology embedded in a new constitution, the way was now open to proposals emphasising how this ethos would be applied to policy. It was outlined in a series of statements. In *Let Us Face the Future* (1995), Blair (p. 5) stressed the task was to provide a 'broad consensus for change…as in 1945'. A consensus built on a national purpose and 'core Labour values', not just policies, reaching beyond its traditional base as a true 'people's party' (ibid., pp. 6 and 9). A 'governing consensus' with a hegemonic programme of interdependence and 'sharing of responsibility' to tackle decline; 'one nation' politics, 'Attlee's kind of socialism, and it is also mine' (ibid., pp. 9 and 12). At the Brighton Conference (3 October 1995) 'stakeholding' was postulated. A new 'civic society' could be built, 'a new social order, where everyone has a stake and everyone plays a part' (Blair,1995, Brighton Conference speech). The central theme was tackling social exclusion. By casting out the old prejudices, a new spirit of 'solidarity' and 'partnership' could be imbued into society (Blair, Brighton Conference, 1995). Stakeholding also had an economic aspect, community was to be linked with efficiency (Gould, 1999, pp. 254-255). Later, in Singapore (8 January 1996) Blair explained:

It is a stakeholder economy in which opportunity is available to all, advancement is through merit and from which no group or class is set apart or excluded. This is the economic justification for social cohesion, for a fair and strong society (Blair, Singapore, 1996).

The speech gave New Labour its 'defining idea' (Gould, 1999, p. 255). Again, at the Southwark Cathedral speech, it was stressed that individuals having a stake in employment, housing, education and the reinvention of community were part of a combined assault on social disaffection and the disintegration of society as in the US, the 'Blade Runner' scenario. Work, opportunities and a new sense of community would create a unified society. He again asserted, 'Our values do not change....But the way of achieving that vision must change' (Blair, Southwark Cathedral speech, 29 January 1996). On community, Blair continued:

For myself, I start from a simple belief that people are not separate economic actors competing in the market place of life. They are citizens of a community. We are social beings, nurtured in families and communities and human only because we develop the moral power of personal responsibility for ourselves and each other. Britain is strongest as a team than as a collection of selfish players (Blair, Southwark Cathedral, 1996).

This is New Labour's 'one nation, one community' Third Way politics (Blair, Southwark Cathedral, 1996). A stakeholder society is one with greater inclusion and mutual responsibility (Deacon, 1996, p. 3; Clarke and Newman, 1997, pp. 136-137; White, 1999). This credo allows New Labour to avoid the old Labour politics of class affiliations and exclusive politics and reach other social groups. It provides an argument that eschews Tory market individualism though not social markets. Collective action is accepted and encouraged but not solely state action (Driver and Martell, 1998, pp. 28 and 33). Clarke and Newman (1997) also note that it 'identifies the realm of the 'social', insisting that society is composed of more than an aggregate of self-willed individuals and their families.' (Clarke and Newman, 1997, p. 131). This is what Blair calls 'social-ism' (Blair, 1994, p. 4). Within this communitarian paradigm are three elements, social cohesion, economic efficiency and morality. This domino effect Driver and Martell (1997) explain thus:

Economic success – particularly more jobs – will bring greater social cohesion, which is further strengthened by a more dutiful and responsible citizenry, and more social cohesion will in turn create a more viable market economy (Driver and Martell, 1997, p. 34).

The Third Way is a moral code also. Christian socialism is at the heart of this paradigm. Christian socialism has more influence than any other core idea. It is the genesis of the Third Way and forms its guiding ethos. This is New Labour's meta-narrative. It is seen in its communitarianism, stakeholding and inclusive initiatives. This philanthropic Christian ethos of the nineteenth and early twentieth century has been, almost subliminally, reaffirmed and placed at the centre of the Party's thinking. It forms the Party's moral mindset. The future 'New Britain' with its progressive and inclusive socio-economic system is entirely inspired from the Christian socialist ethos that inspired Tawney, Hardie, Attlee, Green, Temple, Scott Holland and Beveridge (Wilkinson, 1999, p. 40; Foote, 1997, pp. 42-44 and 73). Blair (like John Smith) is a member of the Christian Socialist Movement (affiliated to Labour in 1986), so are Straw and Field (Wilkinson, 1999, pp. 45-47). From the early 1990s Blair expressed overtly Christian socialist values. In 1993, as Shadow Home Secretary, he stated that people cannot exist in 'a moral vacuum' (Blair, cited in Sopel 1995, pp. 154-155). Blair sees it as a direct counter to Thatcherism's divisive individualism. As the original Christian socialist, F. D. Maurice (1805-72) believed, Christianity was a 'communal not individualistic faith' (Wilkinson, 1999, p. 39). It is compatible with communitarian ideas. It is also a counter to Left-wing utopianism and can appeal across political boundaries. At the 1995 Party Conference, Blair expressed this moral code, 'Socialism to me was never about nationalisation or the power of the state....It is a moral purpose in life...I am my brother's keeper. I will not walk by on the other side....This is my socialism' (Blair, 3 October 1995, Labour Party Conference). This is where Blair's view on community and mutuality stem from, a 'something for something' society (Blair, 29 January 1996, Southwark Cathedral speech). Such statements and the Third Way ethos can be traced to the writings of Tawney and early Christian socialists (Tawney, 1921 and 1926; Temple, 1942; Wescott, 1890). For Tawney, Christian morals and socialism were the same thing (Foote, 1997, p. 74). The primary problem socially was the loss of Christian moral direction in communities, leaving only selfish acquisition (Tawney, 1921, p. 32).

This moral code is at the heart of New Labour thinking, effectively inculcating a Christian socialist consensus into peoples' lives and communities by actively encouraging a new moral code and communitarian structure, 'changing the mindset' (Blair, 1996, p. vi). This is to be achieved via policies that positively change peoples lives, based on social democratic Christian values. This Third Way moral ethic is the thinking of New Labour. Christian socialism was arguably communitarianism before communitarianism. Such a community web of mutual obligations and duties form the basis of a cohesive society, which the government then actively maintains. A dynamic project that, New Labour argues, would alleviate socio-economic problems and carry people with them. On 1 May 1997, New Labour won a landslide of 419 seats (44.4% of votes, an increase of 148 seats) a majority of 179 seats (Fielding, 1997b, p. 23; Geddes and Tonge, 1997, p. 1; Sanders, 1997, p. 47; Dunleavy, 1997, p. 3). Notably, three quarters of unskilled, over half of skilled, almost half of office workers and almost a third of professionals voted New Labour (Fielding, 1997b, p. 23). Blair had changed the 'mindset' (Blair, 1996, p. vi). After the election, in Malmo, Blair stated:

> Our task today is not to fight old battles but to show that there is a third way, a way of marrying together an open, competitive and successful economy with a just, decent and humane society (Blair, 6 June 1997, Speech to the European Socialist Congress, Sweden).

The shape of things to come had arrived. This was the new politics of the new times.

The Originality of the Third Way

'Blairism' is a response to fundamental political and socio-economic changes and a seeming decline in the social democratic consensus. It is a programme of pragmatic policies to achieve social democratic objectives and not 'righteous aspirations' (Commission on Social Justice, 1994, p. 17) to reverse socio-economic decline, to rebuild society and move out of the impasse that Britain had been in. New Labour is the fruition of these conditions and policy imperatives. New Labour represents a significant evolution in the Party's politics and agenda, that owes more to its old Labour revisionist and Christian socialist past. New Labour's ideas can be traced directly to the debates of the 1950s and 1960s and the genesis of democratic socialism with the Fabians and Independent Labour Party of the 1880s to 1900s (Vincent, 1998, p. 51). Out of a need to re-emphasise the meaning and purpose of the Third Way, Blair (1998, p. 1) asserted it stood for a modernised social democracy and the 'goals of the centre Left', but 'flexible, innovative and forward-looking in the means to achieve them'. It was not an attempt to 'split the difference' between Left and Right, but a 'serious reappraisal of social democracy, reaching deep into the values of the Left to develop radically new approaches' (ibid.). Pragmatism was necessary to put social democratic values into effect: 'what matters is what works to give effects to our lives....I believe that a critical dimension of the Third Way is that policies flow from values, not vice versa' (ibid., p. 4). Accordingly, the Third Way is an approach is 'permanent revisionism', a continued search for better means to meet our goals, based on a clear view of the changes taking place in advanced industrialised societies' (ibid.). The Third Way is a 'modernised social democracy for a changing world', built on unshakable values of community and mutuality and a commitment to modernization, 'to shape the future by embracing change not seeking to defy it' (ibid., p. 20).

Blair is keen to ally New Labour's paradigm with past socialist, social democratic and Liberal figures like Crosland, Keynes and Beveridge (Blair, 1996, p. 7; Freeden, 1999a, p. 43 and 1999b, p. 151; Gould, 1999, p. 234). New Labour's pragmatic stance is seen in its underlying Christian socialist ethic and 'new dynamic economy' (Blair, 1998, p. 8). The post-1983 Kinnock and Smith era was like that of the 1950s. Labour realised it had to broaden its electoral base. Merely keeping the faith was not enough, as with the 1950s, one last 'big push' would not achieve a Labour government. Politics had fundamentally changed, the Labour Party had not changed with it. Likewise, the intense infighting that consumed the Labour Party throughout the 1980s was a repeat of those damaging debates between the Gaitskell and Bevan wings of the 1950s. While it is true that comparative prosperity did exist during the 1950s, rather as Crosland (*The Future of Socialism*, 1956) argued, many of Labour's agendas were becoming irrelevant. In the 1980s this was not the case, endemic deprivation being widespread. Labour continued to be unelectable however. This is the determining point that proved Labour had not modernised with society and its former supporters. Again, as with Gaitskell's amendments to Clause IV in 1960 (Labour Party, 1960, p. 12), Kinnock was only able to put forward compromises, reflected in the 1987 manifesto *Britain Will Win* and *Meet the Challenge, Make the Change* (1989), endorsing a qualified market economy – a pragmatic centrist direction though without a 'central theme' (Kinnock, 1994, p. 545). The Smith era after 1992 reflected a more concerted effort to modernise and a realisation that society and politics had changed and that if Labour continued as it was it would be in opposition permanently. As Crosland had contended decades before, there was a need to reassert social democratic thought into mainstream politics (Crosland, 1956). The Party's constitution had 'failed to keep pace' with social changes (Straw, 1993, p. 4) and the inadequacy of the one big push strategy was shown in the 1992 defeat, as it had in 1955 and 1959.

Fundamental and faster change was essential, which is reflected in the arguments of Blair, Brown, Straw, Mandelson, Gould and others. Labour had lost because it had not modernised completely. There was, after July 1994, with Blair, the opportunity for more dynamic and faster change, the emphasis again inspired by revisionist and pragmatic ideas of ethical socialism (Crosland, 1956, p. 116). Consequently, debates over economic organisation theories were dead, or 'relegated to means, not ends' (Blair, 1991, p. 33). This is a theme of Crosland's, the 'confusion between ends and means' (Crosland, 1956, p. 100). Much of this ethical socialism is not based around class or sectional interests or economic proscriptions but, it contends, had learned from history (Blair, 1994, p. 4). Out of this it was possible for Blair and the modernisers, unlike Gaitskell, to put forward a broader-based agenda and rewrite Clause IV, out of which came New Labour. This was the triumph of ethical socialist revisionism.

White Heat of a Knowledge Economy

New Labour's economic argument is arguably post-Fordist/post-industrial. It is contended that the politics of the Left was an expression of this old economic order and that the Right 'retained a strong aristocratic and paternalistic streak as late as the 1960s' (Blair, 1998, p. 8). Both were seen as inadequate for economic sustainability. The new economy (like the politics) is fundamentally different, wherein knowledge, skills, innovation, enterprise and technology are the cornerstones of the economy. It is argued that its most valuable assets are 'knowledge and creativity', a successful economy will 'excel at generating and dissemination knowledge, and commercially exploiting it' (ibid.) This echoes post-industrial concepts of a 'knowledge society' (Bell, 1974, pp. 189 and 212). It is also similar to Wilson's 1963 speech on harnessing the 'scientific revolution' and that this 'white heat' of technological change would require a new ethos for government, business and unions and an end to 'practices' or 'outdated methods' (Wilson, 1963, Scarborough, Labour Party Conference). It is contended that New Labour's partnership with business is critical for material prosperity, wealth generation and development (Labour Party, 1994, p. 21 and 1995b, p. 4). This is new Keynesian 'Implicit Contract Theory'. The economy, business and the achievement of the government's objectives have to be based in an environment of sustainable economic growth, a new Keynsian concept of 'market equilibrium' wherein government and its agencies have an active role (Shaw, McCrostie and Greenaway, 1997, pp. 298-299). The role of the state is that of facilitating economic sustainability, investment (publicly and economically), growth, encouraging re-skilling, educational and training opportunities and life-long learning. In co-ordinating tax and benefit changes (Working Families Tax Credit, New Deals and a minimum wage etc.), the Third Way identifies an approach to economic reality (Kelly, 1999, pp. 103-104; Dept. of Social Security, 1998).

This is seen as essential due to the realities of the late modernity period, where, in macro-economic policy terms, medium-sized nations cannot 'go it alone' (Blair, 1998, p. 8). Again, the government's role of equipping individuals and communities for the future is like the 1964 'New Britain' vision of harmonising talents, skills and technology to reverse the decline of the pre-1964 regime; new opportunities that would be economically necessary and socially just (Labour Party, 1964, pp. 3 and 23-24). Renewal, then as now, would be via ending stop-go economics for stability that is intrinsic to social development. The importance of sustainability is continually stressed 'The Left can only be successful if it demonstrates economic competence' (Blair, 1998, p. 9). It is also electorally expedient. It now fully accepts that 'Whereas capitalism may be impossible without markets, socialist markets can function without full-blooded capitalism' (Vincent, 1998, p. 53). Such an economic paradigm and set of policies are far from being a continuation of Thatcherite free market economics. It recognises sustainability is essential, without which any social democratic objectives of wider equality, opportunity and maintaining progressive politics generally is unachievable (Brown, 1994; 1997; 1999; Thompson, 1996, p. 278). It also offers, 'a stronger counterbalance to contemporary conservatism' (Hutton, 1999, p. 98). It is greatly influenced by past revisionist sentiments and agendas. The approach of Blair and New Labour of permanent revisionism represents arguably a consolidation of Croslandite revisionist politics.

The Class War is Over, Social-ism Won

New Labour does have a 'radical centre' pragmatism (Giddens, 1998, pp. 44-45). It has to be pragmatic to achieve its core social democratic objectives. Driver and Martell (1998, p. 3) believe New Labour has attempted to strike a balance between economic success and social inclusion, the market and the community. New Labour offered a greater popular sensitivity in politics, and a concern for those left behind. With regard to the political landscape, they stress (1998, p. 3) that there

> is no going back to the pre-Thatcher era... . But on this ground changes have to be made, often guided by sentiments which are far from Thatcherite. What New Labour has become is defined by Thatcherism. But the new Labour government is post-Thatcherite.

Driver and Martell also believe it is wrong to say Left and Right influences are now gone, they are still relevant and still there. The old ideologies that formed and guided the Left and Right are still present politically, economically and culturally. Though they are less overtly utilised they continue to have influence on perceptions of social problems and policies. They may be 'echoes' of the past 'crashes' of both old social democracy and Thatcherism (Mulgan, 1997, p. xviii), but they are still relevant and observable in political discourses and paradigms.

There is certainly no 'end of ideology', despite the changes internationally with the end of Stalinism, collapse of neo-liberal conservativism and globalisation. While New Labour attacks the Tories as being an ideological party led by dogma and claims itself to be beyond Left and Right (Labour Party, 1997, p. 19), the Labour Party still has a belief system behind it (Wright, 1999, pp. 193-201). The communitarianism embraced is a break with neo-liberal conservatism and is a reassertion of Christian socialism. This is a departure also from 'statist' social democracy; however, it is more interventionist than Thatcherism (Driver and Martell, 1998, p. 181). New Labour's project is cleverly designed, taking account of socio-economic change and political realities. Labour has reformed old social democracy and has accommodated itself to the changes in politics of the past thirty years. However, New Labour is a distinct reaction against

Thatcherism. Driver and Martell (1998, p. 184) believe that New Labour combines Left and Right rather than transcending them, concluding that

> while pragmatic, it is not just that: it is driven also by ideological belief. It is defined by, but departs from, Thatcherism – moved to the Right but with anti-Thatcherite emphasis. New Labour's politics are defined both by Right and by Leftwards inclinations which are beyond old Left. These are the politics of post-Thacherism.

In the 2001 election campaign Blair again asserted the need to move beyond Thatcherism and a 'clean break with the politics of the 1980s' and juxtaposed Thatcherism's 'no such thing as society' with Labour's communitarian paradigm (Blair, Moving Beyond Thatcherism speech, South Yardley, Birmingham, 5 June 2001). Thatcherism did change the language of consensus to a reciprocal relationship of consumers and deserving poor. New Labour's Third Way Christian socialism and pragmatic approach in achieving its objectives is a different language, one that does strive to be consensual and inclusive. While morally prescriptive, New Labour's initiatives for the unemployed and dependent communities and its holistic approach are fundamentally different from the past, both Thatcherism and old Labour, though inspired by its past.

The Future of Ideological Politics in the UK

Ideologies will play a part in politics, as Blair said, 'politics is first and foremost about ideas' (Blair, 1998, p. 1), but the way this will happen will be different. This will be a post-industrial politics wherein government is broadly 'liberal', as Bell postulated (Bell, 1974, p. 164). The socio-political changes of the last thirty years and eighteen wasted Tory years have had a significant impact on society, vast tracts of it impoverished and endemically fractured. Many of the past changes, while not irreversible, will take time and political dexterity to resolve. Consequently, New Labour's policies, particularly on welfare and public policy will still have ideological underpinnings that are distinct from the Tory years.

Looking at the main parties, while New Labour has captured and consolidated its position on the centre-Left of consensual, social democratic politics, the Tories are moving towards divisive political objectives. This will continue, a form of Right-wing populism that just is not popular. After two crushing election defeats, seeing widespread tactical voting against them, the Conservatives are in political meltdown. The strength of the New Labour position has enormous implications for Blair's goal of a centre-Left coalition to keep conservatism out of office permanently. The desire to have a broad coalition and entrench a centre-Left hegemony was expressed in *Leading Britain into the Future*, stating, 'We seek the broadest possible support for this vision of a new Britain' (Labour Party, 1997, p. 19). It is feasible that a coalition or even merger between Labour and the Liberal Democrats could emerge in the future (Dunleavy, 1997, pp. 12 and 14; Wheen, 1999, p. 5). Philip Gould, Blair's former senior adviser, argued for a 'progressive coalition' to dominate the twenty-first century, this offering greater radical change. Gould believes this to be inevitable due to 'all-embracing' global change and its social impacts, an age of 'permanent revolution' (Gould, 1999, pp. 393-395). A 'new middle class' of 'aspirational working class' and insecure middle/low-income white-collar groups are 'the key to the progressive century', as they share a commitment to the NHS, education and the family, and will increasingly support parties that equip them to 'manage change' (ibid., pp. xix and 396-397). Gould asserts that, to resolve the 'progressive dilemma', the new alliance has to endure, the party has to be 'one broad, pluralist political grouping' (ibid., p. 397). To build this 'progressive alliance' Labour and the Liberal Democrats have to converge, 'effectively becoming one party' (ibid., pp. 398-399) With Labour's domination of the centre-Left, the Liberal Democrats will be pushed towards acceptance of many of its policies and objectives. It is likely that Labour and the Liberal Democrats will co-operate in future elections. It is highly likely that constitutional changes, devolution and regional assemblies will result in a dominant social democratic politics; wherein the battle of ideas is not a battle between capitalism and socialism, but rather between 'the forces of progress and the forces of conservatism' (Blair, Bournemouth conference speech, 28 September 1999).

There is indeed a need to move on into the new political terrain, make the vision a reality and make social democratic politics irreversible (Wright, 1999, pp. 193-201; Gould, 1999; Wilkinson, 1996, pp. 226-252). Far from accepting New Right ideology, social democratic politics has emerged stronger than ever. As Gamble and Wright (1999, p. 4) state,

> Far from dying with the twentieth century, social democracy has now opportunities and new challenges, with Left of center thought having a new vibrancy, freed from the straightjackets of the cold war and the long division of the socialist movement between state collectivist and social democrats.

Sharper issue politics will continue to be seen, particularly on globalisation, racism and specific policy minutiae. However, minority politics is not important to most people and the government knows this (Gould, 1999, pp. 158-159 and 257-259). The future of ideological politics, at least in a UK context, is one where it will be dominated by consensual social democratic all embracing paradigms, that are pragmatic to maintain political power. As Blair has argued 'We must remain the party of progress, of the future. Our values matter. Believe in them. But the means of realising them is not a question of ideology, but of what works' (Labour's 100th anniversary speech, Old Vic Theatre, London, 27 February 2000). New Labour is implementing reforms that will significantly alter the social structure and future of politics. New Labour's Third Way paradigm can become the eradicator of conservatism. After 1 May 1997 Britain did indeed enter a new political era.

Conclusion

In conclusion, it is clear that the Labour Party's ideology has changed. Certainly after 1987, electability was a primary goal in policy formulation, to counter the seeming hegemony of Thatcherism, post-Fordist globalisation and its socio-political impacts – all apparent in the rethinking, from Kinnock to Smith and culminating with the Blair reformation. There were within these debates, however, concerns for social renewal. With Blair and increased modernisation it is clear that the core values of social democracy and Christian ethical socialism are increasingly reaffirmed to emphasise the socially progressive Third Way ethos of Blair's New Labour. Re-establishing its core identity by redefining Clause IV was a seminal event. There emerged a re-emphasis of community, mutuality, inclusion, interventionism and an economy of opportunity for stability and cohesion. This transformation and consensus building was a distinct hegemonic project and paradigm shift that looked to its origins for inspiration. It is a political shift, but the shift is in its pragmatism to achieve its goals. New concepts, that emerged with this paradigm, are attempts to change the social mindset and are a new way of re-conceptualising socio-economic problems for strategies to reverse decline. The government is aware that it has a responsibility and interventionist role to provide for society, unlike Thatcherism. This was to connect with people.

New Labour is more than image, its modernisation was the key. Its all-embracing paradigm is a consolidation of 1950s agendas, were the means of achieving objectives have changed. New Labour owes much to the ideas of Crosland and Christian socialist ethics. Past values and ideas have inspired and define New Labour, it has understood what is necessary to achieve its objectives and modernised accordingly. New Labour is far from being postmodern and rootless, it is not Thatcherism by other means. It is pragmatic, but not valueless. The Third Way is a response to a disintegration of social structures, identities and economic certainties, a set of solutions out of this impasse, underpinned by a Christian socialist moral ethos that itself can appeal to Left and centre perspectives to cut across political boundaries. New Labour will dominate mainstream politics with this all-embracing Third Way. It will stay on the centre-Left ground indefinitely. Progressive politics is all about 'progress', New Labour has learned the lessons of the past and moved on.

References

Abrams, M., Rose, R. and Hinden, R. (1960), *Must Labour Lose?*, Penguin, Harmondsworth.

Allen, J. (1992), 'Post-Industrialism and Post-Fordism', in S. Hall, D. Held, and T. McGrew (eds), *Modernity and its Futures*, Open University Press, Cambridge, pp. 169-204.

Baldwin, T. (2000), 'Lib-Lab Pact Paves Way for New Voting System', *The Times*, 2 June 2000, p. 1.

Bell, D. (1974), *The Coming of Post-Industrial Society*, Penguin, Harmondsworth.

Blair, T. (1991), 'Forging A New Agenda', *Marxism Today*, Oct, 35, pp. 32-34.

Blair, T. (1994), *Socialism*, Fabian pamphlet No. 565, Fabian Society, London.

Blair, T. (1995), *Let Us Face the Future*, Fabian pamphlet No. 571, Fabian Society, London.

Blair, T. (1996), *New Britain*, Fourth Estates Ltd, London.

Blair, T. (1998), *The Third Way: New Politics for the New Century*, Fabian pamphlet No. 588, Fabian Society, London.

Braverman, H. (1974), *Labour and Monopoly Capital: The Degradation of Work in the Twentieth Century*, Monthly Review Press, New York.

Brown, G. (1994), *Fair is Efficient*, Fabian pamphlet No. 563, Fabian Society, London.

Brown, G. (1997), 'The Iron Man', *Fabian Review*, 109, (1), pp. 1-2.

Brown, G. (1999), 'Equality – Then and Now', in D. Leonard (ed.), *Crosland and New Labour*, Macmillan in association with the Fabian Society, Houndmills, pp. 35-48.

Burrows, R. and Loader, B. (eds) (1994), *Towards a Post-Fordist Welfare State?*, Routledge, London.

Butler, D. and Stokes, D. (1974), *Political Changes in Britain*, Macmillan, London.

Clarke, J., Cochrane, A. and Smart, C. (1987), *Ideologies of Welfare*, Routledge, London.

Clarke, J. and Newman, J. (1997), *The Managerial State*, Sage, London.

Commission on Social Justice, (1993a), *The Justice Gap*, Institute for Public Policy Research, London.

Commission on Social Justice, (1993b), *Social Justice in a Changing World*, Institute for Public Policy Research, London.

Commission on Social Justice, (1994), *Social Justice: Strategies for National Renewal*, Vintage, London.

Coxall, B. and Robins, L. (1998), *Contemporary British Politics*, Macmillan, London.

Crosland, A. (1956), *The Future of Socialism*, Cape, London.

Deacon, A. (ed.) (1996), 'Editorial Introduction', in F. Field, *Stakeholder Welfare*, IEA Health and Welfare Unit, London, pp. 1-6.

Department of Social Security, (1998), *New Ambitions for our Country: A New Contract for Welfare*, (Cm. 3805), Dept. of Social Security, London.

Driver, S. and Martell, L. (1998), *New Labour: Politics After Thatcher*, Polity Press, Cambridge.

Dunleavy, P. (1997), 'Introduction: "New Times" in British Politics', in P. Dunleavy, A. Gamble, I. Holliday, and G. Peele (eds), *Developments in British Politics 5*, Macmillan, London, pp. 1-19.

Fielding, S. (1997a), *The Labour Party: Socialism and Society since 1951*, Manchester University Press, Manchester.

Fielding, S. (1997b), 'Labour's Path to Power', in A. Geddes and J. Tonge (eds), *Labour's Landslide*, Manchester University Press, Manchester, pp. 23-35.

Foote, G. (1997), *The Labour Party's Political Thought: A History*, Macmillan, Houndmills.

Freeden, M. (1999a), 'The Ideology of New Labour', in *Political Quarterly*, 70, (1) pp. 42-51.

Freeden, M. (1999b), 'True Blood or False Genealogy: New Labour and British Social Democratic Thought', in A. Gamble and T. Wright (eds), *The New Social Democracy*, Blackwell, Oxford, pp. 151-165.

Gamble, A. (1990), 'The Thatcher Decade in Perspective', in P. Dunleavy, A. Gamble and G. Peele (eds), *Developments in British Politics 3*, Macmillan, London, pp. 333-358.

Gamble, A. (1994), *The Free Economy and the Strong State*, Macmillan, London.

Gamble, A. and Wright, T. (eds), (1999), *The New Social Democracy*, Blackwell, Oxford.

Geddes, A. and Tonge, J. (eds), (1997), *Labour's Landslide*, Manchester University Press, Manchester.

George, V. and Wilding, P. (1992), *Ideology and Social Welfare*, Routledge, London.

Giddens, A. (1998), *The Third Way: The Renewal of Social Democracy*, Polity Press, Cambridge.

Goldthorpe, J., Lockwood, D., Bechofer, F. and Platt, J. (1968), *The Affluent Worker: Political Attitudes and Behaviour*, Cambridge University Press, Cambridge.

Gould, P. (1999), *The Unfinished Revolution: How the Modernizers Saved the Labour Party*, Abacus, London.

Grice, A. (2001), 'Blair and Kennedy thrash out PR deal', *The Independent*, 23 March, p. 4.

Hall, S. (1988), *The Hard Road to Renewal*, Verso, London.

Heath, A., Jowell, R., Curtice, J., Evans, G., Field, J. and Witherspoon, S. (1991), *Understanding Political Change: The British Voter 1964-87*, Pergamon, Oxford.

Hutton, W. (1999), 'New Keynesianism and New Labour', in A. Gamble and T. Wright (eds), *The New Social Democracy*, Blackwell, London, pp. 97-102.

Jessop, B. (1994), 'The Transition to Post-Fordism and the Schumpterian Workfare State', in R. Burrows and B. Loader (eds), *Towards a Post-Fordist Welfare State?*, Routledge, London, pp. 13-37.

Johnson, N. (1990), *Reconstructing the Welfare State*, Harvester Wheatsheaf, Hemel Hempstead.

Jones, T. (1996), *Remaking the Labour Party: From Gaitskell to Blair*, Routledge, London.

Kelly, R. (1999), 'Response to Will Hutton', in A. Gamble and T. Wright (eds), *The New Social Democracy*, Blackwell, London, pp. 103-104.

Kinnock, N. (1985), *The Future of Socialism*, Fabian pamphlet No. 509, Fabian Society, London.

Kinnock, N. (1994), 'Reforming the Labour Party', in *Contemporary Record*, 8 (3), p. x.

Kolberg, J. E. and Esping-Anderson, G. (1992), 'Welfare States and Employment Regimes', in J. E. Kolberg (ed.), *The Study of Welfare State Regimes*, Sharpe M. E., New York, pp. 3-36.

Labour Party (1960), *Report of the Fifty-Ninth Annual Conference of the Labour Party*, Labour Party, London.

Labour Party (1964), *Let's Go with Labour. The Labour Party's Manifesto for the 1964 General Election*, Labour Party, London.

Labour Party (1987), *Britain Will Win*, Labour Party, London.

Labour Party (1989), *Meet the Challenge, Make the Change*, Labour Party, London.

Labour Party (1994), *Rebuilding the Economy*, Labour Party, London.

Labour Party (1995a), *Constitution: Labour's Aims and Values*, Labour Party, London.

Labour Party (1995b), *A New Economic Future for Britain*, Labour Party, London.

Labour Party (1997), *Leading Britain into the Future*, Labour Party, London.

Marquand, D. (1991), *The Progressive Dilemma*, Heinmann, London.

Moran, M. (1989), *Politics and Society in Britain*, Macmillan, London.

Mulgan, G. (1997), *Life After Politics: New Thinking for the Twenty First Century*, Fontana, London.

O'Gorman, F. (1986), *British Conservatism: Conservative Thought from Burke to Thatcher*, Longman, London.

Peele, G. (1990), 'Parties, Pressure Groups and Parliament', in P. Dunleavy, A. Gamble and G. Peele (eds), *Developments in British Politics 3*, Macmillan, London, pp. 69-95.

Pelling, H. and Reid, A. J. (1996), *A Short History of the Labour Party*, Macmillan, London.

Penna, S. and O'Brien, M. (1996), 'Postmodernism and Social Policy: A Small Step Forward?', *Journal of Social Policy*, 25 (1), pp. 39-61.

Rentoul, J. (1995), *Tony Blair*, Little Brown and Co, London.

Robins, L. and Savage, S.B. (1990), *Public Policy Under Thatcher*, Macmillan, London.

Sanders, D. (1997), 'Voting and the Electorate', in P. Dunleavy, A. Gamble, I. Holliday and G. Peele (eds), *Developments in British Politics 5*, Macmillan, London, pp. 45-74.

Shaw, E. (1994), *The Labour Party since 1979*, Routledge, London.

Shaw, E. (1996), *The Labour Party since 1945*, Blackwell, Oxford.

Shaw, G.K., McCrostie, M.J. and Greenaway, D. (1997), *Macroeconomics: Theory and Policy in the UK*, Blackwell, Oxford.

Sopel, J. (1995), *Tony Blair: The Modernizer*, Michael Joseph, London.

Straw, J. (1993), *Policy and Ideology*, Blackburn Labour Party, Blackburn.

Tawney, R. H. (1921), *The Acquisitive Society*, G. Bell and Sons, London.

Tawney, R. H. (1926), *Religion and the Rise of Capitalism*, John Murray, London.

Temple, W. (1942), *Christianity and the Social Order*, Penguin, Harmondsworth.

Thompson, N. (1996), *Political Economy and the Labour Party*, University College London, London.

Tomlinson, J. (1997), 'Economic Policy: Lessons from Past Labour Governments', in B. Brivati and T. Bale (eds), *New Labour in Power: Precedents and Prospects*, Routledge, London, pp. 11-27.

Vincent, A. (1998), 'New Ideologies for Old?', *Political Quarterly*, 69, (1), pp. 48-58.

Westcott, B. F. (1890), *Socialism*, Guild of St. Matthew, London.

Wheen, F. (1999), 'In Search of Liberals Past', *The Guardian*, 1 Dec, p. 5.

White, S. (1999), ' 'Rights and Responsibilities': A Social Democratic Perspective', in A. Gamble and T. Wright (eds), *The New Social Democracy*, Blackwell, Oxford, pp. 166-179.

Wilkinson, H. (1996), 'The Making of A Young Country', in M. Perryman (ed.), *The Blair Agenda*, Lawrence and Wishart, London, pp. 226-252.

Wilkinson, A. (1999), 'New Labour and Christian Socialism', in G. R. Taylor (ed.), *The Impact of New Labour*, Macmillan, London, pp. 37-49.

Wright, T. (1999), 'New Labour, Old Crosland?', in D. Leonard (ed.), *Crosland and New Labour*, Macmillan in association with the Fabian Society, Houndmills, pp. 193-200.

6 Northern Ireland: Plenty of Problems for the Future

MARK COWLING

Introduction

This chapter discusses the major background considerations which will influence developments in Northern Ireland over the next few years. Current issues in the politics of Northern Ireland have long historical roots, and the chapter therefore starts with a brief review of the historical background. It discusses the major parties and organisations involved, arguing that they make better sense if it is assumed they represent two nations. The chapter concludes by discussing the four main issues likely to dominate the next few years: the limited value of the Good Friday Agreement to Northern Ireland's Protestants, decommissioning, demographics and the role of cross-border institutions. It is argued that in the long term the evolution of the Republic into a more affluent and secular society and the deepening of the European Union may somewhat defuse the issue of the border.

Historical Background

As Irish nationalism developed in the nineteenth century, its proponents tended to talk of an Irish race and depict the Northern Protestants as an alien race introduced by the Plantation of 1607 (see below).

Settlement, 'invasion', Plantation, division

The racial and cultural origins of contemporary Irish people are, however, much more complex. The westward movement of peoples across Europe had to stop at the Atlantic, so that any group which reached Ireland stayed there. The Gaels or Celts may have been the last of four waves of invaders (Stewart, 1977, p. 29), arriving in 'a few centuries B.C.' (Kee, 1972, p. 9).

It was, however, Gaelic culture which prevailed, undisturbed by the Romans, who never invaded Ireland. This culture managed to absorb many Norse invaders, although the high point of the Gaelic tribes politically was the defeat of invading Norsemen by the High King Brian Boru in AD 1014. After Boru the clans fell apart again, and his successors were known as 'King with opposition'. The 'English invasion' of Ireland, which occurred in 1170, and started '800 years of oppression', was actually the result of Norman adventurers, speaking Norman French, and seeking land, accepting the invitation of an Irish chief, Dermot MacMurrough, to help in his fight against other Irish chiefs (Kee, 1972, p. 10). The Norman chiefs had feudal obligations to the English King Henry II, hence the 'English' invasion. In fact the Norman Lords largely merged into Gaelic society.

In the North East of Ireland there had for a long time been migrations to and from South West Scotland (at this stage to talk of 'Scots' or 'Irish' would be misleading). This tradition was continued in the thirteenth century with a migration of Scottish mercenaries to North East Ireland (Stewart, 1977, p. 36). These 'wild Scottish' were an obstacle to attempts to assert the authority of the English crown in Ireland.

During the Middle Ages English authority in Ireland was nominal, except for the small area of the Pale around Dublin, where English laws usually prevailed. This position altered from 1541, when Henry VIII decided to impose an effective administration on the chiefs. He got them to surrender their lands to him, and immediately regranted them, only now under English laws of succession. Other Tudor monarchs continued this policy. Objections to 'grant and regrant' were met with confiscation, and some attempts at plantation were made under Queen Mary. The most effective resistance to the Tudors came from the O'Neills of Ulster. Hugh O'Neill, Earl of Tyrone, was actually only defeated just after the death of Elizabeth I. O'Neill stayed in Ulster until 1607, hoping his fortunes would change, but then gave up hope, and fled to the Continent with his allies and followers ('The Flight of the Earls'). This was seen as treachery, and the Earls' lands were confiscated. Plantations were established in Armagh, Cavan, Coleraine (Londonderry), Donegal, Fermanagh and Tyrone (i.e. six of the nine Ulster counties, excluding Antrim, Down and Monaghan). A small part of each county was reserved for deserving natives; some given to people who were allowed to take Irish tenants at high rents; and much to 'undertakers' who had to settle their land with Protestant English or Scottish farmers, Scots settlers now being acceptable because James I had succeeded Elizabeth and was also king of Scotland.

Large numbers of planters came over, but not enough to completely settle the plantation areas, and the 'undertakers' accepted Irish tenants in breach of their contracts. In fact, it seems, 'a very substantial proportion of the original population was not disturbed at all' (Stewart, 1977, p. 25), and it seems that many of these were ultimately assimilated into the Protestant, British culture the settlers brought with them – hence the Gaelic family names of many Protestants: first names are a good clue to religious identity in modern Northern Ireland, but surnames are not. Nevertheless, the Gaelic lords and their followers took refuge in the mountains, and engaged in lamentations and raiding.

Modern Northern Ireland is based on the counties which, in 1919, had Protestant majorities or slight Catholic majorities. It can readily be seen that it is not solely based on plantation. Four planted counties became part of what is now the Republic, whereas the counties closest to Scotland, Antrim and Down, did not require plantation as they already contained many Scots settlers, and it was on these that the success of plantation elsewhere in Ulster depended. In fact Stewart argues that 'the real Scots plantation' was the gradual settlement of Eastern Ulster over the rest of the seventeenth century (Stewart, 1977, pp. 38, 81).

The industrial revolution must have encouraged a great deal of additional migration of Protestant skilled workers from the mainland to the Belfast area, attracted by good rates of pay (Bell, 1976, p. 18). Indeed, today almost two thirds of the population of Northern Ireland live within 30 miles of Belfast. At that time migration would have simply been from one country of the UK to another, on the lines of an English person going to work in Swansea or Glasgow today. The plantation of Ulster may have been artificial, but survived only because it had natural foundations.

Bitterness and division between Protestant and Catholic in Northern Ireland was frequently reinforced. The Rising of 1641 in the North took the form of massacres of Protestant settlers by Catholics seeking the return of their lands. It was brutally put down by Cromwell, a third of the Catholic Irish being killed and many sold into slavery during the eleven years of war. Cromwell's settlement left only a quarter of Ireland's cultivable land in Catholic hands, down from two thirds before the rising (Kee, 1972, p. 16).

A further divisive episode was the Glorious Revolution of 1688. In England this took the form of a coup in which the Catholic James II was replaced by the Protestant William of Orange. The military events were mainly in Ireland, notably the Battle of the Boyne in 1690 in which

William of Orange defeated James's forces – still celebrated by Orangemen on July 12th each year – and the siege of Londonderry, where the apprentice boys closed the city gates against James's forces. They were largely motivated by fear of another Catholic attempt to reclaim their land. A noted event of the siege, which was eventually broken, was the defection of Governor Lundy, who was afraid of defeat and its consequences. He plays a significant part in the Ulster Protestant mentality - a community under siege is particularly endangered by betrayal from its leaders, the more so as it has a Catholic fifth column in its midst (Stewart, 1977, pp. 47-8). This legacy is important today, as English politicians are inclined to think that if they win over the leaders of Ulster Protestants the rest will follow. In fact any deal which departs too far from the views of rank and file Protestants leads to accusations that the leader is a Lundy and his replacement, as Northern Ireland Prime Ministers Terence O'Neill and Brian Faulkner learned to their cost.

William's victory led to further land confiscation, and the Penal laws imposed early in the eighteenth century in its wake also impeded Catholic land holding, so that by 1750 only 7 per cent of Ireland's land was held by Catholics. Catholics were also excluded from political life (Stewart, 1977, p. 104).

Towards the end of the eighteenth century there was a Protestant-led movement for independence culminating in the rising of the United Irishmen in 1798. Although seen by nationalists as a precursor of modern Republicanism the movement was largely inspired by the ideas of the French and American revolutions, and would have led to a secular republic more on the lines of the United States than of today's Republic of Ireland. This explains the paradox that many of the United Irishmen welcomed the Union of Great Britain and Ireland in 1801 in which the corrupt Irish parliament was abolished and 100 Irish MPs were incorporated into the Westminster parliament.

Economic division

Over the nineteenth century the North East of Ireland underwent spectacular economic development, linked to the industry of Southern Scotland and Northern England. Two Irish economies developed over the nineteenth century, both linked to England, but largely separated from each other. In the North, Belfast came to function as part of the North of England/South of Scotland industrial framework of textiles, shipbuilding and engineering, indeed, part-finished products were often shifted across the water for completion. The economic ties with the mainland included the supply to Northern Ireland of coal and iron, neither of which existed there in exploitable form, and the dependence of Northern Ireland on the UK market, and through it the Empire, for the sale of ocean liners, the output of the largest rope and tobacco works in the world, or the output of the Northern Ireland linen industry (by 1907 Belfast had more linen spindles than any other *country*) (BandICO 1972, McLaughlin, 1980, p. 21). In contrast the South developed as an agricultural society with only three relatively large industries, i.e. biscuits, Guinness and whiskey.

This economic division reinforced a political division on national lines. In the South there was a persistent demand for greater independence from England, be it in the form of demands for Home Rule or Fenian agitation, leading ultimately to the founding of Sinn Fein and the Irish Republican Army, and to effective independence from Britain under the Anglo-Irish Treaty of 1921. Episodes included O'Connell's campaign for repeal of the Union from 1832 onwards, Smith O'Brien's 'rising' of 1848, Fenian attempts at a rising in 1867, the campaign of the Home Rule League from 1873 onwards, the campaigns by Irish nationalists in the House of Commons which led to the three Home Rule Bills, the Easter Rising of 1916, the Sinn Fein victory in the 1918 general election, and the Anglo-Irish war of 1919-20. A desire for land reform provided much impetus: under the system of rack renting prevalent in the South any benefit from agricultural improvements was absorbed by the landlord, frequently a degenerate Anglo-Irish absentee, and land was sub-let amongst large numbers of tenants who farmed small plots. The potato famine of the 1840s was a consequence, and the laissez-faire indifference of the Westminster parliament as a million Irish people starved and another million emigrated in dreadful conditions fuelled nationalist aspirations. The lack of a middle class in the South increased the leadership role of the Catholic Church, which became strongly ultramontanist (i.e. subordinated to the Pope) in the 1840s, and Catholicism became a central feature of Irish identity (Larkin, 1987, 1975; Blanshard, 1972; BandICO, 1973). Beyond this as the nineteenth century progressed there was a revival of the Irish language and the culture associated with it. Thus independence for Ireland as a whole would have led to a strongly Catholic country dominated by small farmers. Tariffs would probably be imposed on imports to develop industry. The Irish language might become a requirement for public service jobs. There might also be moves to tax or even expropriate the industries of the North for the national benefit.

The measures described at the end of the last paragraph would be anathema to the Northern Protestants. They were comfortable with a British identity, or if they thought of themselves as Irish they did so in the way a Unionist Scot would describe him or herself as Scottish. The northern industries needed free trade or, at minimum, free trade with the British Empire, as the Irish market for ocean liners would be limited. They would benefit from cheap food, whilst the southern farmers would prefer food to be dear. They were not Catholic, and felt threatened by Papal edicts such as Ne Temere, which insisted the children of mixed marriages be brought up as Catholics, contrary to the traditions of Northern Ireland. They did not have a cultural background of Irish language, which they would at very best learn out of polite curiosity. The Protestants thus resisted moves to Home Rule *en bloc*, eventually forming the Unionist party and arming themselves before the First World War to resist the third Home Rule bill. Thus the partition of Ireland has democratic origins even if the boundary is irrational and Fermanagh and Tyrone had slight Catholic majorities.

A divided island

The state that emerged in the South fulfilled the Unionists' nightmares. In Articles 2 and 3 of the 1937 Constitution it laid claim to the whole island of Ireland. Article 8 gives Irish as the first national language, while English is 'recognised' as *a* second official language. The Constitution was plainly Catholic. Sections of the Constitution which referred to fundamental rights (Articles 41 to 44), namely those relating to the family, education, private property and religion, followed the encyclicals of Pope Pius XI and the summary of Catholic social principles in the Social Code of 1927. Article 41 declared that divorce is unconstitutional. Article 44 recognised the special position of the Holy Catholic Apostolic and Roman Church as the guardian of the faith professed by the great majority of the citizens. If we add to this the prohibition of the import and sale of contraceptives in 1935, the inclusion in the Constitution of the principle of censorship, which had been heavily enforced from 1930 onwards (see Adams, 1968), and the celebration of Catholic power at the Eucharistic Congress held in Dublin in 1932, the Catholic character of the state becomes apparent (Whyte, 1972, Blanshard, 1972, Chubb, 1970, p. 54; Schmitt, 1973, p. 48).

The Unionists were left in charge of a devolved parliament they did not initially want, and with one third of the population being Catholics, many of whom saw Northern Ireland as an institutionalised gerrymander and were loyal to the South instead. Where Catholics formed the majority on local councils they flew the tricolour, sent their minutes to Dublin and entered their schoolchildren for Dublin examinations. This problem was basically solved by the Leech Boundary Commission of 1922 which gerrymandered local government wards to produce Unionist majorities on the council, leaving only two Catholic dominated councils (Buckland, 1981, p. 60). Moreover, the Westminster exchequer in its settlements with Northern Ireland during the 1920s and 30s continued the traditional stingy provision for Irish needs despite Northern Ireland being hit very badly by the slump. Northern Ireland only started to be funded according to its needs after the Second World War (Lawrence, 1965). Thus politicians who had started with relatively generous instincts reverted to sectarian patterns. It is hardly surprising that Northern Ireland's Catholics remained sullen, not accepting the Northern Ireland state and resenting the gerrymandering of local government boundaries, unfair allocations of council housing and job discrimination. Politics under the Stormont Parliament, which lasted from 1921 to 1972, was always dominated by the Unionists, as one might expect given that the population was divided between Unionists and Nationalists. There was no outlet for Catholics wishing to make a constructive contribution to political life.

When the civil rights movement started in the late 1960s, the Northern Ireland government moved fairly rapidly to deal with the worst of the abuses. Unfortunately, however, the civil rights movement also led many in the Protestant community to fear that the Northern Ireland state itself was under attack. This led to assaults on peaceful demonstrations and to burning Catholics out of their homes, which culminated in the largest forced movement of population in Europe up until then since the Second World War. The revival of the IRA, and particularly of the Provisionals, was initially a response to attacks on Catholics and their homes. However, the IRA soon moved on to its traditional aim of removing the British from Ireland by force of arms, and the contemporary round of the Troubles began. By the 1990s both the security forces (i.e. the British army, the Royal Irish Regiment, the Royal Ulster Constabulary, and the RUC reserve) and the Provisionals concluded that a stalemate had been reached: the security forces could by no means eradicate IRA activity; on the other hand, the Provisionals were too small and weak to win by force of arms.

This in turn led on to the peace process, the Good Friday Agreement and the Northern Ireland Assembly.

Two Irish nations?

This breathless thumbnail sketch of the history of Northern Ireland is intended to show a number of things. It highlights quite how far apart are the two communities on the island of Ireland, and how much the politics of Northern Ireland are a zero-sum game in which what one side gains the other side loses. It suggests that of the very many theories put forward to explain the politics of Northern Ireland the two nations theory goes a long way to make sense of many phenomena, with the Unionists seen as a part of the British nation that lives on the island of Ireland. Theorists are divided on whether a nation is mainly identified by the subjective determination of its members to live together, or – at least partly – by objective factors such as geography, language, a common history, and economic cohesion. Whichever way this is played, Northern Protestants and Irish Catholics come out as the most sharply divided national groupings in the British isles (Protestant version) or these islands (Catholic version). We have seen above a long history of conflict, often armed, and a sharp economic division for most of the nineteenth and twentieth centuries. Add to this different flags, songs, heroes, newspapers, sports and above all religion, and a picture which looks very like a national division emerges. (For a comprehensive discussion of theories to explain the conflict see McGarry and O'Leary, 1995; for a specific discussion of the two nations theory see Gallagher, 1995.) It also offers a background to the very extensive segregation between Catholics and Protestants in Northern Ireland. Each community has its own housing, shopping, sports, education and newspapers. For many people there is very little mixing with members of the other community (Darby, 1976, p. 29; Boal et al., 1982).

Parties and Organisations

Parties and political organisations in Northern Ireland have occasional nuances of the standard left-right divisions characteristic of capitalist societies, but make much better sense when classified in relation to the national division in the province. We thus start with Unionist parties and move on to Nationalist ones.

The official Unionists, the Ulster Unionist Party (UUP), remain the largest of the Northern Ireland parties, holding 6 of the Westminster seats on 27 per cent of the vote in the 2001 Westminster general election. This is seriously down from its 34-38 per cent of the vote and 9-11 Westminster MPs the party achieved between 1983 when Northern Ireland was allocated 17 seats, and 1997. In the 1998 Assembly election (see below) the party obtained 21 per cent of the vote and 28 seats. The Unionists were effectively founded in 1886, their initial core comprising Irish Conservatism and Orangeism (Harbinson, 1973, pp. 8-10). The Unionist party is a thoroughly democratic party. Its governing body is the Ulster Unionist Council of almost a thousand members, which represents all the major unionist associations and the eighteen constituency bodies, and meets annually to elect a leader and an executive and to determine policy. The party ruled Northern Ireland from 1921 to 1972, and remains the largest unionist party despite several splits in the 1970s. Its majority has gone along with the peace process and its leader, David Trimble, was the First Minister of the Northern Ireland Assembly when that body was not suspended. However, a significant minority opposes collaboration with Sinn Fein in the power-sharing executive, leaving Trimble vulnerable and making him more intransigent about any issues of the day for fear of sharing the fate of Lundy.

The other main unionist party is the Democratic Unionist Party (DUP). Founded and led for many years by the Reverend Ian Paisley it has consistently opposed the Good Friday Agreement, arguing instead for a devolved assembly based on straightforward majority rule. Currently the party has five Westminster MPs with 22 per cent of the vote, in comparison to 14-20 per cent of the vote and two or three MPs since 1983. In the 1998 Assembly election the party received 18 per cent of the vote and 20 seats. The party developed from the Protestant Unionist Party formed to oppose the liberalising tendencies of Northern Ireland Prime Minister Terence O'Neill at the Stormont election of 1969, in which they won 38 per cent of the vote. Following from this very impressive result for a new party the DUP was launched in 1971. Although the party has flirted briefly with the idea of integrating Northern Ireland more fully with the UK, it has generally stood for majority rule devolution, and for resistance to political or cultural advancement for republican ideas.

There are other small Unionist parties: the UK Unionist Party (UKUP), comprising followers of Robert McCartney MP and which rejects the Good Friday Agreement; the Northern Ireland Unionist Party, a small breakaway from the UKUP; and the Progressive Unionist Party linked to the Ulster Volunteer Force, and which has been generally supportive of the peace process and the Good Friday Agreement. None of these are electorally significant.

The Alliance party is specifically neutral in the conflict. It is 'union-minded' because most people in Northern Ireland wish to retain the Union, but is not an advocate. Instead it wants people from both sides of the sectarian divide to work together, and is thus delighted with the development of the peace process and the Assembly, but concerned at the grudging way it has been implemented. The party is parasitic on the conflict, as it makes sense only in an electoral spectrum which ranges from orange to green. In recent elections it has gained from 2 to 8 per cent of the vote, 8 per cent being about the best the party could hope for. In elections for local government or the Assembly, which are held on a Single Transferable Vote (STV) proportional representation basis, the Alliance is normally the sticking point for voters from each side. Thus Unionists will number preferences on a list until they get to the Alliance but then will not express a preference between the Catholic parties; the same holds in reverse for Catholic voters.

The Social Democratic and Labour Party (SDLP), formed in 1974, was until 2001 the largest Catholic party in Northern Ireland. Despite the 'Labour' in its title, at various crunch points it clearly emerged as the moderate Catholic party, attracting virtually no Protestant votes and standing for a united Ireland by consent. In Westminster elections since 1983 it typically gained 21-24 per cent of the vote and three or four seats. It was supportive of the peace process and gained 22 per cent of the votes and 24 of the seats in the Assembly, where at the time of writing its leader since November 2001, Mark Durkan, was Deputy First Minister prior to the current suspension. In the 2001 Westminster election it was overtaken by Sinn Fein, who gained 22 per cent of the vote to the SDLP's 21 per cent and four MPs to their three.

Sinn Fein is the electoral wing of the Provisional IRA. Up to 1981 it took an abstentionist line on electoral politics on the grounds that it should not participate in illegitimate institutions which flout the will of the Irish people as manifest in the General Election of 1918 in which Sinn Fein, the electoral ancestor of the main parties in the Republic, won a majority of the seats. In that year the PIRA decided to move forward with 'an Armalite in one hand and a ballot paper in the other'. Initially it stood for the removal of British troops from Ireland and for reunification by physical force. It would typically win a third of the Catholic vote and gain one Westminster MP, who did not take his seat. Since the IRA ceasefire of 1994 its vote has gone up and in the 2001 Westminster election it overtook the SDLP, gaining 22 per cent of the vote and four MPs.

The Conservative Party is organised in Northern Ireland. After a promising start in 1992, when it fought 11 seats and gained a large vote for Lawrence Kennedy, the Conservative candidate in North Down, who came a good second, it has not been promoted with enthusiasm by Central Office and has not been electorally significant. Until October 2003 the Labour Party was not organised in Northern Ireland for reasons which are unclear, nor would it accept individual members from the province despite accepting them from, say, Kabul, Baghdad or Tehran. There is an undertow of feeling that the Party should be organised in an area of the UK with a large working class and where many trade unionists opt in to pay the political levy.

Paramilitary organisations are, of course, divided on sectarian lines. The most important is the Provisional IRA (PIRA), founded at the beginning of 1970 in a split with the more political and now defunct Official IRA. The PIRA initially got going to provide armed defence of Catholic areas against Protestant mobs, but soon switched to attempting to get rid of the British. Tactics have included bombings and shootings against the security forces, against 'collaborators' who provide services to the security forces (e.g. doing building work or delivering milk at police barracks), against economic targets in Northern Ireland, against outside businessmen (soon abandoned because of unpopularity in Catholic areas), against military targets on the mainland and in Europe, and, best of all in propaganda terms, against political and economic targets on the mainland: the 1984 Brighton bomb, which nearly killed Mrs Thatcher, the rocketing of 10 Downing Street, the Baltic Exchange bomb, the Canary Wharf bomb and the destruction of central Manchester. Despite being vastly outnumbered and outgunned by the security forces the PIRA managed to carry on a highly effective armed struggle from 1970 to its ceasefire in 1994. Apart from the Official IRA, rivals to the PIRA include the Irish National Liberation Army and splinter groups unable to stomach aspects of the peace process such as the Continuity IRA and the Real IRA.

People in the Nationalist community who want to advance its cause in arms or to defend the community have no legal options. They have to join the PIRA or one of its rivals. This in turn helps to maintain a high standard of idealism in many activists even though there must be some level of personal gain from racketeering intended to finance the armed struggle. This is less true in the Protestant community, where joining one of the security forces run by the state, the Royal Ulster Constabulary (RUC), now Police Service of Northern Ireland (PSNI), or the Royal Irish Regiment is a realistic and respectable option. There might still be a case for joining the paramilitaries because they are independent of the state. Thus they could not be made to do something inimical to the Unionist cause, such as stopping an Orange parade from taking a particular route, unlike the PSNI. Certainly, more suggestions of people feathering their own nests are applied to the Protestant paramilitaries. Another difference concerns the selection of targets. For the PIRA there are fairly credible legitimate targets readily available, as listed in the previous paragraph. For the Protestant paramilitaries the only fully legitimate targets are Republican paramilitaries, who are difficult to find for obvious reasons. This in turn points to two possibilities. One is getting information on supposed Republicans from members of the security forces, perhaps Protestants who are sure they know who the Republicans are, but cannot currently make any charges stick. A major scandal is emerging in the Stevens enquiry, which has concluded that the RUC Special Branch and Army's Force Research Unit was involved in arranging the murders of innocent Catholics. The other is simply targeting random Catholics in the hope that the terror caused to the Catholic community generally will lead the PIRA to ease off on its current activities. The main Protestant paramilitary organisations are the Ulster Defence Association (UDA), which at one stage numbered 40,000 and functioned as an umbrella organisation and dabbled in the idea of an independent Northern Ireland, but is now much depleted, and smaller bodies such as the Ulster Volunteer Force, Ulster Freedom Fighters and the Red Hand Defenders, who run the rackets in particular areas and engage in sectarian assassinations.

The other organisation which should be mentioned is the Orange Order. The Order was founded in the aftermath of a particularly violent rural battle between the Catholic Defenders and the Protestants of Armagh, organised as the Peep O'Day Boys at Diamond Hill in 1795 (Dewar, 1967, p. 85). Lodges spread rapidly, and Orangemen played a significant part in the militia which put down the United Irishmen (Dewar et al., 1967, p. 109). Sporadically banned from 1825 to1870, the Order tended to lose its members from the gentry, but the Order finally came to include most of respectable Protestant society at the time of the first Home Rule Crisis (Dewar, 1967, pp. 128-144). From that stage onward the Order was always ready to help with the organisation of resistance to Home Rule, and, because of this, came to play an institutional role in the Unionist party. The Order is officially represented in the constitution of the Ulster Unionist Party. More significantly, an Orangeman could be relied upon to be a solid Unionist, rather as feminists rely on lesbians to represent their interests, and it was – and, apparently, still is – difficult for non-members of the Order to get a Unionist nomination. Between 1921 and 1966 only 11 out of 149 Northern Ireland MPs were not Orangemen at some stage of their parliamentary career, although the numbers declined towards the end, and in 1970 seven of the 37-strong Unionist Parliamentary Party were not Orangemen. Nonetheless, with 125-130,000 members in Northern Ireland in 1969, the Order was not to be lightly disregarded by Unionist politicians.

The 1994 IRA Ceasefire

On 31 August 1994 the IRA unilaterally announced a 'complete cessation' of its military operations because of the 'potential of the current situation and in order to enhance the democratic peace process'. On 13 October 1994 the UVF and UDA followed suit, indicating that their violence was a response to IRA violence, and that their ceasefire was dependent upon the IRA ceasefire holding.

Precisely why the IRA did this needs much discussion. Possible factors include:

- a feeling, with the defeat of Gerry Adams in the 1992 General Election, that their electoral strategy was getting nowhere;
- worries about the unpopularity of the long war in their own community;
- secret low-level talks with the British government;
- talks between Adams and John Hume, leader of the SDLP;
- talks between the government of the Republic and the British government, concluding with the Downing Street Declaration of 15 December 1993, which includes specific pledges: i. that Britain has no selfish strategic or economic interest in Northern Ireland; ii. that should the people of Northern Ireland wish to become part of the Republic the British government would not stand in their way; iii. a reiteration of the pledge in the Anglo-Irish Agreement of 1985 that such a move would only be by majority consent in Northern Ireland;

- a possible reason is that the IRA think demographics are on their side.

None of the above can be seen as decisive, and the IRA obviously went through a long period of thought before making its announcement, involving a limited ceasefire and clarifications of the Declaration from the Irish and British governments.

The immediate question following the cessation was whether it was permanent. Despite the odd hiccup, and the continuation of punishment beatings by both the IRA and the Protestant paramilitaries, there were no major or serious violations of the ceasefire for 18 months until the Canary Wharf bomb in February 1996, followed by the bomb that destroyed a large part of central Manchester. Despite these major bombings and a bomb at British Army HQ in Belfast the IRA did not seem to have gone to war again in a major way, and a second ceasefire was announced on 20th July 1997, followed by Sinn Fein being admitted to the talks on the future of Northern Ireland on 8 September 1997.

The Good Friday Agreement (Belfast Agreement)

Following discussions with the Irish government the British government issued, on 22 February 1995, a Framework Document offering a possible model of government. Its main features were ultimately embodied, somewhat modified, into the Agreement. Following the election of a Labour government with a massive majority in 1997 it became possible for the parties in Northern Ireland to return to the peace process, resulting in the election of a Forum and of negotiators. This in turn produced the Good Friday Agreement, signed on Good Friday, 10 April 1998. Referendums were held in both Northern and Southern Ireland. In the North the referendum attained a substantial majority overall and a slight majority in the Unionist community. In the South the changes to Articles 2 and 3 (see below) were approved. The main features of the Agreement were:

- a province-wide Assembly of 108 members in six-member constituencies under the STV system elected for a five-year term;
- a system of assembly committees, appointed in line with party strengths, to oversee the work of Northern Ireland departments. Concretely the Assembly would deal with education, health,

agriculture, housing and tourism. Contentious matters would require weighted majorities;

- a North/South Ministerial Council, accountable to the new Assembly and the Irish parliament with limited and agreed executive, consultative and harmonising powers to be designated by the two governments, which is to discuss, for example, animal and plant health; education, including teacher qualifications and exchanges; strategic transport planning; environmental protection, pollution and inland waterways; social security entitlements of cross-border workers; tourism; relevant EU programmes; inland fisheries; cross-border emergency health services;
- a British-Irish Council (BIC) will be established under a new British-Irish Agreement to promote the harmonious and mutually beneficial development of the totality of relationships among the peoples of these islands; it will have members from the British and Irish governments and devolved institutions throughout the UK;
- the Irish government to hold a referendum on Articles 2 and 3 of the Constitution, altering them to an aspiration to unity by consent;
- Secretary of State to remain in charge of security (but policing might be handed to the Assembly once it became clear that peace looked permanent), overall accountability to Westminster, negotiating with Westminster about funding and co-chairing the proposed new inter-governmental conference.

Following the referendums to ratify the Agreement, elections were held to the Assembly on 25 June 1998, resulting in a composition where Unionists supportive of the Agreement were in a majority. The Assembly was then supposed to work towards the appointment of an Executive in early 1999, but a major stumbling block emerged. David Trimble, the new Chief Executive, had been given to understand by Tony Blair that some IRA decommissioning would be a prerequisite of the setting up of an executive. The Agreement itself merely binds Sinn Fein to facilitate decommissioning within two years of the setting up of an Executive. This type of problem has led to two short suspensions of the Assembly plus one of three months and the current one of over eight months.

A further stumbling block was Chris Patten's report on the future of the RUC. He recommended that its name should be changed to the Police Service of Northern Ireland, its badge changed, an oath affirming human rights rather than loyalty to the crown should be introduced; the Union flag should no longer be flown at police stations. The 3,000 strong full-time RUC reserve should be phased out, and the force cut from 12,700 to 7,500. Recruitment procedures should ensure one Catholic joins the force for every one Protestant. The force should not, however, be disbanded. These recommendations include something to offend everyone, but offending the Unionists worst. On the other hand, the confirmation by Stevens of collaboration between the FRU and Special Branch and loyalist paramilitaries has greatly heightened Catholic suspicions of the police.

Problems for the Future

The balance of advantage

Journalistic coverage tends to start from the optimism of 1998 and to treat the abandonment of the peace process and of the Assembly as a disaster. It is worth asking if this is entirely true. Put yourself for the minute in the position of a Protestant who hesitates at election times between Ulster Unionists critical of the Agreement and the DUP. You do not like the Agreement much to start with. You think that IRA prisoners should not have been released to help along the peace process. You hate Martin McGuinness, former Chief of Staff of the IRA Army Council, being in charge of your children's education. You do not want closer links with the Republic of Ireland. You take note of all the evidence below about decommissioning and think that Unionists who support Trimble are allowing themselves to be deceived by the IRA. You were proud of the name RUC and think it an insult to the memory of over three hundred members of the police who died in the Troubles to change the name to Police Service of Northern Ireland. Your nephew, who wanted to join the RUC, may well now not get in to the police because numbers are shrinking and 50 per cent of new recruits have to be Catholics. Your cousin who is a glazier is on short time now that few windows are getting broken by bombs. Your other cousin is about to lose his job as a private security guard now that security is much less of a problem. You reflect that, whatever the political situation, deaths from the Troubles have been below 100 each year since 1982 (http://www.psni.police.uk/stats/data/deathscy.doc). Life with the Troubles was not intolerable for most people. Belfast did not look like West Beirut at the height of the conflict there; public housing has been well maintained in Northern Ireland, and the area around the Malone Road in

Belfast looks like the better parts of Hampstead. Most of the deaths associated with the Troubles were suffered by people who deliberately put themselves at risk in some way, by joining the paramilitaries or the security forces. Northern Ireland residents who want a long life should first attend to health matters and avoid animal fat and smoking and take regular exercise, and make sure they obey the rules of road safety; worries about the Troubles rank well below these. You are deeply sceptical that it is worth paying large salaries to members of the Assembly. Your interests were catered for fairly well under Direct Rule, and reversion to Direct Rule and the Troubles would not upset you unduly.

Even Protestants supportive of the Agreement are likely to find some of the above arguments tempting. Moderate members of the Catholic community obviously have most to gain from the Agreement: their representatives have a real role in the Assembly, something that was last briefly achieved in the power-sharing executive of 1974. On the other hand since the Anglo-Irish Agreement of 1985 the Irish government had a formal consultative role in the direct rule framework, so the status quo ante would be better than a really badly working Assembly. Less moderate members of the Catholic community might well have sympathies with the dissident Republicans and feel that the Sinn Fein leadership had given up too much to make the Assembly work: instead of pursuing a constitutionally sanctioned claim to Irish unity in arms they are striking compromises with the Unionists.

A further point for people on either side of the divide living in more hardline areas is that the Agreement has changed everyday life less than one might imagine: insults and bricks still get thrown across peace lines; they still experience paramilitary policing rather than normal policing; there is still some danger of random sectarian assassination. (On the transmission of bitterness from one generation to another see Hayes and McAllister, 2001; on problems around peace lines see Conservative Shadow Secretary of State for Northern Ireland Quentin Davies, *The Guardian,* 6 December 2002.)

Thus for many ordinary people in Northern Ireland the Agreement represents the hope of a brighter future rather than the only lifeline to a tolerable present. This is less true for the British government. One of the great benefits of the 1920 Government of Ireland Act, which set up the Stormont government, was that if anything went wrong in Northern Ireland it was the Unionists' fault, not theirs. American accusations that Britain was holding on to part of Ireland against the will of its people could be countered by pointing to the composition of Stormont. A convention developed that the House of Commons was not allowed to discuss Northern Ireland. This was untrue, but reflected the underlying reality that if the British government did anything to upset the Unionists excessively they would call and win a Northern Ireland general election, i.e. the choice would be either to give in or to revert to direct rule. Closer British involvement in Northern Ireland affairs from 1969 onwards was very reluctant, and when it was felt necessary to abolish Stormont in 1972 the constant and bipartisan aim of British policy has been to restore devolved government. Attempts have included the power-sharing executive of 1974 (brought down by the Ulster Workers' Council strike of that spring), the Constitutional Convention of 1975, the Constitutional Conference of 1979 under Humphrey Atkins, the Northern Ireland Assembly and rolling devolution under Jim Prior from 1982-6, the provision in the Anglo-Irish Agreement of 1985 that matters dealt with in joint consultations with the Irish government could perhaps go to a power-sharing Northern Ireland Assembly instead, and finally the current peace process, which was started under Major but carries on in much the same way under Blair.

British governments are thus very keen for the Assembly to succeed. The benefits are that they no longer bear immediate responsibility for 'holding on to part of Ireland' or for bad things which happen there; with a bit of luck Irish terrorists stop blowing up parts of English cities; and in the longer term it might be possible to get shot of the place altogether, complete with the £4 billion subsidy it requires every year as the poorest part of the UK. Whatever happens readers should not expect British governments to give up on the peace process and devolution.

Decommissioning

This is the most fraught immediate area. The issue has been behind the suspensions of the Assembly. As we saw above, Tony Blair led David Trimble to believe that some decommissioning would occur before the setting up of the power-sharing executive, while Sinn Fein stuck to the letter of the Good Friday Agreement. It is plainly asking a lot of politicians whose community has been a terrorist target for twenty-five years to settle down to peaceful-power sharing with people who directed military operations, particularly when they still hold on to many of their weapons.

There is obviously a major issue of confidence building. On the acid test of not engaging in active military operations the IRA have thus far met their obligations. Beyond this there are inevitably plenty of grounds for suspicions. The IRA have shown General de Chastelain's commission five arms dumps, two of which they have put beyond use. Have they shown the commission everything? Given the secretive nature of their operations, do they have a comprehensive list of their munitions? They started in 1970 with virtually no weapons, and ended with a substantial supply. Can they be trusted not to re-arm? Not very much equipment is needed to do straightforward terrorism, and the IRA have a good base of knowledge for obtaining or making weapons. A further worry concerns the breakaway groups such as the Real IRA. Might not the Unionists find they had done a deal with the Sinn Fein leadership, but that most of the activists had regrouped in a different organisation, taking large quantities of weaponry with them? The Sinn Fein/IRA leadership share this worry in the sense that they want to take their followers with them. Inevitably this means moving slowly and avoiding any suggestions that they are surrendering. In turn this inevitably augments Unionist suspicions that they are not sincere.

These issues are not discussed by impartial people in calm circumstances. The DUP and the anti-Agreement Ulster Unionists have an obvious interest in exaggerating every incident. There are plenty of incidents to keep the question on the boil. Incidents in 2003 included the IRA members who took their holidays with the FARC guerrillas of Columbia, possibly testing new weapons with their friends; the break-in at the Special Branch office at Castlereagh police barracks, which may have been an IRA hunt for information; the discovery of apparent lists of people targeted for assassination; suggestions that the IRA is orchestrating sectarian street violence, notably in North Belfast; and suggestions that Sinn Fein officials at Stormont were drawing up targeting information on Unionists.

There is no ready solution to this problem. Over a number of years in which there are no major military incidents confidence will hopefully grow, perhaps enhanced by the recognition that there were similar problems in the South following the civil war and also following the call for the IRA to dump arms with the founding of Fianna Fail in 1926.

Demographics

Two issues need to be considered under this heading. The big issue is whether demographic shifts might not spell the end of Northern Ireland altogether. In the 2001 census, 40.26 per cent (1991: 38.4 per cent) of the population of Northern Ireland regarded themselves as Catholic, 45.57 per cent (1991: 50.6 per cent) as Protestant while 13.88 per cent (1991: 11.1) professed no religion or refused to say. Sadly Jedi were at under 1 per cent (http://www.nisra.gov.uk/census/pdf/Key%20Statistics%20ReportTables.pdf). Catholic numbers are plainly rising, although estimates they could hit 51 per cent by 2011 look on the high side. Thus the peace strategy involves telling Sinn Fein supporters to 'go home and bonk', and the current peace process could be seen as a gentle way of preparing the Unionist population for united Ireland achieved by referendum in the foreseeable future.

This simple scenario begs four important questions. To start with, people across Europe have been reproducing less in recent years, probably because opportunities other than motherhood have opened up for women. Why should Northern Ireland's Catholics be immune from this trend? Further, Northern Ireland Catholics have outbred the Protestants ever since the founding of the state. Conditions in Northern Ireland have been harsher for Catholics than for Protestants, while emigration has been relatively easy, helped by the diaspora that started with the famine, and a higher rate of Catholic emigration has largely counteracted their higher birthrate.

Third, the scenario assumes that being a Catholic means you vote for a united Ireland. It is difficult to get a grip on this issue through opinion polls. The big problem is what assumptions people have in mind when they answer. A Catholic might favour a united Ireland if it could be achieved with no bloodshed and with no economic sacrifice, and therefore answer 'yes' at the level of ultimate ideals. However, realistically a united Ireland might meet with armed resistance from the Protestants among Northern Ireland's 100,000 licensed shotgun holders, and from members of the police, police reserve and Royal Irish Regiment who managed to retain their weapons. Levels of violence could be considerable. What is more, the security forces might now be reduced to the small Irish army, and the rules of engagement would allow loyalist gunmen to fire from crowds and urban locations, confident that a vigorous response would lead to civilian casualties. What would happen to the £4 billion annual subvention that Northern Ireland currently receives from the British exchequer? Even given the rate of growth of the Irish economy in recent years, it would cripple the Celtic tiger to match it. One cannot simply assume, therefore, that Catholics would automatically vote for a united Ireland in realistic circumstances. For what they are worth, opinion polls back up this reasoning. For example, Duffy and Evans found that whereas under 10 per cent of Protestants favoured a United Ireland, only around 60 per cent of Catholics supported this, with some 25 per cent of Catholics wanting to remain part of the UK (for details see Dowds, Devine and Breen, 1997 – see http://cain.ulst.ac.uk/othelem/research/nnnisas/rep6c6.htm).   Previously Breen found that the overall constitutional preference of people in Northern Ireland was that between 60 and 70 per cent wanted to remain with the UK and about 25 per cent favoured a United Ireland (for information on this issue see Breen in Dowds, Devine and Breen, 1996 at: http://cain.ulst.ac.uk/othelem/research/nisas/rep5c2htm#chap2).

Fourth and finally, Northern Ireland exists because Protestants had a local majority in the North East corner, in spite of Sinn Fein's overall victory in terms of seats in 1918. The argument was that it would be oppressive for them to live in a state they so vehemently rejected. It is not impossible that a version of the same argument might be used again, although the form of words in the Good Friday Agreement appears to rule this out.

There is a smaller set of demographic issues that will continue to afflict Northern Ireland. The population mix in particular areas continues to shift. This in turn upsets existing assumptions. Thus an Orange march down the Ormeau Road or the Garvachy Road was not originally provocative, but became so because the area in question became a nationalist one. Marches in Northern Ireland are intensely territorial, and there is a long tradition of marches triggering off riots at times of political tension. Incidents based on local territorial disputes can thus be expected to recur regularly, and to be approached in a spirit of ill will.

Relations with the Republic

Part of the Catholic population of Northern Ireland wishes to move towards Irish unity; almost all the Protestants are opposed to such a move. The third strand of the Good Friday Agreement relates to this issue. Obviously Nationalists will wish to expand the proposed co-operation with the Republic and Unionists to contain it to a minimum of pragmatic issues. This section discusses two background factors which may have an affect on the working out of these rival aims.

The first is the nature of the state in the South. As indicated above, the state that emerged following partition was overwhelmingly Catholic and Irish. It is obvious that this has been eroded to some extent over the years. Article 44 of the Constitution, recognising the position of the Catholic Church, was dropped in 1972. The family clauses have been somewhat diluted; notably divorce is now permitted in the Republic, although the divorce law is one of the most restrictive in Europe; abortion remains illegal but the extreme harshness of the specific laws against it have been somewhat reduced by allowing information about abortion facilities abroad and permitting Irish women to travel abroad for abortions. Catholic principles are implemented less aggressively in the wider society: censorship is much relaxed, although the entertainment listings magazine, *In Dublin*, was banned for six months from 10 August 1999; contraception is more widely available, and a full range of methods including male and female sterilisation and the morning-after pill are offered by the Irish Family Planning Association, although the health service is still dominated by a Catholic ethos; homosexual sex is legal from the age of 17. The Irish Film Board was a major sponsor of the film *When Brendan met Trudy* (2001), which must have the old censors rolling in their graves, with its script by Roddy Doyle, copious swearing, drugs and sex including one scene where Trudy imitates a nun or the Blessed Virgin whilst squatting on Brendan. The position of the Church in the wider society has been weakened by some growth of secularism and by scandals involving priestly child sexual abuse. Weekly attendance at mass has declined from 84 per cent in 1991 (World Values Survey: http://www.umich.edu/~newsinfo/Releases/1997/Dec97/r121097a.html) to between 50 and 60 per cent today (poll by Irish Marketing Surveys December 1999: http://www.religoustolerance.org///rel_rate.htm). This contrasts with weekly mass attendance at 25 per cent in Spain in 1995-7 or 45 per cent in Italy in 1990-1 (World Values Survey: http://www.umich.edu/~newsinfo/Releases/1997/Dec97/r121097a.html).

Belief in God remains high but: only 40 per cent believe that abortion is always wrong, 30 per cent that premarital sex is always wrong, and 60 per cent that same-sex relations are always wrong. Only 7 per cent of those born in the 1970s had a great deal of confidence in the church, but 70 per cent had high confidence in their local priests (Peter Gould, 2001 using information from Father Andrew Greeley, BBC News Online: http://www.bbc.co.uk///1/hi/world/eeeurope/1203314a.stm) (6 March 2001).

That said, much of this apparent growth of secularism is pretty recent, and Ireland remains a Catholic country to a surprising extent compared to other Catholic countries in Europe, which have much more permissive divorce and abortion laws and censorship. The Church retains control of 94 per cent of the country's primary schools and two thirds of secondary schools, despite all staff wages and 90 per cent of building costs coming from the state (http://flag.blackened.net/revolt/ws91/ccchurch32.html).

Ireland still lacks an anti-clerical political party. It has a very long way to go before becoming a state and society that could attract Northern Ireland's Protestants.

Although Irish remains the official language it is not promoted with anything like the former vigour. The claim on the North in Articles 2 and 3 of the Constitution was dropped in the 1998 referendum in the Republic in favour of an aspiration. The Republic used to be poorer than Northern Ireland and the UK, but according to World Bank figures its gross national income per capita is either marginally above or marginally below that of the UK depending on which of two methodologies is used (http://www.worldbank.org/data/databytopic/GNPPC.pdf). As income per capita in Northern Ireland is the lowest of any UK region, per capita income in the Republic can be taken to be well above that in Northern Ireland. This still does not, of course, take care of the £4 billion subsidy from the UK, which provides Northern Ireland with a generally superior infrastructure and welfare state, even if it lags behind on the new cars and bungalows front.

The second background factor is whether the division between North and South might not be undermined by the decline of the nation state, notably in the context of the EU. An independent state controls its own financial affairs. As Parnell put it, 'An Irish custom-house is really of more importance to Ireland than an Irish parliament' (Lawrence, 1965, pp. 188-9). Today, however, the tax regime of both the UK and Ireland is partly determined by the EU, which is one important reason that both levy VAT. Part of the purpose of the EU is to create a free market in goods and services, driving a coach and horses through member states' custom-houses. Similarly, both are covered by personal import regulations decided at the European level which allow individuals to bring with them from other EU countries large quantities of alcohol and tobacco for personal consumption, thus creating pressures towards the harmonisation of duty. An independent state issues its own currency, but Ireland is in the Euro zone and the UK may well soon follow. States which use the Euro as their currency have to follow various regulations which constrain their fiscal policy. An independent state issues its own passports and driving licences, but both the UK and Ireland issue EU documents. An independent state controls its citizens, but EU states are constrained to subscribe to the European Convention on Human Rights. We are by no means as yet in a European superstate, but some of the point of struggling for an independent Ireland has been eroded, with more to follow.

Conclusion

This chapter has shown that Northern Ireland's divisions have long and deep historical roots. Although some recent developments, for example the relative decline of Catholicism in the South, greater affluence in the South and a degree of convergence via the EU may be helpful in the long term, the small industry of research into ethnic conflict which has developed in Northern Ireland has a healthy future for some years to come.

In the short term a particular source of difficulty may well be the dominance of Provisional Sinn Fein on the Catholic side of the political divide in Northern Ireland. The major objection which some Catholic voters had to Provisional Sinn Fein was its link to the armed struggle. Catholic voters are likely to be more readily convinced than Protestants that the armed struggle is effectively over. If both Provisional Sinn Fein and the Social Democratic and Labour Party represent a peaceful claim that Ireland should be united, then Sinn Fein's presence on the ground, its militant past and its effectiveness on grassroots issues should stand it in a very good stead. It may very well become established as the leading Catholic Party. In this situation it would hardly be surprising if many Unionists became more vigorously anti-Agreement and supported either DUP or anti-Agreement UUP candidates, as has indeed happened in the Assembly elections of 26th November 2003 in which the DUP topped the poll with 30 seats, the UUP came second with 27 (subsequently weakened by defections to the DUP), Sinn Fein became the leading Catholic party with 24 seats to the SDLP's 18. This would lead to a degree of polarisation in the North which would cause grave difficulties for the institutions set up under the Good Friday Agreement. Although the British press currently sees this as a nightmare scenario for Northern Ireland I am inclined to think that there might simply be a few years during which the peace process stalled. Indeed, if Republicans refrained from going back to the armed struggle in this difficult situation it might help to build confidence in the long term.

References

Adams, M. (1968), *Censorship, The Irish Experience, 1922-63*, Irish Academic Press, Dublin.

Bell, G. (1976), *The Protestants of Ulster*, Pluto Press, London.

BandICO (1972), *The Economics of Partition*, Athol Books, Belfast.

BandICO (1973), *Ulster As It Is*, Athol Books, Belfast.

Blanshard, P. (1972), *The Irish and Catholic Power*, Greenwood Press, New York, NY.

Boal, F. W., Neville, J., and Douglas, H. (1982), *Integration and Division: Geographical Perspectives on the Northern Ireland Problem*, Academic Press, London.

Buckland, P. (1981), *History of Northern Ireland*, Gill and Macmillan, Dublin.

Chubb, B. (1970), *The Government and Politics of Ireland*, Longmans, London.

Darby, J. (1976), *Conflict In Northern Ireland*, Gill and Macmillan, Dublin.

Dewar, M., Brown, J. and Long, S. (1967) *Orangeism: A New Historical Appreciation*, Grand Orange Lodge of Ireland, Belfast.

Dowds, L., Devine, P. and Breen, R. (1996), (eds), *Social Attitudes in Northern Ireland: The Fifth Report*, Appletree Press Ltd, Belfast.

Dowds, L., Devine, P. and Breen, R. (1997) (eds.), *Social Attitudes in Northern Ireland: The Sixth Report*, Appletree Press Ltd, Belfast.

Gallagher, M. (1995), 'How Many Nations Are There In Ireland,' *Ethnic and Racial Studies*, 18, (4), pp. 715-739.

Harbinson, J. F. (1973), *The Ulster Unionist Party, 1882-1973: Its Development and Organisation*, Blackstaff, Belfast.

Hayes, B. C. and McAllister, I. (2001), 'Sowing Dragon's Teeth: Public Support for Political Violence and Paramilitarism in Northern Ireland', *Political Studies*, 49, pp. 901-922.

Kee, R. (1972), *The Green Flag*, Wiedenfeld and Nicholson, London.

Larkin, E. (1987), *The Consolidation of the Roman Catholic Church in Ireland, 1860-70*, Gill and Macmillan, Dublin.

Larkin, E. (1975), *The Roman Catholic Church and the Creation of the Modern Irish State*, Gill and Macmillan, Dublin.

Lawrence, R. J. (1965), *The Government of Northern Ireland, 1921-64*, Clarendon, Oxford.

McGarry, J. and O'Leary, B. (1995), *Explaining Northern Ireland*, Blackwell, Oxford.

McLaughlin, J. (1980) 'Industrial Capitalism, Ulster Unionism and Orangeism: An Historical Re-appraisal' *Antipode*, 12, (1), pp. 15-28.

Police Service of Northern Ireland, available at http://www.psni.police.uk/stats/deaths2.htm (Accessed 2 March 2003.)

Schmitt, D. E. (1973), *The Irony of Irish Democracy*, Lexington Books, New York.

Stewart, A. T. Q. (1977), *The Narrow Ground, 1609-1969*, Faber, London.

Whyte, J. H. (1971), *Church and State in Modern Ireland, 1923-1970*, Gill and Macmillan, Dublin.

7 Regionalism: A Response to Globalisation?

HOWARD ELCOCK

Introduction

Regionalism is an idea whose time appears to have come. Stateless nations and regions within the European Union have increasingly asserted both their identities and their interests, both in negotiations with their state governments and in seeking financial and other support from the European Union (EU), especially its Structural Funds. Local and regional authorities have opened offices in Brussels in order to lobby 'Europe' more effectively. Associations of European regions, such as the Atlantic Arc (for details see http://www.arcat.org/Anglais/arcanet.html), the Four Motors (comprised of Baden-Württemberg, Rhone-Alpes, Lombardy and Catalonia) and associations of frontier regions associated with the INTERREG programme (an EC Community Initiative to promote inter-regional co-operation), have proliferated. The importance of regions was recognised in the Treaty of European Union of 1992 by the creation of the Committee of the Regions, which has the same advisory status within the Union as the older Economic and Social Committee.

Between 1945 and the mid to late 1990s, the fate of regional governance in Britain was determined largely by shifts in domestic policy and ideology. The creation of the modern town and country planning system in 1947 was one of the major achievements of the Attlee, post-war Labour Government. It included an attempt to ensure that increases in land values, which resulted from the decisions of local planning authorities, should accrue to the community rather than to the landowners, although the Conservative Governments of the 1950s eliminated this aspect of the scheme. It was briefly revived in the 1970s by the passage of the Community Land Act but this piece of Socialism was again firmly squashed by Margaret Thatcher's Conservatives after 1979.

In the United States and Canada too, regionalism and regionalisation have become increasingly active political issues. Quebec has periodically demanded independence and in 1997 its people came close to giving it majority support in a referendum. The Harris Government in Ontario, Canada, imposed a merger on seven municipalities in the City of Toronto in order to create an efficient metro government (Boudreau, 2000). An elected regional government was established in Portland, Oregon by State legislation in 1979 and confirmed in 1992. In other cities similar efforts have been made to create regional institutions to co-ordinate development and planning, with varying degrees of success (Rusk, 1999; Orfield, 2000). Thus, in other US regions efforts are being made to develop inter-municipal co-operation together with negotiating partnerships with the business community and other regional actors (Foster, 2000). Regionalism is on the move, despite the removal of much economic power to multi-national corporations and international agencies such as the World Bank, the International Monetary Fund and the World Trade Organisation. Globalisation and regionalisation appear to go hand in hand, rather than the one eliminating the other.

Ideologies, Interests and Regionalism

However, the pace and nature of regionalisation are strongly affected by which ideology is dominant within a particular country's government, as the example of England demonstrates. During the 1960s, the importance of the regional dimensions of economic and spatial planning became increasingly recognised. Local authority consortia were created in the South-East and North-East in the early 1960s. In the South-East, SERPLAN (South East Regional Planning Conference) was created to cope with increasing problems of overcrowding and the consequent increasing stresses imposed on that region's infrastructure. In the North-East a regional consortium of local authorities was created as part of the first recognition of and attempt to deal with the increasingly severe unemployment and social problems resulting from that region's industrial decline (Chapman, 1987). This effort was led by Quintin Hogg after his appointment by the then Prime Minister, Harold Macmillan, as Minister for the North-East. His main achievement was to secure major improvements to the North-East's highways.

Then, in 1965, the Labour Government under Harold Wilson created the Regional Economic Planning Councils (REPCs) as part of the structure for developing and implementing its National Plan. They were made up of members from business, trade unions, local government and other figures, who were appointed to them by the First Secretary of State and charged with the preparation of Regional Strategies (Hogwood and Keating, 1982). These strategies had to be taken into account by local planning authorities framing the new Structure Plans, which were to be prepared as part of a radical revision of the planning system also carried out by the Wilson Government in the 1960s (Crossman, 1975; Cherry, 1982; Cullingworth and Nadim, 1997). The formation of the REPCs and the Regional Advisory Planning Boards (RAPBs), made up of regional civil servants whose function was to advise the REPCs and co-ordinate central government policies and activities in their regions, in turn encouraged the formation of local authority planning consortia or regional planning conferences in most of the English regions. However, the North-West Regional Association was not established until 1993, because of political divisions and local rivalries within that region (Burch and Rhodes, 1993; Jenkinson, 1999). Some REPCs became vigorous advocates for their regions' needs and interests, notably the Northern REPC under the chairmanship of T. Dan Smith, which brought the North-East's problems to national attention but also vigorously promoted a positive image for its region. However, the demise of the National Plan at the hands of the 'gnomes of Zurich' in the summer of 1966 blunted their impact. Mr. Smith was eventually imprisoned for corruption, thus ending his influence on the future of the North-East.

The election of Margaret Thatcher's Conservatives in May 1979 led quickly to the abolition of the REPCs in the autumn of that year. The RAPBs followed soon after, victims of a new dominant ideology which proclaimed that the way to improve Britain's economic performance and hence her prosperity was to liberate markets and entrepreneurs from state control. The State's role should be reduced to performing those residual tasks such as defending the country from its external and internal enemies, which could not be turned over to private enterprise.

At the same time, the effectiveness of the planning system was extensively reduced. Its regional component was virtually abolished (Cherry, 1982), while the preparation and revision of Structure Plans were accorded low priority. Structure Plans were almost abolished during the tenure of office of Nicholas Ridley, a disciple whom Thatcher loved and who was a particularly forceful advocate of the primacy of the market (Thornley, 1991). Furthermore, Enterprise Zones and Simplified Planning Zones were established where entrepreneurs could secure permission for development with little or no let or hindrance from the planners. In a number of decaying inner city areas, the local authorities' planning powers were transferred wholesale to the Urban Development Corporations (UDCs) created from 1982 on, which were charged with the physical redevelopment of decayed inner cities, dockland areas and riversides. Spectacular results were sometimes achieved, such as the Docklands development in East London and the MetroCentre near Gateshead but the main effect was to transfer jobs into these Zones from elsewhere in their localities. During the same period too, the local authorities responsible for the strategic government of England's seven largest conurbations, the Greater London Council and the metropolitan county councils, were abolished. The true reason was that they had all become Labour controlled centres of opposition to the government's free market policies but the Government argued that their abolition was timely because they had been the creations of 'a fashion for strategic planning whose time has now passed' (DoE, 1982). The market ruled, OK?

Furthermore, the Thatcher Government fanned regional discontents by refusing to acknowledge the problems faced by those English regions, as well as Scotland and Wales, which are peripheral to the European Union's centres of wealth and have suffered rising unemployment and poverty as a result of the decline and disappearance of their people's traditional sources of employment (Hudson, 1989). By 1982 Sir Keith Joseph had abolished most of the industrial support which had formerly existed to shore up declining industries or enable the regions to attract new industries by making grants to entrepreneurs to encourage them to locate there. Complainers who argued that this constituted unfair treatment were dismissed as 'moaning Minnies' by the Prime Minister personally. Many regional officials would have agreed with the one who declared that 'Policies are South-Eastern policies' (Fenwick et al., 1989). John Tomaney (2000, p. 384) suggested that there was a growing disenchantment with 'the way we are governed'. Peter Roberts (2000, p. 262), recorded that 'the Thatcher Government helped to germinate the seeds of devolution through its scant regard for constitutional conventions and the abolition of regional local government in the English metropolitan areas and Scotland'. Not only were market-oriented policies rigorously enforced, sources of opposition and effective lobbying against the effects of those policies were suppressed.

Since 1990, however, the ideological climate has changed again in favour of regionalism, at first incrementally and then more radically under Tony Blair's Labour Government. Also, the Conservative Government once more acknowledged the value of planning after 1990. In the 1990 Town and Country Planning Act, the desirability of enforcing Structure and Local Plans was once more accepted; Section 54A provides that planning decisions 'should be taken in accordance with the plan, unless other material considerations indicate otherwise', which was 'in many ways a statement of continuity but seen as a triumph for planning at the time' (Hull and Vigar, 1998, p. 117). It also became apparent that there was a need to establish some kind of regional government structures, in order to permit the English regions to compete for European Community's (EC) Structural Funds under the new regime established by the Community's reform of its regional policy in 1989. An EC Regional Affairs Directorate official told a conference in Manchester that 'the mere existence of resources in Brussels can be a catalyst which changes the way in which a region regards its future'. He also cautioned that a region must decide 'where it wants to go before considering how the European Community can help' (McIldoon, 1993; Elcock, 1997a). In consequence, local authorities and the business community in the North-East established a Northern Development Company, partly as a vehicle to lever Structural Funds from the Community. Similar bodies were created in other regions.

In 1993, John Major's Conservative Government made its own contribution to the developing English regionalisation by announcing its intention to establish ten Government Offices for the Regions (GORs), later reduced to nine by merging the Merseyside and North-West Offices. They began operating in April 1994. Initially these Offices, each headed by a Regional Director, were responsible for co-ordinating the regional work of four government Departments: Trade and Industry, the Environment, Transport and Employment. Since then, their remit has been gradually extended for two reasons. The first has been changes in the configuration of the central departments themselves, for instance the merging of Education and Employment in 1995. The second has been deliberate decisions to extend to scope of the GORs' work; thus they now include the Department of Environment and Rural Affairs (DEFRA) and aspects of the Home Office's regional work. Further extensions to their role and the enhancement of the Regional Directors' status in order to give them a role analogous to that of the French Prefects, were recommended by the Performance and Innovation Unit of the Cabinet Office in early 2000 (Cabinet Office, 2000). The government has largely accepted these recommendations and one regional planner argued that the Regional Directors were already acquiring the status of regional Prefects (interview data).

By May 1997, then, several components of a developing system of regional governance were in place in England. All the regions had established regional local government associations, albeit under a variety of titles. Several of them had also created development companies or regeneration agencies in partnership with their regional business communities and other social partners. The Labour Party under Tony Blair was committed to offer devolution to Scotland and Wales – an offer quickly and eagerly grasped by the Scots, if much more hesitantly by the Welsh once Labour won election to government (Elcock and Parks, 2000). For the English, the Labour Party had promised the establishment of Regional Development Agencies (RDAs), which could, if the region's governors so chose, be partly supervised by Regional Chambers. The members of the RDAs' boards were to be predominantly business people appointed by the relevant Secretary of State, together with representatives of the trades unions, higher education and volunteer groups. The Chambers were also to be made up of Ministerial appointees, a majority of whom would be councillors nominated by the local authorities in the region, the remainder being representatives of business, education and the voluntary sector. Significantly, despite the refusal to create directly elected assemblies, the Chambers were quickly established in all the English regions. Hence the machinery of English regional governance was considerably extended but it does not include representative elected assemblies, although these were created in Scotland and Wales, as well as in Northern Ireland as a result of the Good Friday Agreement of April 1998 (Sandford and McQuail, 2001).

Scotland and Wales achieved their long-standing ambitions for devolved government relatively quickly. Referenda in both countries were held in September 1997. The Scots voted by three to one for the restoration of their own Parliament and by almost as large a number to give it a tax-varying power which might hurt their pockets. Wales, divided both vertically between the agricultural North and the industrial South and horizontally between the Welsh-speaking West and the anglicised East, supported the creation of its own Assembly but by only the narrowest of margins (Elcock, 1997b; Elcock and Parks, 2000). Elections for the new Scottish Parliament and Welsh Assembly were held in 1998 and the two institutions are now firmly established. They are in the process of developing not only distinctive policies for these two countries but also leading to the growth of increasingly distinctive polities there (Wright, 2000). Alice Brown (2000,

p. 44) has declared that 'the Scottish Parliament is going its own way on policy matters', including student tuition fees, land reform and care for the elderly. Scotland's politics is also developing 'a growing distinctiveness' which means that 'No longer will it be tenable for books on British politics to be published which assume the homogeneity of the British state and the British political system' (ibid., pp. 46-7). Devolution has been achieved too, if more shakily, in Northern Ireland as a result of the Belfast Good Friday Agreement (Elcock and Parks, 2000).

In England the new regionalism has been reflected in the creation by 1999 of four bodies in each region with extensive responsibilities for government and governance. The establishment of local government regional consortia began in the early 1960s and reached full fruition in the early 1990s. The Major Administration created the Government Offices for the Regions in 1994 to co-ordinate central government regional policies. To these institutions the Blair Government has added the Regional Development Agencies and Regional Chambers. However, to date there are no elected assemblies able to hold these agencies to account for their deeds and misdeeds before the representatives of the regions' citizens, either in general or in the context of specific public services (Ross and Tomaney, 2001; Sandford and McQuail, 2001). However, the recent The Regional Assemblies (Preparations) Bill (May 2003) has prepared the ground for referenda in the regions, and it is anticipated that the North-East of England will be the first region to hold a referendum.

Apart from the questions of democratic government and accountability, three other major issues remain. The first is the fragmentation of regional governance and the need to co-ordinate the plans, policies and activities of the various regional and local agencies involved in regional or sub-regional strategic planning. The Performance and Innovation Unit (2000) identified 43 strategic plans which local authorities are required to prepare. Several devices have been developed to reduce this fragmentation or at least to ensure that undesirable consequences, such as squabbles over regional priories, lack of co-ordination of regional strategies and conflicting actions that cancel one another out, can be avoided.

Some regions, notably the East Midlands, have resorted to preparing over-arching strategies within whose parameters the various governance organisations agree to prepare their own strategies. Other regions have seen the adoption by some or all of the 'peak' regional governance organisations of regional Concordats binding them to co-operate in the achievement of agreed visions and policy objectives. However, the remainder are relying on establishing networks of communication and co-ordination without preparing over-arching strategies or agreeing formal Concordats. In these regions, network management or reticulist skills (Friend, Power and Yewlett, 1974) are at a premium. In some there are indications that the Regional Chambers in particular have had difficulty in defining and articulating their roles within the regional governance structure (Saunders and Mawson, 2000). The Performance and Innovation Unit (2000) has proposed more powerful co-ordination by national and regional civil servants by enhancing the roles and status of the Regional Directors and the Government Offices for the Regions. In all these ways it seems likely that means to improve regional partnership and co-ordination will become increasingly important if consistent policies and plans are to result from the present fragmented structures.

A second issue is the allocation of resources among the regions and stateless nations of the United Kingdom. The Barnett Formula gives more generous allocations to the Celtic Fringes than to the English regions, giving rise to widespread feelings of injustice, especially in those regions such as the North-East which have borders with Scotland or Wales. The *Newcastle Journal* has published a long series of reports highlighting the higher levels of public money spent in South-East Scotland compared to Northumberland and the North-East of England more generally. Reallocation of resources both across the UK and within England itself is controversial. Further controversies have been generated over the distribution of responsibilities such as the need for more housing units as households become smaller and more numerous, therefore demanding greater numbers of houses and apartments although the total population is not rising. This has been the cause of a major dispute between the Government and the South-East of England Regional Assembly (SEERA) (Ward, 2000). Those regions with borders on the over-crowded South-East, the East and West Midlands and the South-West have been compelled to decide either how to resist suburban encroachment on their flanks which border the South-East, or how to cope with the demands of immigrants from that region, especially if they are elderly or otherwise economically inactive (interview data). A new distributive analysis is urgently needed to develop a fairer and more efficient allocation of housing numbers.

The last and most fundamental unresolved issue is the existence of a widely recognised democratic deficit at the regional level in England, which is only partially filled by the developing regional Chambers or Assemblies with their councillor majorities. In several regions, this has given rise to increasing demands for the establishment of directly elected regional assemblies to provide full democratic legitimacy and accountability for the increasingly numerous and significant regional governance agencies that now exist in England (Sandford and McQuail, 2001). The North-East has had a Campaign for a Regional Assembly since 1993. A North-East Constitutional Convention has also been established under the chairmanship of the Bishop of Durham, to prepare a blueprint for a North-East Assembly in the hope of repeating the eventual success of the Scottish Constitutional Convention in achieving devolution (Tomaney, 2000). Similar campaigning organisations and constitutional conventions now exist in the South-West, the West Midlands, the North-West and Yorkshire and Humberside. A national lobby group, the Campaign for the English Regions (CFER), has been established to stimulate Parliamentary support for English regional assemblies, with its headquarters in Newcastle. Peter Roberts (2000, p. 262) has suggested that the choices on offer include 'two-speed regional governance, regional governance à la carte, inner and outer regions, etc.'. Scotland is 'the pacemaker and the test case' but one question is where Scotland will evolve to next, including the possibility of its seeking and gaining full independence as an EC Member State.

In Scotland and Wales there are demands for increased powers to be granted to the devolved assemblies, together with increasingly credible demands for independence within the EU, especially in Scotland. Robert Hazell and his colleagues at the Constitution Unit have argued that, in consequence, the devolution settlement is itself inherently unstable (Hazell, 2000). The United Kingdom is already an asymmetric democracy (Keating, 1998): the long-term question is whether it will ultimately become a federal state or even break up altogether. This may both depend on and reflect wider international trends in favour of regionalisation in both Europe and North America.

Regionalism as an International Phenomenon

This progression towards what might (perhaps daringly) be described as a form of crypto-federation in the United Kingdom is part of an international movement towards the creation of stronger regional governments in response to globalisation and the growing power of international government agencies, notably the European Union. For Trevor Salmon (2000, p. 165), 'in an era of globalisation, the local is increasingly international and vice versa'. Stein Rokkan's centre-periphery analysis, based on his extensive studies of European political history from the Renaissance onwards, demonstrated the tendency for centres to dominate the government of peripheries. Centres are 'privileged places', while peripheries are necessarily characterised by 'distance, difference and dependence' (1999, p. 64). The peripheries tend therefore to become subordinate to the centre, although 'for each process of centralisation there is a corresponding effort of boundary accentuation, of attempting to preserve peripheral attributes' (ibid.). However, this essentially bipolar analysis must now be modified to reflect the establishment of multiple centres at the supra-national, national and sub-national levels, together with multiple peripheries, consisting of nations, regions and local communities. They possess and assert their own needs, interest, and desires and possess constitutional, financial and political resources which they can deploy to protect and promote them. Peripheries may combine in consortia or networks to influence or oppose one or more centres.

The extent to which regions seek to assert their interests and promote their identities will depend on the extent of the resources available to them and the willingness of the people of the region to assert their regional identity, interests and demands. Kathryn Foster (1997; 2000) suggests that the effectiveness or otherwise of moves to establish regional institutions depends on the extent of regional impulses or regional capital, offset by anti-regional impulses or capital. The question is 'what accomplished regions may have that less accomplished regions do not have' (Foster, 2000, p. 83), which enables them to develop levels of inter-municipal and cross-sector co-operation and in turn promulgate coherent regional plans and policies. The answer lies in part in political institutions, as well as - significantly – achieving 'a shift of attention from *government* - that is the public sector – to *governance* – which encompasses an array of public, private, nonprofit, academic and civic interests' (ibid., p. 85, author's italics). This is also what many of the new English regional governance agencies are seeking to achieve: maximum collaboration both among themselves and with their social partners, including business, labour, academe and the non-profit sector. Specific factors conducive to regionalism are, according to Foster, 'a progressive state legislative framework....political alignment of city, county and state officials,...common heritage, socioeconomic composition, growth patterns.....and active support from public corporations and civic leaders' (ibid.). Foster wrote in the American context, where regionalisation occurs primarily through local initiatives, albeit that state legislatures and governors need to encourage them and enable them to happen, by passing the relevant legislation and allocating resources to support regionalisation initiatives.

In Europe, however, an additional factor in the development of regionalism has been the revival of minority languages and cultures which, perhaps paradoxically, has accompanied European integration (Keating, various; Parks and Elcock, 2001; Parks, forthcoming). Welsh, Breton, Scots and Irish Gaelic cultures and the Catalan language are all more significant sources of identity for these stateless nations than was the case twenty or thirty years ago. The existence of a common culture, especially a minority language, is a powerful force reinforcing functional demands for regionalisation, including recognition of a region or stateless nation's functional problems, such as agricultural poverty, industrial decline or environmental degradation: the problems the EU's Structural Funds were intended to address (Parks and Elcock, 2000).

Regions, then, have impulses which drive them towards seeking more coherent and powerful governments, possibly including demands for autonomy or independence from an existing national or multi-national state but there are also counter-influences which may reduce the credibility of claims that a regional culture exists, render regional consensus difficult to achieve and hence reduce the credibility of the region's demands in the eyes of national or supra-national policy-makers. Parks and Elcock (2000) propose a four-fold classification of regions according to the credibility of their demands for recognition of their cultural and functional identities. Definite regions or stateless nations possess both a cultural identity, often including a minority language, as well as economic and social interests which require regional solutions, plus sufficient political consensus to support regional institutions. As stateless nations, both Scotland and Wales fall into this first category and significantly, both have achieved a degree of devolution in recent years. Much the same could be said about Catalonia and the Basque Country in Spain.

A second group of regions also both possess regional cultures and have functional needs at the regional scale but neither is strong enough to be unchallenged. Thus the North-East of England has a recognisable cultural identity reflected in its distinctive accents and local arts, together with a political identity founded on its relatively solid support for the Labour Party. It is 'a region with a characteristic history and identity' (Tomaney, 2000, p. 384). It also has a social and economic heritage based chiefly upon the former domination of the region's economy by heavy industries with large plants and mass workforces, including shipbuilding, coal-mining and steel-making (Hudson, 1989), although large areas of the region are rural, possessing very different interests and attitudes. In consequence, the North-East has a long tradition of regional consensus: it 'has a distinct identity and interests within the region are perceived as working together pursuing the common cause' (Robinson, 1993, p. 58).

Campaigners in the North-East seek recognition of the region's identity and collective interests by the form of regional institutions, including an elected assembly, together with more effective remedies to deal with the economic decline and environmental degradation which have resulted from the decline and demise of its traditional heavy industries. However, until recently national governments have been reluctant to entertain the region's claim for greater political autonomy. Between 1979 and 1997 the government's responses to its economic difficulties were notoriously unsympathetic. The new regional institutions offer the North-East new opportunities to assert its interests but the Labour Government has been slow to enable the region to express its political will through an elected assembly. This must therefore be regarded as a problematic or contested region.

Still more doubtful must be the claims to regional identity and hence the credibility of demands for regional autonomy from marginal regions such as the South-West of England, where identities are multiple and confused. Cornwall claims to be a cultural region on its own with its own language but it is too small to be accepted as a region in terms of economic regeneration or other policy issues – although its separation from Devon in the collection of EU statistics enabled Cornwall and the Isles of Scilly to obtain Objective 1 status, because on its own, their domestic product per head of the population was sufficiently low to justify Objective 1 status, which had not been the case when the figures were returned together with wealthier Devonshire (Parks and Elcock, 2001). There is a Cornish language but the extent to which it is in everyday use is disputed. Further East, Bristol, Exeter and Plymouth contest the status of regional capital, although some of the regional institutions have avoided this issue by locating themselves in the smaller market town of Taunton. A negative but important source of regional identity is its need to address the problems caused by the South-East. One regional planner stated that 'we are strongly tied together because we are all fighting the same battle against the concentration of prosperity in the South-East' (interview data). On the one hand, the South-East possesses economic resources and facilities which the South-West needs but on the other hand, immigration from the South-East may threaten the South-West's attractive environment, which is the main reason for retirees and workers to move there from the South-East in the first place. Hence one factor unifying the South-West is a common foe (Elcock, 2001; interview data).

Lastly, some regions are purely functional, lacking a distinctive cultural identity. This applies especially to American regions such as Western New York State, which have no distinctive cultural or popular identity but which increasingly seek to establish regional institutions in order to reverse economic decline and its inevitable accompaniments, poverty and environmental degradation. Both Western New York and Southern Ontario need to exploit the tourist attraction of the Niagara Falls. Efforts have therefore been made by political office-holders, academic institutions, business partnerships and some local governments in Western New York to create regional alliances and municipal co-operation, which have met with some success. However, these fall a long way short of creating regional governance institutions, let alone an elected regional government. Indeed, there is only one elected regional or metro-government in the entire USA, in the region centred on Portland, Oregon. This has extensive transportation and planning functions. It was created by State legislation which originated in an alliance between urban environmentalists and farmers who were both concerned about urban sprawl (Rusk, 1999). Portland's metro-government is viewed enviously by politicians, administrators and business people in other American regions but nowhere else has the local and state-wide consensus behind regionalisation developed sufficient force to secure the creation of an elected regional or metro-government.

Conclusions

Two conclusions can be drawn from this analysis. The first is that there are rising demands for regional government throughout the Western world, stimulated in part by the injustices perpetrated by globalisation as industries are moved from country to country as a result of decisions made in remote international headquarters. The need for regional approaches to regeneration have increased as heavy industries have been replaced by light industries and service providers as the principal sources of employment and incomes in the developed countries of North America and Europe. Regions therefore must be able to campaign for new investment and press their cases for support effectively in supranational as well as national fora. Such functional demands for development aid and investment will become more varied and more strident in Europe when the EU expands to embrace the new democracies of Central and Eastern Europe, many of which have acute problems of industrial decline and environmental degradation which will require extensive EU funding to address. Many impoverished regions in the present EU Member States feel themselves threatened by enlargement, because the EU's Structural Funds are likely to be concentrated on the new, poor democracies of Eastern Europe at the expense of the peripheral regions of Western Europe.

Secondly, minority identities and cultures have been encouraged to assert their political needs for autonomy and representation by the development of international trading blocks such as the EU and NAFTA, because the existence of these supranational agencies reduces the costs of secession from existing states (Keating, 1995). The Scottish National Party now campaigns on a slogan of 'independence within Europe' because with five million people and its oil revenues, Scotland would be by no means the smallest or poorest Member State in the EU. Hence, an independent Scotland could survive politically and prosper economically within the European Single Market. Equally, Quebec's claims for independence have been rendered more credible by NAFTA, because an independent Quebec could trade freely as a partner within the NAFTA zone (Martin, 1997). Similar arguments can be deployed by Catalans, Basques and other stateless nationalities and may even be beginning to stir among the minority nations within France, including the Bretons, Occitans and Catalans. Hence centres have become multiple, peripheries are multiplying and traditional notions of orderly hierarchies among states, nations, regions and communities are becoming increasingly outdated.

References

Boudreau, J. A. (2000), *The Megacity Saga*, Black Rose Books, Montreal.
Burch, M. and Rhodes, R. (1993), *The North-West R egion and Europe: Development of a Regional Strategy*, Department of Government, University of Manchester.
Cabinet Office, Performance and Innovation Unit (2000), *Reaching Out: The Role of Central Government at Regional and Local Level*, The Stationery Office.
Chapman, R. (ed.) (1987), *Public Policy Studies: The North-East of England*, Durham and Edinburgh University Presses, Durham and Edinburgh.
Cherry, G. E. (1982), *The Politics of Town and Country Planning*, Fontana/Collins, London.

Crossman, R. H. S. (1975), *The Diaries of a Cabinet Minister:* volume 1, *Minister of Housing and Local Government*, Hamish Hamilton and Jonathan Cape, London.

Cullingworth, J. B. (1997), *Town and Country Planning in the United Kingdom*, Routledge, London.

Elcock, H. (1997a), 'The North of England and the Europe of the regions: or When is a region not a region?' in M. Keating and J. Loughlin (eds), *The Political Economy of Regionalism*, Frank Cass, London, pp. 422-436.

Elcock, H. (1997b), 'Unity in diversity: the changing United Kingdom polity', in W. H. Field and I. Holliday (eds), *Labour and the Union: Managing subnational and supranational pressures*, Centre for European Studies, New York University, New York, pp. 40-51.

Elcock, H. (2001), *Singing from the Hymnsheet but Varying the Harmonies: Regional Strategies in England*, The Constitution Unit, University College London, London.

Elcock, H. and Parks, J. (2000), 'The English imperium reversed? Devolution sought and (partly) achieved', in *Developments in Politics,* volume 11, Causeway Press, pp. 75-98.

Foster, K. (1997), 'Regional impulses', *Journal of Urban Affairs,* 19, (4), pp. 375-403.

Foster, K. (2000), 'Regional capital', in R. Greenstein and W. Wievel (eds), *Urban-suburban Interdependencies*, Lincoln Institute of Land Policy, Cambridge, MA., pp. 83-117.

Friend, J., Power, J. M. and Yewlett, C. J. L. (1974), *Public Planning: The Inter-Corporate Dimension*, Tavistock Press, London.

Hazell, R. (ed.) (2000), *The State and the Nations*, Imprint Academic, London.

Hogwood, B. and Keating, M. (eds) (1982), *Regional Government in England*, Oxford University Press, Oxford.

Hudson, R. (1989), *Wrecking a Region*, Pion Press, London.

Hull, A. and Vigar, G. (1998), 'Development Plans', in P. Allmendiger and D. Thomas (eds), *Urban Planning and the British New Right*, Routledge, London, pp. 114-136.

Jenkinson, I. (1998), MA thesis, University of Manchester.

Keating, M. (1995), 'Europeanism and Regionalism', in B. Jones and M. Keating (eds), *The European Union and the Regions*, Clarendon Press, Oxford, pp. 1-22.

Keating, M. (1998) 'What's wrong with asymmetrical government?' in H. Elcock and M. Keating (eds), *Remaking the Union: Devolution and British Politics in the 1990s*, Frank Cass, London, pp. 195-218.

Martin, P. (1997), 'When nationalism meets continentalism: the politics of Free Trade in Quebec', in M. Keating and J. Loughlin (eds), *The Political Economy of Regionalism*, Frank Cass, London, pp. 236-261.

McIldoon, D. (1993), 'Development of a regional strategy: the view from the EC', in Burch, M. and Rhodes, R. (eds) *The North-West Region and Europe: Development of a Regional Strategy*, Department of Government, University of Manchester, pp. 7-10.

Orfield, M. (1997), *Metropolitics: A Regional Agenda for Community and Stability*, The Brookings Institution, Washington, DC, USA.

Parks, J. M., forthcoming: Ph D thesis, University of Northumbria.

Parks, J. and Elcock, H. (2000), 'Why do regions demand autonomy?', *Regional and Federal Studies*, 10, (3), pp. 87-106.

Kuhnle, S., Flora, P. and Urwin, D. (eds) (1999), *State Formation, Nation Building and Mass Politics in Europe – The Theory of Stein Rokkan*, Oxford University Press/European Consortium for Political Research.

Roberts, P. (2000), 'Setting the pace: Scotland and the UK Devolution Project', in A.

Wright (ed.) *Scotland: The Challenge of Devolution*, Ashgate Press, Aldershot, pp. 249-265.

Ross, W. and Tomaney, J. (2001), 'Devolution and health policy in England', *Regional Studies*, 35, (3), pp. 265-270.

Rusk, D. (1999), *The Inside Game and the Outside Game*, Brookings Institution Press, Washington, DC.

Salmon, T. (2000), 'An Oxymoron: the Scottish Parliament and foreign relations?' in A. Wright (ed.) *Scotland: The Challenge of Devolution*, Ashgate Press, Aldershot, pp. 150-168.

Sandford, M. and McQuail, P. (2001), *Unexplored Territory: Elected Regional Assemblies in England*, The Constitution Unit, University College London.

Thornley, A. (1991), *Urban Planning under Thatcherism: The Challenge of the Market*, Routledge, London.

Tomaney, J. (2000), 'Democratically elected regional government in England: the work of the North-East Constitutional Convention', *Regional Studies*, 34 (4), pp. 383-8.

Ward, L. (2000), 'Accusations fly after south-east councils reject homes blueprint', *The Guardian*, 13 June.

Wright, A. (ed.) (2000), *Scotland: The Challenge of Devolution*, Ashgate Press, Aldershot.

PART III
EUROPEAN AND
GLOBAL ISSUES

8 The Economics and Politics of Economic and Monetary Union (EMU)

STEPHEN JAMES AND JULIAN GOUGH

Introduction

The aim of this chapter is to offer a balanced and largely non-technical explanation of the economic effects of the European Single Currency, the Euro, and to consider some of its political implications. For member countries, the Euro has changed fundamentally the way in which governments conduct economic policy. It has not only affected the scope of policy but also governments' freedom of action and the effectiveness of existing policy measures. It is also a wide-ranging change. There is a tendency for economic and financial commentators to focus on currency matters and inflation control. In particular, attention is devoted to the performance of the Euro on the foreign exchange markets and the interest rate decisions of the European Central Bank (ECB). In Britain the emphasis is on the continued existence of the pound. This is far too narrow a focus, however, since Euro membership affects all major aspects of policy from public spending and taxation decisions, to labour market policy and social protection. In many of these areas decision making will pass up to the European level, or at the very least will be constrained by Euro-zone agreements, with decisions inevitably being taken on the basis of their Euro-zone effects rather than their national implications. From the point of view of economics, a crucial issue is not just how and whether the policy instruments work, but whether they promote increasing convergence between the Euro-zone economies. As we will consider later, the arguments are not all one way, and there are strong advocates of the view that the single currency will exacerbate the divergent tendencies that already exist in national economies (Thirlwall, 2000). The question of whether there are convergent or divergent economic effects also has serious political implications. They will have an impact on the cohesiveness of the EU countries and perhaps on the legitimacy of the whole EU project. Just as important is the accountability of the decision-taking process. The so-called 'democratic deficit' and the apparent remoteness of EU institutions has been a problem that has rumbled on for many years, without being satisfactorily resolved (see Cohn-Bendit, 2000 for a recent proposal). The greater centralisation of the major economic policy decisions may well bring this into sharper focus.

These issues are explored at greater length in the following sections. We commence by outlining the transition to the Euro, and then address the extent of popular support. Following this the effects of the Euro on the conduct of economic policy are discussed. Next consideration is given to the implications of enlargement. The final part offers a brief summary and some conclusions.

Transition to the Euro

Economic and Monetary Union (EMU) is the adoption of a single common monetary unit by participating members of the European Union. Twelve countries have adopted the Euro, these being Austria, Belgium, Finland, France, Germany, Greece, Ireland, Italy, Luxembourg, Netherlands, Portugal and Spain. This currency area is now conventionally known as the Euro-zone. The remaining three countries of the EU, Denmark, Sweden and the United Kingdom, decided not to join at the outset, but may do so at a later date.

The single currency, the Euro, was introduced as a unit of account in January 1999 in eleven of the countries, and this number was brought to twelve in January 2001 with Greece joining the group. The currency, in the form of credit balances in Euro-denominated bank accounts, was used initially by governments and large businesses as a means of payment and as the basis of accounting. During this period, the Euro was also established as a major new international currency to be held by individuals, companies and governments around the world. The introduction of the currency for general circulation, in the form of notes and coins and retail bank balances, was delayed for a period of three years, during which ordinary citizens in the countries in the Euro-zone would still use their national currencies. The final changeover to the Euro and the phased withdrawal of national currencies took place in the months following 1 January 2002.

The exchange rate at which each national currency converted to the Euro, and hence each other, was fixed at the outset. These rates superseded the exchange rate bands of the previous Exchange Rate Mechanism (ERM) that existed through the 1990s. In that system exchange rates were allowed to vary within a fairly narrow band around a central rate, the variations reflecting the impact of supply and demand factors in the market at any given time. The fixed exchange rates were set at the ERM central rates and announced in May 1998 prior to the final locking of the exchange rates on 1 January 1999. This was to minimise potentially destabilising speculative activity in the months preceding the start of Stage 3 of EMU.

For some the introduction of the single currency makes a fitting completion to the process of integration in Europe over the last half century. In economic terms the European Union is a regional trading group, sometimes called an economic bloc. These economic groups tend to move from a process of loose economic collaboration to progressively more integrated structures. There are conveniently divided into four main stages:

- Free Trade Area – members of the regional group agree to lower or abolish tariffs and quotas on traded goods and services between nations. Individual nations reserve the right to set their own tariffs and quotas on imported goods and services with countries outside the group. The free trade area is therefore likely to have the effect of diverting trade from the outside world to within the group.
- Customs Union – the nations in the regional group agree a common tariff on imported goods and services entering the group. They may also agree physical quotas on such imports from outside.
- Common Market – the nations agree to the removal of all barriers to the movement of inputs within the group – notably the free movement of labour and capital between countries. It also entails the removal of the remaining non-tariff barriers to trade in goods and services and agreements on common standards.
- Economic Union – the nations complete the integration by becoming a single economy with common monetary arrangements and enhanced fiscal arrangements. In effect the nations lose much of their remaining sovereignty and become states within a larger, possibly federal, state. Such a move to full economic union clearly has more profound political implications than the other stages, as the use of the word 'federal' in the pervious sentence indicates.

With the two World Wars of the twentieth century emanating from Europe, there were moves in the 1950s to try to maintain peace, increase prosperity and promote democracy within Europe. The European Economic Community (EEC) was formed in 1957 and effectively provided a Free Trade Area for the six participating countries in central Europe. This, rather confusingly in terms of our above terminology, was commonly called the 'Common Market'. Subsequently a second economic grouping was formed – the European Free Trade Association (EFTA), containing seven countries mainly on the outer fringes of Europe. Its name was more accurate in terms of its function. The UK was originally a member of EFTA but moved to become a member of the EEC in 1973, with membership confirmed following a referendum on the issue in 1975. As a regional economic grouping EFTA never seriously challenged the EEC, and as the latter grew in number to nine, 12 and then 15 members, it became the dominant economic and political force in Europe.

Over time a set of common tariffs and quotas with the rest of the world were agreed so that the regional group moved to our second category, the Customs Union. As integration increased beyond the economic sphere the name of the group changed to become the European Community (EC) and more recently changed again to become the European Union (EU). During the early 1990s a large effort was made to increase competition in the EU and increase the mobility and labour and capital between member states. This culminated in the formation of what was known as the Single European Market (SEM), which was completed by the end of 1992. This effectively brought it to the third stage in economic terms of being a Common Market.

During the 1990s, following the Maastricht Treaty in 1991, it was agreed to move towards further economic integration by introducing a single currency for the group. This was seen by many as the logical next step to the achievement of the SEM in 1992. For others it seemed an unnecessary, costly and risky move which pushed the integration process too fast or too far and deprived individual nations of much of their remaining sovereignty. As a result some members of the Union opted out of the single currency project, at least in the short term.

The current position is that Europe is poised to move to stage four of economic integration and become an Economic Union. It already has the word Union in the title of the regional group, but does not yet have the complete integration of a true Economic Union. Over the years, while much of the power has moved to the European Commission and the Council of

Ministers, nation states still retain some sovereignty. However, speeches by the German Chancellor Gerhard Schröder and the French Prime Minister Lionel Jospin in mid 2001 suggested a reformed European Union with a strengthening of the powers of the EU and its Commission relative to those of national governments. The Commission President Romano Prodi, in a speech in November 2001, also proposed similar reforms, mainly affecting budgetary, foreign and defence policy, and policing. These suggestions have been criticised by a number of EU states, notably by the UK, for the threat they pose to national sovereignty. Indeed, they indicate a sharp division of opinion on the future of the EU, with France, Germany and the Commission pushing for further integration, and the UK acting as the main source of resistance.

Public Opinion and the Euro

The introduction of the Euro is a bold, ambitious but potentially risky monetary experiment. There is no precedent for the scale of its implementation through twelve national countries simultaneously, covering an estimated population of about 250 million people. For it to succeed it must command the confidence of governments, businesses and ordinary citizens both in the short and long term.

From a political and constitutional point of view, of great significance is that the introduction of the currency was not put to the popular vote in any of the participating countries before a decision was taken to proceed, with the exception of France, which had a referendum on the Maastricht Treaty as a whole (1992). In essence the decision to go ahead with the project, first contained in the Maastricht Treaty of 1991, was taken by governments without specific referenda in their respective countries. They took the view that, as they had all been democratically elected, it was perfectly proper to proceed with this issue, as they had done on many other policy initiatives.

That most of the participating governments did not seek the views of their respective electorates can be regarded as taking a major risk on the successful implementation and acceptance of the Euro. Money is defined as anything with is generally accepted as a payment for a debt, so in the last analysis is subject to the confidence of the people. There are many instances in history of currencies failing and it cannot be taken for granted that this huge European experiment is 100 per cent assured of success. The fact remains that if individuals reject the currency, then it will fail whatever governments may exhort. While it may be argued that the 250 million or so have had no option about their currency in that the Euro has replaced their national currencies, it may still rankle with many that they were not consulted. This may be made worse by a comparison with Denmark, Sweden and the UK where the decision-making process put an effective veto in the hands of the electorate. For example, the Danish solution has been to have a regular referendum on the issue. In the UK the Government has been able to postpone a referendum until it is satisfied that the economic conditions for joining are met. These are set out in the so-called 'Five Economic Tests' specified by the Chancellor of the Exchequer, Gordon Brown, in 1997. In effect, therefore governments in the Euro-zone have taken a risk that they can impose the single currency on their nations, and the likelihood is that they will succeed. But it if were to fail in the short or medium term, this lack of consultation would come back to haunt the politicians. The fall-out of failure in political, economic, financial and business terms would be truly catastrophic for Europe and the world.

Nevertheless, the risk of failure because of widespread rejection by the population at large is negligible. It is certainly true that for many people their country's currency is an important national symbol, often representing a long history of political independence or hard-won liberty from an oppressive political power. In the case of Britain for example, there has been the continuous use and evolution of the coinage since the 670s when the Anglo-Saxons minted the silver denarius, with a pound of silver divided into 240 denarii. This formed the basis of the currency accounting system until decimalisation in 1971. Interestingly for the Euro-sceptics, the early Anglo-Saxon currency system was imported from the Frankish Kingdoms (see Weale 2000 for details). The British Conservative politician John Redwood has argued that a national currency acts as one of the ways of creating a strong 'sense of nationhood' (Redwood, 1997, p. 36). Consequently, moves to a single currency, along with greater emphasis on regionalism (see below) in the EU, are likely to upset 'the sense of nationhood that binds us together and…accept mutual obligations'. He goes on to argue that since the sense of accountability and acceptance developed over a thousand years, people in Britain are unlikely to feel the same obligations to others elsewhere in the EU. As Redwood states:

> if by virtue of a currency union I then had to accept obligations to pay higher taxes to look after unemployed people in Sicily, or women on maternity leave in France, I would disagree. I do not have that shared

purpose I feel with fellow countrymen in the United Kingdom (Redwood, 1997, p. 41).

Further, he maintains the currency union runs the risk of increasing regional and separatist tensions, especially in areas less stable than the UK.

In passing, it is worth remarking that Redwood's reluctance to support income transfers from one part of the EU to another is more of an argument against the EU as a whole rather than the single currency per se.

While Britain provides a case of a strong attachment to a national currency because of a long and continuous history, the former communist states of Eastern Europe offer a contrasting illustration. On the collapse of their economies and political system, these countries broke their link with the Rouble and asserted monetary independence. Even with the separation of the Czech Republic from Slovakia in 1993 the countries opted for separate currencies, once again demonstrating that a national currency can be regarded as part and parcel of the assertion of national identity.

But is it necessarily the case that replacing a country's money with the Euro will undermine national unity and lead to possible rejection by the population? In the case of some of the Eastern European states, it likely that breaking with the rouble was sensible given the state of the Russian economy and financial system. Moreover, the national currencies may well be a first step to joining the Euro at some future date. From a purely economic angle the crucial point is not whose head appears on the notes and coins, but their real value in exchange for goods and services. The control of inflation is the critical factor that will determine the ultimate acceptance of the Euro, both nation by nation and internationally. It is perhaps no coincidence that some of the strongest support for the Euro comes from the countries that have had persistent inflation problems – Greece, Italy, Belgium – and the least support from low inflation countries – Germany and most recently the UK. Perhaps it is a question of whether people trust their governments and central banks rather than whether they have their own distinctive currency.

This last point seems borne out by recent surveys, with a high degree of acceptance of and confidence in the Euro project. According to the European Commission's Eurobarometer poll, on the eve of the final changeover support for the Euro was less than 50 per cent only in the UK, Denmark (non-participants) and Finland (Table 2 below). In nine out of the 12 members support was over two-thirds of the sample, and across the EU support was around 60 per cent. Interestingly, in the survey conducted a year later (autumn 2002), some ten months after the introduction of the Euro as a circulating currency, support seems to have risen in the majority of countries, including the most sceptical members (Germany and Finland) and the non-members (Denmark). Other opinion surveys from the Commission (Flash 139) show that the changeover has been remarkably smooth, with about 50 per cent 'happy' that the Euro has become their country's currency and just over 50 per cent over believing that it will be 'advantageous overall'. This is notwithstanding some concern about upward price adjustments and the initial weakness of the exchange rate against the US dollar.

Table 2   Support for the Euro (%)

	2001 (Autumn)	2002 (Autumn)
Belgium	72	81
Denmark	47	55
Germany	60	62
Greece	79	71
Spain	69	77
France	63	71
Ireland	73	80
Italy	79	76
Luxembourg	84	89
Netherlands	71	67
Austria	68	75
Portugal	67	70
Finland	49	66
Sweden	51	51
UK	27	28
EU	61	63

Source: Eurobarometer No. 56 and No. 58

The ECB, Inflation and Monetary Policy

At the core of any modern currency system is the central bank, the ECB in the case of the Euro. Its main role is to maintain internal value of the currency, i.e. to keep inflation low. It has one principal policy instrument, the ability to set short-term interest rates in the financial markets and thus to influence the level and structure of other interest rates across the Euro-zone. This in turn affects the overall level of expenditure in the Euro-economies as well as the Euro exchange rate, both of which are important elements in the transmission of inflation. The inflation-control role for the ECB is set out in the Maastricht Treaty (1993), Article 105 of which states: 'The primary objective of the ESCB (European System of Central Bànks) shall be to maintain price stability'. Moreover, in pursuing price stability the ECB is independent of political interference from the European Commission, and member governments (Article 107).

In economic parlance, the ECB is instrument independent since it is able to choose the level of interest rates it believes necessary to meet its inflation target. In addition, as Bean (1998) points out, because the Maastricht Treaty did not specify exactly what was meant by price stability, the ECB was able to choose its own definition and thus set its own target. At present this is a 0-2 per cent range for the inflation rate. It can therefore be described as goal independent as well. This contrasts with the UK where the Bank of England is set a target by the government, currently 2.5 per cent.

The underlying logic of an independent central bank rests on a model of inflation that is prevalent in mainstream macroeconomics and macro-econometric forecasting. It is a natural rate of unemployment – a rational expectations model in which there is a unique rate, or narrow range, of unemployment that is consistent with stable inflation. Equivalently, there is a level of potential output consistent with stable inflation. Reductions in unemployment below this natural rate, and increases in output above potential, give rise to accelerating inflation. Conversely, increases in unemployment above, and falls in output below, their natural/potential rates result in decelerating inflation. In brief, output and unemployment in the long run are determined by supply-side factors – productivity and the operation of the labour market – and demand determines prices and inflation. This is not to say that demand has no effect on output or unemployment; rather it is a transitory, short-run effect. Depending on the structure of the economy, such demand effects on output may persist for a considerable length of time, and where there is a greater degree of persistence, there is increased scope for traditional Keynesian demand management policies. Nevertheless, once all the demand effects have worked through, output and unemployment return to their long-run levels, or more accurately for output, to its underlying growth path.

The speed with which the economy returns to its long-run position depends on the way in which people's expectations of inflation are formed. Most economic models assume that people make best use of all the available information and do not make consistent errors in their forecasts. This is the famous rational expectations hypothesis. Its significance lies in the fact that if a rise in demand is anticipated, then people adjust their expectations of inflation instantaneously, inflation rises and the economy moves to its long-run position immediately without there being any short-term effect of demand on output or unemployment.

The implications of this model were analysed by Kydland and Prescott (1977) and Barro and Gordon (1983). They suggested that if monetary policy were in the hands of the government, it would suffer from a lack of credibility, known as time inconsistency. The problem arises because in the short run the authorities are able to obtain reductions in unemployment and increases in output by cutting interest rates and thus raising demand unexpectedly. Over time, however, the gains disappear as people begin to anticipate higher inflation and consequently output falls back to its potential, long-run level. Whether a government is tempted to do this depends on whether the short-term gains are sufficient to offset the long-run costs, and thus depends on the weight it places on reductions in unemployment now relative to losses resulting from higher inflation in the future. A classic scenario is a government reflating shortly before an election and deflating to control inflation immediately after – the political business cycle. With rational expectations, people come to anticipate reflationary actions by governments, and build higher inflation-expectations into their actions, hence inflation rises. Even a commitment by the monetary authorities (government/central bank) to price stability in the form of an inflation target lacks credibility because, having convinced the public of the commitment, there is always the incentive to 'cheat' and inflate for short-term advantage.

The conclusion of this analysis is that monetary policy lacks credibility and that whatever the authorities say, they will not be believed. Either inflation is higher at potential output or to control inflation the level of interest rates will have to be higher. The importance of separating the monetary authorities from the government, giving the central bank independence and setting an inflation target, is that it adds credibility to inflation control policy. As long as there are constitutional constraints preventing political interference in central bank decisions and sufficient sanctions for policy failures, inflation expectations are reduced and actual inflation falls. In fact the circle is even more virtuous than this. Interest rates will be lower, investment higher and thus growth faster.

The relevance of the time consistency approach for the Euro issue is that joining the single currency is one way of importing credibility. Of course, for Germany, which had a central bank with a credible inflation policy for many years, this argument did not apply. It has also become irrelevant for the UK since the Bank of England was given instrument independence in 1997 (see Balls, 2001 for an assessment of the new UK arrangements). For other countries with poor records on inflation, however, it may be argued that it is a rather less painful way of acquiring credibility. Granting their own central bank independence would be one way, but may require an extended period of recession for inflationary expectations to adjust downwards, i.e. actual inflation has to be below expected inflation. Delegating inflation control to a supra-national body such as the ECB may well be a way of acquiring a credible policy while avoiding the worst of the adjustment costs. Moreover, with the country tied into the single currency, there is no prospect that a future government will be able to compromise central bank independence as it could with a national central bank, say through the appointment of a sympathetic head of the central bank or a change in the legislation (also see Ardy, 2001).

Despite the benefits of independence, some concern has been expressed over the concentration of the ECB on the inflation target, with fears that it will be to the exclusion of other objectives such as GDP growth and unemployment. It has, for example, been compared unfavourably with the US Federal Reserve because of the latter's greater flexibility in the pursuit of its objectives. Indeed, the fact that the Fed is not tied to a specific inflation target means that it is able to respond to adverse shocks more rapidly and with greater concern for the effects on output and unemployment. A recent example is in the way in which the US Central Bank cut interest rates rather more aggressively than the ECB in response to the slowdown in the world economy during 2001, and particularly in the aftermath of the World Trade Centre terrorist attack. The alternative point of view is that Article 107 of the Maastricht Treaty (see above) does permit the ECB to consider other objectives besides inflation, just so long as the inflation target is not compromised. Moreover, since the ECB is a new institution, a concentration on gaining credibility for its anti-inflation stance is an important short-term investment; once gained, the Bank will have greater flexibility in the future. The Federal Reserve also is not without its critics. A recent study has suggested that it would be more effective if it set out its objectives more clearly rather than let the financial markets and general public have to guess the strategy (Blinder et al. 2001).

Another cause of concern with the ECB is in the area of democratic accountability and the transparency of the decision-making process. To some critics, it is a classic case of a remote EU institution. The conditions and framework under which the ECB operates are set out in the Protocol (No. 18) on the Statute of the European System of Central Banks and of the European Central Bank. They represent an attempt to balance accountability and democratic control on the one hand with the need to maintain political independence of the Bank on the other. Thus day-to-day control of the ECB is in the hands of the President and Vice President working as part of the Executive Board and decisions on the setting of interest rates are made by the Executive Council. The latter comprises the Board, including President and Vice-President, and the heads of the central banks of the Euro zone countries.

In terms of democratic control, the ECB is not unlike other aspects of the EU. Overall control is in the hands of member states' governments either in their appointments to head national central banks or through the European Council for the appointment of the President, Vice-President and Executive Council. It is distant, tenuous and operates indirectly through national political institutions. Unlike the US system, where the Chairman and members of the Board of Governors of the Federal Reserve are confirmed by the Senate, elected representatives to the European Parliament are unable to scrutinise, and certainly cannot veto, appointments. There is clearly the potential for horse-trading over the selection of the President, as happened in the appointment of the first President, Wim Duisenberg. The eventual agreement, or perhaps understanding, was that he would serve for four years instead of the usual eight, and be replaced by J.-C. Trichet, the French central banker (though this is now in doubt because of fraud allegations against Trichet). Moreover, there is the criticism that the system is open to manipulation through the appointment of heads of national central banks with a particular outlook or brief. This problem, however, is probably overstated. Each member of the executive has only one vote, thus minimising the likelihood of any one country's outlook prevailing, and that is without considering the fact that ECB independence is protected by statute and Council and Board members can only be removed for serious misconduct (Articles 14 and 11.3 respectively).

Perhaps of greater concern is that there are no provisions in the statutes for the disciplining of the ECB President, Board or Council for a failure to perform their primary task, that is to maintain price stability. In the UK for example, the Governor of the Bank of England is required to write an open letter to the Chancellor of the Exchequer if the UK inflation rate deviates by more than one per cent from the 2.5 per cent target. Such a letter explaining why inflation is away from the target, the action the Bank proposes to take and how long the adjustments will last is clearly an ignominious act for a central bank governor, and one that may well force resignation. The toughest regime facing central bankers is perhaps the New Zealand system introduced in 1989. Here the Governor can be sacked by the government if the Reserve Bank's performance has been inadequate in terms of achieving price stability (RBNZ, 2001).

A comparison between the ECB and other central banks also indicates that accountability and transparency are limited. The ECB does publish an annual report and explanatory notes accompanying interest rate changes, but little else apart from presidential speeches. It publishes no record of discussions or voting in the Executive Council, and explanations of interest rate decisions are usually extremely terse. By contrast, the Bank of England has to give evidence and answer questions to the House of Commons Treasury Select Committee (TSC) four times a year, it publishes a quarterly Inflation Report and the Annual Report is debated in the Commons. Interestingly, the Bank is also required to publish the minutes and voting of the Monetary Policy Committee, the committee that decides on interest rates. Although the minutes have to be published within six weeks of the MPC meetings, the average time was five weeks until recently, and has been reduced to within two (October 2001) following a recommendation by the TSC in July 2001. Moreover, there are clear explanations of interest rate decisions following the monthly MPC meetings. In the US the Federal Reserve publishes a semi-annual report and the Chairman is required to testify before two Congressional Committees, the Senate Committee on Banking, Housing and Urban Affairs and the House Committee on Banking, Finance and Urban Affairs.

In general, therefore, the framework within which the ECB operates has major shortcomings in the three areas that are generally regarded as crucial for the legitimacy and efficient operation of institutions in democratic societies – democratic control, accountability and transparency. It may be argued, for example by Christopher Huhne (passim), that surrendering democratic control is a small price to pay for a credible, independent central bank that is able to ensure price stability. Inflation, after all, is often regarded as not only as an impediment to the efficiency of an economy, but also as a threat to the fabric of society. And certainly, there are few who would argue that a central bank's decisions on interest rates should be put to a parliamentary vote or plebiscite. However, there are even fewer who would argue that institutions in a democratic system should not be directly answerable for their decisions, and not have to justify them both to elected organisations and the public at large. This is not to say that the ECB decisions have so far suffered from the excessive secrecy of the institution. On the other hand, in the long term to ensure good decisions and public support, especially in times when difficult decisions have to be made (e.g. world recessions), one would anticipate, and hope for, the development of a system with greater openness and transparency. From an economics point of view, as recent research shows (Blinder et al., 2001), transparency also brings more effective and efficient policies. Since economic instability may result from sharp changes in expectations, clear and regular explanations of central bank policies are necessary to ensure smooth adjustments to changing economic circumstances.

Turning to more specific economic policy issues, we now consider some questions concerning the determination of the exchange rate and the choice of interest rates. At the strategic level, the Euro exchange rate is not in fact an objective for the ECB, with responsibility for decisions on the exchange rate system taken at head of state/government level at the European Council. The ECB's role is operational; that is to hold and manage foreign exchange reserves of member states, and to conduct foreign exchange market operations. Given the interdependence between the exchange rate and interest rates, however, the ECB's targeting of inflation using interest rates effectively means that the Euro must float against other currencies such as the US dollar and the yen. Clearly, therefore, any change in the Council's decision on the appropriate exchange rate regime will have major implications for ability of the ECB to set interest rates. For example, a shift towards an exchange rate target or fixed rate against the dollar would mean that the ECB would have to set interest rates at a level required to meet the target. It would mark a major shift in policy, and whilst it does not necessarily undermine the ultimate target of price stability – and may be an alternative way of meeting it – it would result in a fundamental change in the way in which the ECB operates. Consequently, it is a decision that is unlikely to occur without close consultation with the Bank.

The reason for the interdependence between interest and exchange rates follows from the fact that in financial markets capital tends to flow to those countries offering the highest return (risk and other factors equal). Thus differences in interest rates between countries will give rise to significant shifts in the allocation of capital. This in turn involves the buying and selling of currencies on the foreign exchange markets, and thus movements in exchange rates. This effect is summed up in the generally accepted result that it is not possible for the monetary authorities to control both the domestic interest rate and the exchange rate. Consequently, in a single currency area there will be a single interest rate or, to be precise, a single set of interest rates, the level of which is determined by the ECB. It is a major concern of the critics of the Euro that the level of interest rates chosen by the ECB will not suit all countries. This is the famous 'one size fits all' problem. It is explored in more detail in the next section.

Economic Policy Choices – the Sovereignty Issue

In the previous section it was shown how a single currency operating across a number of countries results in the loss by each country of the principal instrument of monetary policy – the rate of interest. This raises the question of whether this loss of sovereignty actually matters. That is, will it be possible to operate an effective common economic policy across the Euro-zone?

For the new currency to work effectively it was thought essential that the economies in constituent countries of the Euro-zone should be performing similarly. To this end, there was a process of 'convergence' undertaken for a number of years prior to the adoption of the Euro in 1999. This was used to encourage countries to formulate the same economic policies and as a formal test as to whether they qualified for entry into the Euro-zone. The five tests of convergence used referred to inflation, interest rates, public sector borrowing, government debt as a proportion of GDP and the exchange rate. The aim was to ensure a starting pattern for the new currency of low inflation, low interest rates, stable exchange rates and a manageable level of government debt. In the event the test were not so rigorously applied as was initially proposed and there were several accusations that the data for some countries on particular tests had been manipulated. There were also several instances of non-compliance, particularly on total government debt, and the criteria were set aside for particular countries on the grounds that they were making progress to their achievement. Only Greece failed to pass the tests in 1999. This prompts one of two conclusions: either political considerations took precedence on the final decisions; or wise economic judgement was used to override what were essentially rather arbitrary measures of convergence.

This approach to convergence has become known as nominal convergence – i.e. it concerns a fairly narrow band of tests concerned with monetary factors. What it did not do was to test more widely for the performance of the applicant countries in terms of economic growth, stage of the business cycle, level of unemployment or state of the balance of payments. This is known as real convergence. As a result it was possible for countries to meet the nominal tests whilst being out of line with each other on a wider dimension. Indeed this appears to have happened since 1999, with countries like Ireland and Spain on the outer fringe of the zone experiencing an economic boom, while Germany and France were struggling to pull out of recession. The ECB had the unenviable task of trying to formulate an economic policy that was appropriate to these differing circumstances. In the case of Ireland, the rise in inflation and rapid growth in the economy warranted a rise in interest rates to contain the boom, while in Germany the sluggish growth of manufacturing industry led to pressures for decreased interest rates to promote recovery. The ECB has to decide between these conflicting requirements, resulting from diverging economic conditions in member states. Inevitably, it had to compromise, bearing in mind that some countries were 'more important' than others – Germany is the largest economy in the Euro-zone while Ireland is one of the smallest.

But inflation and growth were not the only complicating factors. The international trading value of the Euro collapsed by 20 per cent against the dollar in its first two years – hardly the game plan of the ECB at its triumphal launch of the currency. Rather than being as good as the German Bundesbank, the ECB presided over a huge devaluation that was inflationary, due mainly to the rise in the price of imported oil which is denominated in dollars. Partly for this reason, the ECB failed to meet its inflation target and has therefore faced a lack of credibility from the world at large. Furthermore, it is possible that due to the impact of missed targets on the credibility of its anti-inflation policy the Bank has been slow to reduce interest rates despite the sluggish performance of many of the Euro-zone economies.

The underlying problem therefore when trying to design a single interest rate policy to cover the whole of the Euro-zone is the lack of real convergence between the countries. A principal source of this divergence stems from the fact that the economic structure varies from country to country. This may be in terms of the balance between the broad economic categories of primary, manufacturing and service sectors, or the relative importance of different industries within each. Also of importance is the degree to which each country is integrated into the EU and world economies. The significance of these types of differences between countries is that unexpected changes in economic conditions affecting the economies, 'shocks', will not have the same effect in one country as they will in another. There are two possibilities here. One is that a shock will affect one economy but not another; more likely is that the impact of the same shock will vary from one country to another according to its economic structure. For these reasons they are known as asymmetric shocks. A classic example of an asymmetric shock is the effect of a rise in the world price of oil, which for an oil producer and exporter (e.g. the UK) will be markedly different than for a non-producer and importer (continental western Europe).

The conditions under which these shocks actually cause problems have been explored in the optimum currency area literature. Following Mundell (1961) and McKinnon (1963), economic differences would not constitute a problem if the economies in a single currency area were sufficiently flexible, i.e. they can be regarded as being part of an optimum currency area. Adjustment to shocks would not only be rapid but also produce convergence. Where the conditions for an optimum currency area are not met, however, the internal mechanisms within each country or region may not be sufficiently strong to prevent a greater divergence in economic performance and an exacerbation of the existing problems, such as regional and localised unemployment. Some fairly straightforward economic analysis can be used to illustrate the problems.

Insufficient factor mobility between countries is one of the main reasons why asymmetric shocks will cause persistent difficulties in a single currency area. Consider a country that has a sizeable motor industry. A substantial negative demand shock due to, say, a decline in the world demand for cars, will raise unemployment in that country. This rise in unemployment will be mitigated if factors, especially labour, are mobile between countries and industries since workers will look to another country and industry to find employment. In the absence of factor mobility, unemployment will persist. Policies will therefore have to be devised to deal with inter-country disparities in much the same way that national regional policies are aimed at intra-country ones.

An alternative, or additional, adjustment mechanism to factor mobility is through changes in factor prices. Keeping with the motor industry example and concentrating on the labour market, the decline in the world demand for cars will tend to have a depressive effect on wages in the car industry. Under competitive conditions this would induce both an outflow of workers from the industry and a restoration of its competitiveness. A general presumption by economists, however, is that in the short term wages are relatively inflexible, especially in heavily unionised sectors or economies. The adjustment to the shock therefore will be mainly through a contraction in the industry and rise in unemployment. Real wages may fall over the longer term, restoring competitiveness of the industry and region/country, but this may take a number of years and leave the country with prolonged and possibly chronic unemployment.

These kinds of problems are all too evident in national economies where regional disparities have shown a marked persistence over time. This suggests that the normal market mechanisms are rather slow to operate, or are impeded in some way. Another possible explanation is that the regional disparities are less to do with shocks, which may be reversed, but more likely to be the result of long-run structural changes in demand. This appears to be the case with coal, shipbuilding and other heavy industries that are usually associated with the depressed regions of advanced economies. It also indicates another related source of economic difficulties that can arise in a single currency area, that of a lack of diversity in an economy. It should be evident that the greater the diversity in a regional or national economy, the more able it may be to withstand and adapt to changes in the economic environment.

One adjustment mechanism open to national economies with their own currency that is not available to their regions is the ability to change the external value of the currency. This may be permissive, allowing the exchange rate to fall or rise with market sentiment, or by engineering a change through action on other policy instruments, notably interest rates. In the case of a country which suffers a negative demand shock, a fall in the value of the currency can act as an alternative to wage flexibility and the adjustment in the labour and product markets. Thus competitiveness can be restored because a depreciation (or devaluation) reduces the overseas price of exports (and raises the domestic price of imports) without requiring the usual domestic price and cost changes. Notably, real wages fall as a depreciation is usually associated with a rise in the domestic price level. Exchange rate changes therefore act as a cushion for the economy when there are short-term inflexibilities. Over the longer-term there may not necessarily be a permanent change in the real exchange rate as domestic wages and prices catch up due to the rise in import prices and the looser monetary policy, and consequently the benefits of the depreciation evaporate. However, the point is not that the exchange rate change necessarily has a lasting effect on competitiveness; it is that it helps the adjustment in the real economy when wages are inflexible and factors immobile. By the time the real exchange rate has been restored, either the asymmetric shock will have been reversed or the necessary real adjustments will have taken place without the painful effects that arise from real rigidities – plant closure, unemployment and the like.

The significance of this analysis is that for a country that is a member of a single currency area, the exchange rate buffer is not available. The burden of adjustment is therefore shifted to other instruments of economic policy. One possible solution is increased use of fiscal policy. The other is to increase the flexibility of product and labour markets, and hence the automatic response of the economies. These are now discussed in turn.

Fiscal policy involves controlling the aggregate economy by altering government expenditure and taxation. Countries that are able to run their own fiscal policy will be able to insure against the risks of an adverse shock by borrowing in the capital markets. Thus, in times of recession, when an expansionary policy is required, deficits can be allowed rise as they can be financed by the capital markets. In inflationary periods on the other hand, deficits will fall, leading to fewer calls on the financial markets, and possibly a net repayment of debt.

The use of fiscal policy, however, poses economic and political difficulties, both of which hinge on the sovereignty issue. For some, there seems little reason why membership of a single currency area should seriously jeopardise a country's control over fiscal policy, and maintain that decentralisation is both feasible and desirable. Allsopp and Vines (1996) have argued that there are two basic benefits of decentralisation. One is that at country, or even at regional level, it has the advantage that the fiscal authorities will have access to better information on which to base their tax and spending decisions. A second is that decentralisation avoids the moral hazard problem. Consider a region that needs to adjust to changing economic circumstances, but which is supported by transfers from the federal authorities (or the European Commission in the case of the EU), and is thus subsidised by other regions. It may be less inclined to adopt policies that are painful in the short term but required for longer-term prosperity. Decentralisation reduces this potential difficulty.

Despite such arguments, it is evident that there will be growing pressure for countries to align, or harmonise, their tax and spending plans. Such a move would significantly reduce a government's control over the national economy since it would be left with little direct power over instruments which governed aggregate expenditure. In the short run this would probably take the form of the limitation of national governments over certain issues – for example, permitted changes to Value Added Tax or the maximum permitted government borrowing as a percentage of GDP (e.g. as in the Stability Pact, see below). In the longer term it may progress to the structure of business and personal taxation and possibly the distribution of government expenditure between alternative uses, though this would depend on the degree of decentralisation. Thus in a future federal EU-wide variations in tax and spending would be feasible as is the case in most federal states.

At present, the principal framework for fiscal policy in the Euro-zone is set out in the Stability and Growth Pact (Amsterdam Summit, 1997). This is designed to counter a number of tensions and difficulties that could arise as a result of countries pursuing different fiscal policies, and is particularly aimed avoiding the problems brought about by excessive budget deficits and high national debt levels. One of the main difficulties is ensuring compatibility between a centralised monetary authority, with a commitment to low inflation (ECB), and decentralised fiscal authorities, national governments. Budget deficits add to demand in the economy and need financing – by a monetary expansion or increased sales of government debt. Either way, interest rates are likely to rise. Where demand and the money supply are rising, the central bank will raise interest rates to counter the potential inflationary effects. In the latter case, to sell more bonds governments have to offer higher returns, again pushing up interest rates. The higher interest rates are in turn likely to raise the exchange rate, causing a reduction in trade competitiveness and ultimately a balance of payments problem. The classic example of these effects was the 'twin deficits' problem in the US in the mid-1980s. A further adverse effect is that high interest rates reduce investment and thus slow growth.

A sophisticated explanation of the difficulties of co-ordinating monetary and fiscal policy is offered by Allsopp and Vines (1998). They see the

Stability and Growth Pact as a solution to a prisoner's dilemma problem. All countries accept the benefits of fiscal restraint but, unless they are compensated by a relaxation in interest rates, regard the costs as too great. Where there is national control over fiscal and monetary policy, it is possible to co-ordinate policy adjustments. In the Euro-zone, however, with decentralised fiscal policy but monetary policy outside the control of each country, co-ordination is more difficult because no individual government can guarantee either that other countries will exercise fiscal restraint, or that the benefits of lower interest rates will be forthcoming. The incentive therefore is to play safe and not co-operate since no country wants to be caught out with restrictive fiscal and monetary policy. An agreement such as the Stability and Growth Pact, which ties all countries to a credible policy of fiscal discipline and which can be enforced, therefore offers a solution to the dilemma, and in return the ECB is more likely to relax monetary policy.

How the Stability and Growth Pact solves the co-ordination problem is not only by encouraging countries to commit themselves to fiscal restraint, but also through the imposition of penalties on countries which do not meet the terms of the agreement (see Buti et al., 1998 for a full discussion). In effect this is a punishment strategy to deter free riders. Essentially the Pact follows the Maastricht convergence conditions by imposing a medium-term objective of a balanced budget, with a deficit ceiling of 3 per cent of GDP in recession. There is monitoring of each country's budgetary conditions to maintain the commitment to the Pact and act as an early warning mechanism for likely breaches in the conditions. Countries in the Euro-zone are required to present stability programmes. These are examined by the European Council, which is also able to recommend that member states make adjustments to their plans. The credibility of the system is ensured by the imposition of sanctions for 'excessive' deficits. There is a two part penalty comprising of an interest-free deposit. The first, fixed component is 0.2 per cent of GDP. The second, variable part is equal to 10 per cent of the difference between the actual deficit and the 3 per cent limit. After the first year, only the variable component is applied, but the deposit is converted to a fine after two years.

Despite its apparent strictness, the Pact does have some flexibility. Deficits above 3 per cent are permitted in exceptional circumstances, defined as a deep and persistent recession. Specifically, 'exceptional' means a fall in real GDP over a year by more than 2 per cent, or by less than 2 per cent if it is particularly abrupt. Nevertheless, the exceptional deficit is only temporary and unless the conditions persist, steps must be taken to reduce it below 3 per cent in the following year. In effect, this means that the deficit has to be reduced two years after its occurrence and a year after its identification if sanctions are to be avoided. Thus there is some leeway for a country to operate its own fiscal policy, but it is severely constrained. Indeed, it is unlikely that countries will be able to use discretionary fiscal policy in a deep recession unless they are starting from a position of substantial budget surplus. Reliance will therefore be placed on the operation of automatic stabilisers provided by the tax and benefit system as well as the actions of the ECB.

There is also some imprecision in the Pact that leaves scope for political conflict and haggling between states. First, there is a provision for the extension of the excessive deficit procedure in special circumstances. While it is accepted that this means a very severe recession, the circumstances are not spelt out in detail. It remains to be seen whether the Stability and Growth Pact is robust enough to survive a deep recession in a major Euro country, or whether it will need to be more flexible, perhaps along the lines of the UK's Code for Fiscal Stability. The recession and growing deficits in 2002-03 in Germany and France may well put the Pact to its first major test.[1] Second, even though the Council can make recommendations to countries to adjust their budgetary programmes before an excessive deficit occurs (part of the early warning system), there is no guarantee that a country will take action. For example, with the rapid expansion of the Irish economy in 2000-01, one response could have been to pursue a more restrictive monetary policy than that being followed by the ECB at the time (see above). The alternative was to tighten fiscal policy by raising taxes or cutting spending. In fact this is precisely what the Council of EU Finance Ministers (Ecofin) recommended when they issued a critical assessment of the 2001 Irish budget. The Irish Government was urged to take 'countervailing budgetary measures', but refused to change their budgetary stance following electoral commitments it had made not to raise taxes.

It is clear from the above discussion that the Stability and Growth Pact is designed to control the overall balance of budgetary policy across the Euro-zone so that it is consistent with the ECB's primary aim of maintaining price stability. It therefore reflects the view that stabilisation policy in general, and inflation control in particular, should be conducted through interest rates rather than through discretionary variations in budget deficits. What it does not do is co-ordinate budgetary policy in a positive way or lead to greater centralisation, though it does constrain individual governments' tax and spending plans (for a further discussion of some of the issues see EC, 2001 and Allsopp, 2002). As yet, given the size of the EU budget and its concentration on Structural Funds, there is little that could be done as regards a centralised counter-cyclical policy. Without a substantial increase in the EU's own resources or very close co-ordination between national fiscal authorities there is little prospect of the EU budget acting like the Federal budget in the US, and this is likely to remain the position for the foreseeable future for two reasons. Firstly, it is highly politically sensitive, especially given the association with the federalist view of the EU's future. Secondly, it runs against the grain of thinking on the appropriate use of fiscal policy. This is the eschewal of tax and spending adjustments as instruments of macroeconomic stabilisation.

With monetary policy assigned to inflation and fiscal policy constrained by the need to keep a firm control over budget deficits, adjustment to shocks in the Euro-zone economies must rely on other mechanisms, notably the automatic operation of the market. It is for this reason that steps to improve the flexibility of the Euro-zone economies is seen as a necessary part of the EMU enterprise. Especially important is flexibility in their labour markets. If labour markets are responsive, so that wages and the allocation of labour to different industries and regions adapt to shocks, the potential for divergence within a single currency area is much reduced. Furthermore, it is argued that competitive market pressures will reduce existing disparities and result in a greater convergence of the Euro-zone economies. It is also maintained that labour market flexibility necessary to deal with the existing persistent unemployment problem in many EU economies. These are considered by many to be largely structural and also likely to be exacerbated by EMU without reform of the labour market.

The appropriate approach is to encourage flexibility is widely accepted to be a policy of deregulation – the so-called supply-side or microeconomic reforms (see the OECD Jobs Study 1994). The UK, as is well known, has been at the forefront of deregulating the labour market, but there have been significant measures taken in other countries. These range from reductions in unemployment benefit entitlements (e.g. in Germany, Italy, Spain and Sweden) to a relaxation of legislation so that firms find it easier to shed workers (e.g. Spain and Italy). Recent UK proposals for the EU are set out in the Treasury paper *Meeting the Challenge: Economic Reform in Europe* (HM Treasury, 2003).

There are, however, some major drawbacks to a wholesale deregulatory approach. As recent experience in the UK and the US indicates, a substantial proportion of the growth in employment has been in low-paid, often part-time, jobs. The studies by Alogoskoufis et al. (1995) and Freeman (1995) suggest that the main results of Anglo-American style deregulation seem to be larger swings in unemployment rather than a lower average level, and that these are accompanied by a widening dispersion of wages. Indeed greater income inequality has been a major feature of both the US and UK in recent decades. Labour market liberalisation will also have political implications as it will fundamentally alter the existing approach to social welfare policy and labour market protection in most continental EU economies. The ending of high levels of protection and generous social welfare provision along with some adverse distributional effects will leave an increased proportion of the EU population more exposed to the vagaries of the market. The greater feelings of insecurity this engenders could well undermine social cohesion and support for the European integration project. Moreover, as Saint-Paul (1996) points out, it is not evident that liberalisation is feasible. The gains tend to be concentrated on a small proportion of the population, while the losses are more widely spread. Consequently, there may be little support of widespread dismantling of social protection.

A further aspect of the deregulation debate is the question of whether it is necessary. There is a general presumption that the US is a great deal more flexible than the European economy. It is therefore more able to withstand shocks and also less likely to suffer problems of persistent unemployment, thus conforming more closely to an optimum currency area. Eichengreen (1990) for example has shown that regional mobility between states in the US is greater than that between EU countries. This is certainly one aspect of flexibility, but not the only one, and there is good evidence that the EU economies are not as inflexible as is often assumed. Alogoskoufis et al. (1995) show that job turnover – the rate at which jobs are created and destroyed – is much the same in the EU as it is in North America, indicating a similar degree of flexibility. The major difference arises in worker turnover, with US workers more likely to experience periods of unemployment than workers in Western Europe, but of shorter duration. This can be explained in part by the higher firing costs in most EU economies, i.e. the employment protection legislation.

The emphasis on free market solutions and dismantling protective legislation may well be excessive. There are good reasons for thinking that the labour market is susceptible to market failure and that regulations improve rather than impede its operation (see Alogoskoufis et al., 1995 and James, 1998). Moreover, the concentration on microeconomic policies tends to mean that macroeconomic policies are given insufficient weight. It could be argued that creating a stable macroeconomic environment is just as, or more, important as a flexible microeconomic one. Shocks are smaller, and as confidence is greater, the adjustment to shocks is speedier. Similarly, persistent unemployment problems are also less likely to arise. As Bean (1997) has demonstrated, part of the blame for the prolonged periods of high unemployment in Europe can be placed on significant demand shocks (e.g. in the early 1990s).

The Euro and Enlargement

A further dimension to the Euro debate is added by the admission of 10 new countries to the EU in 2004, and the possibility of more in the longer term. The move to enlargement has been driven by several factors. Firstly, the Eastern European countries are anxious to tap into European markets in their transition to a market-based system. Meanwhile, countries in Western Europe feel an obligation to assist the transition following the demise of communism, which could otherwise leave a dangerous political and economic vacuum. Further, the political leaders of the EU may have their own agenda in strengthening the European economic and political bloc to balance the power of the US in the world economy. Currently, for example, there is little that can be done to counter US objections on environmental policy. A stronger and more cohesive EU may well have greater negotiating weight. Finally, multinational firms faced with saturation of markets in the developed economies of Western Europe see the new markets of Poland, Hungary and the Czech Republic as a new area for the expansion of export markets and the location of foreign direct investment. As the new member economies catch up they are likely to expand at the high growth rates that have been seen in other formerly lagging economies, e.g. Ireland. With rising living standards and expanding consumer goods markets, they offer attractive prospects for big business.

While none of these new countries will be members of the Euro-zone, at least in the early years of their admission to the EU, the enlargement is going to have profound effects on the EU. Most of the new countries are relatively poor and in the early stages of transition from a communist to a market-based economy. They are therefore quite unlike the existing members of the EU and add greatly to the diversity of the entire group. The new countries will need to re-structure their economies radically and will probably make substantial demands on EU funds in order to do so. This will put the EU budget under severe strain and may require additional funding from the more developed states.

Enlargement will therefore have an impact on the operation of economic policy in the Euro-zone. For example, there is the need for increased funding to boost the EU budget and even the levying of taxes directly from the EU on member states. This has already been suggested (e.g. by Belgium, mid-2001), but has not yet gained acceptance from other member states. The issue will, however, return as the EU develops. The enlargement may also bring a dichotomy within Europe between the whole EU and the inner members of the Euro-zone. This split already exists to some extent, with the UK, Denmark and Sweden marginalised because they have chosen not to be members of the single currency. On the negative side, this is likely to be greatly accentuated by enlargement, with a dangerous economic and political schism between a central powerful inner zone and a wider and weaker fringe of anti-Euro or newly developing countries. The stability of the EU as a whole could therefore be threatened. Looking at it more positively, enlargement provides an incentive for new and potential EU members to introduce the necessary economic reforms as well as to ensure the continued operation of democratic institutions and the entrenchment of democratic values.

Concluding Comments

The introduction of the Euro is the most important step in the EU integration project so far. It will add to and place greater constraints on the actions of national governments that resulted from the Single European Act (1986) and the Single Market (1992).

The earlier Single European Market programme set the EU on the route to a completely free trade zone. Within the Single Market there are supposed to be few if any barriers to trade, including domestic microeconomic policies such as subsidies to troubled domestic industries. It therefore involves both a commitment to a market economy and implies a reduced public sector element in the traditional mixed economies of

Western Europe. There is thus some loss of sovereignty over domestic microeconomic policy.

Free trade is perfectly feasible with separate currencies, and allows countries to maintain significant domestic control over the main instruments of economic management. Once a currency union is formed, however, economic management passes largely out of national hands. Monetary policy (interest rates) are adjusted to meet the inflation or growth objectives for the currency union as a whole, with the appropriate indicators being averages, as in the case of the Harmonised Index of Consumer Prices (HICP). With the introduction of the Euro, it is the ECB that has become responsible for this aspect of policy. Fiscal policy is more flexible, with governments primarily in control of spending and tax plans, and thus of the balance of the budget, though still having to operate within constraints to avoid conflicts with monetary policy. These constraints are set out in the Stability and Growth Pact.

This loss of economic sovereignty associated with the single currency gives rise to a host of economic and political issues. These include: the problems of managing diverse and possibly divergent economies; the degree to which future developments will involve greater harmonisation, (e.g. of tax systems); the extent to which decision taking and economic management will move to the centre, perhaps with greater budgetary control transferred to the European Commission; and the democratic control and accountability of policy makers. Each of these has an economic content. But in all cases there is an underlying question, that of whether the Euro, with its centralised monetary policy, will lead to the parallel development of a centralised fiscal authority. In other words, does a currency union require fiscal federalism? This, of course, is much more than a technical economic issue; it is essentially the major political question that the Euro raises. That is whether the Euro presages a move towards a federal Europe.

Einaudi (2000), in an enlightening paper, documents the long history of the ideas and practice of monetary union in Europe and its close links with political union. But although monetary union is not a new phenomenon, as Einaudi demonstrates, the current project is quite unlike any other in the past. Between the end of the eighteenth century and the mid-nineteenth century the number of currencies in Europe fell from 200 to fewer than 20, rising again to 26 by the mid-twentieth century. In many cases monetary unification tended to follow political unification, which in turn followed wars, as in the case of Switzerland (1850), Italy (1862), Yugoslavia (1919) and Germany (1871). Where centralised government has remained secure, the unions have remained intact; but in cases where the central authority collapsed, it was accompanied by a collapse of the currency union and a proliferation of currencies, e.g. the Austro-Hungarian Empire (1919), Yugoslavia (1991) and the Soviet Union (1991). Other forms of monetary union are what Einaudi calls supranational currency unions. These involve the creation of a stable monetary instrument either with a common coinage in the case where there was no paper money, e.g. Hanseatic monetary league (1379), or with fixed exchange rates as in the Latin Monetary Union (1865-1926), and even a single currency – the Scandinavian Monetary Union (1872-1931). In these cases the principal motivation was to support the development and extension of trade, and there was no relinquishing of political sovereignty by national governments.

The Euro-system most closely resembles the supranational form of monetary union, but differs from earlier arrangements in a number of important respects. Firstly, there are a greater number of countries involved. Secondly, there is far greater diversity in the members. This not only includes economic differences, but also differences in language, culture and social and political institutions. Thirdly, EMU has gone further in creating the institutional framework to support the monetary union. On the economic side there is the single central bank and a formal grouping of member states' finance ministers (Ecofin) as well as the rest of the EU institutions. Fourthly, there is the motivation behind the EMU that is both political and economic, but which is not associated either with the extension of an Empire or simply supporting trade.

On the political side it is possible to view EMU as a further stage in development of a Europe in which peace and stability is ensured. The creation of a supranational system in which nation states voluntarily agree to relinquish power is regarded by some as the appropriate way of avoiding a repeat of the two devastating twentieth-century wars. The idea of a monetary union to promote peace and co-operation is not new and can be dated at least as early as the late sixteenth century. It has been promoted with increasing interest from the eighteenth century and especially since 1945 (see Einaudi, 2000, Table 2, p. 99).

On the economic side the Single European Currency can be seen as a further attempt to create a framework for international monetary relations in an unstable world economy. Early attempts grew out of the problems caused by the competitive devaluations of the 1930s, and were largely conceived on a world scale. Thus there was the Keynes Plan drafted in

1941 that proposed a fixed exchange rate system and a mechanism (the International Currency Union and International Clearing Bank) to rectify balance of payments problems without recourse to deflation (see Skidelsky, 2000). This was the forerunner to the fixed exchange rate system established at Bretton Woods (1944), which lasted until the early 1970s. It may be argued that the floating exchange rates that followed the break-up of the Bretton Woods system were the appropriate monetary regime to cope with the oil shocks and inflation of the 1970s. However, the experience of floating has shown that shocks are just as likely to emanate from the financial markets as they are from elsewhere. Indeed, with the liberalisation and greater internationalisation of capital markets, financial, and especially foreign exchange market volatility is likely to be increased, thus raising the risks of shocks and amplifying their effects. Recent experience has shown that attempts to manage and stabilise currencies in the face of market sentiment almost invariably fails. Speculators win on a one-way bet, and everyone else loses. As McKinnon notes in the opening of his proposal for international currency reform: 'Globalized financial volatility is capitalism's Achilles heel. And nowhere is the problem of controlling such volatility more acute than in monetary and exchange rate relationships across countries' (1996, p. 1). Moreover, one does not have to be a supporter of international capitalism to be concerned about the acute problems caused by financial market turbulence. Susan Strange for example provides an excellent discussion of the political economy of the international financial system in her last book *Mad Money* (1998), although she was sceptical about the prospects for the future of the Euro, as indeed is McKinnon.

EMU may therefore be seen as a rational development of the fixed-but-flexible exchange rate system – the ERM – of the European Monetary System (EMS). In a world of near perfect capital mobility, fixed or targeted exchange rates become unsustainable during times of rapid changes in expectations. This is clearly illustrated by the problems of keeping the pound in the ERM and its eventual exit in September 1992 and also by the widening of the ERM bands a year later. Given the commitment to financial market liberalisation since the early 1980s and its role in the Single Market, few governments seem willing to re-introduce the exchange controls required to keep the system stable. The alternative, a tax on speculative capital flows – the Tobin tax (see Geoff Harcourt in *The Guardian*, 22 October 2001 for a recent proposal) – would require wide international agreement. But this is only a remote possibility given the competition between governments to secure the lucrative international financial business for their financial centres. Consequently, a move to irrevocably fixed exchange rates and thus a single currency seems a logical step.

The authors of this chapter disagree on the desirability and workability of the Euro-zone. One is concerned that it is too big and too diverse for a single monetary policy to work satisfactorily for all member states. In the long run the fixed exchange rate removes an essential tool of adjustment for particular nations in their economic performance. With the surrender of national sovereignty on monetary policy and its erosion on fiscal policy, member countries will have very few economic levers to pull in managing their economies. The enlargement of Europe will increase this diversity of economic performance and there will be an inevitable division between a fast-track, powerful group in the Euro-zone and a marginalized group of weaker countries on the fringes. In the long term this is thought dangerous both for the working of the Euro-zone, and the stability of the wider super-state of the European Union. It is a huge, expensive and unnecessary project involving high economic and political risk. It was forced upon 12 countries involving a population of about 250 million people without consulting public opinion.

The other author places greater weight on creating stable monetary arrangements and developing mechanisms to minimise exchange rate and other financial market shocks that cause major disruption to the real economy. That this seems to result in a loss of sovereignty in economic policy is essentially illusory. Given the interdependence of policy instruments, there is often very limited room for manoeuvre in the modern economy. Furthermore, in a highly integrated world spillover effects are so significant that international co-operation and the co-ordination of policy is essential. One country's devaluation after all is another's revaluation. EMU may well lead to a move towards a federal Europe in order to devise a system of fiscal transfers that offset regional imbalances in the European economy. However, the loss of national sovereignty and currency flexibility will be no bad thing if it results in a more stable environment better insulated from financial market shocks.

What both authors are concerned about, however, is the continued development of EU institutions without the transparency, accountability or direct democratic control usually expected in national democracies. The development of political institutions alongside economic integration would seem to be an essential condition for the future stability and long-term endurance of the Euro-zone.

Note

[1] As it turned out, in 2003 Germany and France exceeded the 3% deficit limit for the second year running, thus breeching the SGP rules. However, Ecofin waived the penalties and gave both countries longer to correct their budgetary problems. This has provoked a furious debate within the EU since not only has the Commission claimed that Ecofin acted illegally, and is considering a challenge in the European Court of Justice, but it is also a clear example how the two largest and most powerful economies have been treated differently from a small one, Portugal, which was previously fined for exceeding the deficit limits.

References

Allsopp, C. (2002), 'The future of macroeconomic policy in the European Union', *External MPC Unit Discussion Paper*, No. 7, Bank of England.

Allsopp, C. and Vines, D. (1996), 'Fiscal policy and EMU', *National Institute Economic Review*, No. 158, October.

Allsopp, C. and Vines, D. (1998), 'The assessment: macroeconomic policy after EMU', *Oxford Review of Economic Policy*, 14, (3), pp. 1-23.

Alogoskoufis, G., Bean, C., Bertola, G., Cohen, D., Dolado, J. and Saint-Paul, G. (1995), *Unemployment: Choices for Europe*, Centre for Economic Policy Research, London.

Ardy, B. (2001), 'British membership of EMU: Why it is a political not an economic decision', *New Economy*, 8 (1), pp. 14-18.

Balls, E. (2001), *Delivering Economic Stability*, H.M. Treasury, London.

Barro, R. J. and Gordon, D. B. (1983), 'Rules, discretion and reputation in a model of monetary policy', *Journal of Monetary Economics*, 12 (1), pp. 101-21.

Bean, C. (1997), 'The role of demand management policies in reducing unemployment', in D. J. Snower and G. de la Dehesa (eds), *Unemployment Policy: Government Options for the Labour Market*, Cambridge University Press, Cambridge, pp. 83-111.

Bean, C. (1998), 'Monetary policy under EMU', *Oxford Review of Economic Policy*, 14 (3), pp. 41-53.

Blinder, A., Goodhart, C., Hildebrand, P., Lipton, D., and Wyplosz, C. (2001) 'How Do Central Banks Talk?', *Geneva Reports on the World Economy*, No. 3, Centre for Economic Policy Research, London.

Buti, M., Franco, D. and Ongena, H. (1998), 'Fiscal discipline and flexibility in EMU: the implementation of the Stability and Growth Pact', *Oxford Review of Economic Policy*, 14 (3), pp. 81-97.

Cohn-Bendit, D. (2000), 'A European Magna Carta', *The Guardian*, 10 November.

EC (2001), 'Public finances in EMU', *European Economy*, No. 3, pp. 1-180.

Eichengreen, B. (1990), 'One money for Europe? Lessons from the US currency union', *Economic Policy*, No. 10, April.

Einaudi, L. (2000), '"The generous utopia of yesterday can become the practical achievement of tomorrow": 1000 years of monetary union in Europe', *National Institute Economic Review*, No. 172, April, pp. 90-104.

Freeman, R. (1995), 'The limits of wage flexibility to curing unemployment', *Oxford Review of Economic Policy*, 11 (1), pp. 63-72.

Harcourt, G. (2001), 'Turn to the Tobin alternative', *The Guardian*, 22 October.

H.M. Treasury (2003), *Meeting the Challenge: Economic Reform in Europe*, H.M. Treasury, London.

James, S. (1998), 'Labour market policy in Europe: how much harmonisation, how much regulation?' in R. Sykes and P. Alcock (eds), *Social Policy in Europe: Patterns of Convergence and Divergence*, Policy Press, Bristol.

Kydland, F. E. and Prescott, E. C. (1977), 'Rules rather than discretion: the inconsistency of optimal plans', *Journal of Political Economy*, Vol. 85, pp. 473-91.

McKinnon, R. (1963) 'Optimum currency areas', *American Economic Review*, Vol. 53, pp. 717-25.

McKinnon, R. (1996), *The Rules of the Game: International Money and Exchange Rates*, MIT Press, Cambridge MA.

Mundell, R. (1961), 'A theory of optimum currency areas', *American Economic Review*, Vol. 51, pp. 657-65.

OECD (1994), *Jobs Study*, Organisation for Economic Co-operation and Development, Paris.

RBNZ (2001), *Central Banking in New Zealand*, Reserve Bank of New Zealand, Wellington.

Redwood, J. (1997), *Our Country, Our Currency*, Penguin, London.

Saint-Paul, G. (1996), 'Exploring the political economy of labour market institutions', *Economic Policy*, No 23, October.

Skidelsky, R. (2000), *John Maynard Keynes Volume 3: Fighting for Britain, 1937-1946*, Macmillan, London.

Strange, S. (1998), *Mad Money*, Manchester University Press.

Thirlwall, A. (2000), *The Euro and 'Regional' Divergence in Europe*, New Europe Research Trust, London.

Weale, M. (2000), '1300 years of the pound sterling', *National Institute Economic Review*, 172, April, pp. 78-89.

9 Economic and Monetary Union: Implications for the European Union's Global Role

CHARLOTTE BRETHERTON

Introduction

> The Union must increase its influence in world affairs, promote values such as peace and security, democracy and human rights, provide aid for the least developed countries, defend its social model and establish its presence on world markets...prevent major damage to the environment and ensure sustainable growth with an optimum use of world resources. Collective action by the European Union is an ever increasing necessity if the benefits of globalisation and if the constraints it imposes are to be faced successfully. Europe's partners expect it to carry out fully its responsibilities (European Commission, 1997a, p. 27).

As the world's largest trading bloc, the sheer size of its internal market gives the European Union enormous potential for influence on international trade issues and beyond. The European Commission, in proposing an ambitious global role for the Union, is explicitly urging that the Union act proactively to realise the potential suggested by its economic weight – in response not only to the patterns of constraint and opportunity afforded by the external environment but also to the expectations of third parties. The global role of the EU, it is implied, entails responsibilities as well as the pursuit of interests.

This chapter seeks to establish, firstly, the extent to which the EU has become a purposive actor in world politics and, secondly, the implications of Economic and Monetary Union, and in particular the introduction of the Euro, for the actor capability of the Union.

Conceptualising Actorness

The Commission's statement, in *Agenda 2000*, contributes to the discursive practices through which understandings about the EU's global role are constructed. In consequence, it closely reflects the concerns of this chapter. The approach adopted builds upon earlier and more extensive work (Bretherton and Vogler, 1999; 2000). It posits a relationship between the evolving internal character and policies of the EU, the changing reactions and expectations of third parties as the significance, or 'presence', of the EU has increased over time, and the development of EU external policy. This relationship can be characterised as a dynamic process of social construction, in which shared understandings evolve over time and play a role in shaping – enabling or constraining – subsequent action. As Alexander Wendt has argued (1994, p. 389) 'Intersubjective structures give meaning to material ones, and it is in terms of meanings that actors act'. Thus it is interesting to observe ways in which the declared objective of the Union 'to assert its identity on the international scene...' (Article 2, Treaty on European Union) is reflected in discourse, and hence in the construction of shared understandings. Here, the potential of political rhetoric to contribute to the evolution of international practices is nicely illustrated in a speech by Alain Juppé to a Conference of Ambassadors in 1994.

> It is your role as ambassadors of France, both to assert the identity of the European Union and to explain the specific positions defended by France within the institutions thereof. It is without reservations, therefore, that you will endeavour, wherever you are, to affirm the political identity of the Union (quoted in de La Serre, 1996, pp. 36-7).

Similarly, of course, third-party perceptions and judgements concerning the EU's external policy role also contribute to the construction of understandings, if not always to the construction of EU actorness. Of significance, here, are the frequently reiterated, and evidently disingenuous, complaints from US policy makers (and others) about the difficulties of interacting with a disaggregated and leaderless entity.[1]

A focus upon the construction of actorness directs attention to internal/external interactions, and to the perceptions and expectations of third parties. It does not, however, obviate the need to examine the nature and capability of the actor 'under construction'. Nevertheless this chapter is not concerned, primarily, to engage in debates about the 'nature of the beast'. While the EU is evidently very much more than a trading bloc, it is neither an over-developed international organisation nor a partly-formed and incompetent state; rather it is considered, here, to be an international actor *sui generis*. Thus the singularity of the EU is recognised in its sole occupancy of the United Nations category of Regional Economic Integration Organisation (REIO), while its complexity is captured by John Ruggie's characterisation of the EU as 'a multiperspectival polity' which perhaps comprises the world's 'first truly postmodern international political form' (1993, p. 140).

An assertion that the EU is unlike *other* international actors, does not, of course, establish that the EU is *itself* an actor. There can be found, within the International Relations literature, a wide range of competing approaches to actorness.[2] Nevertheless, there is some consensus that an entity or organisation, to be considered an actor in world politics, must enjoy some degree of autonomy from its constituent parts – that is, in the present case, the Member States. Thus, in Hopkins and Mansbach's early formulation (1973, p. 36), if the EU is to be considered an actor it must possess 'the ability to behave in ways that have consequences in international politics and cannot be predicted entirely by reference to other actors or authorities'. Here it is interesting to note the conclusion reached, as early as 1977, that the EU met the two most fundamental prerequisites for achieving the status of an international actor – it was 'discernible from its environment' and it enjoyed some degree of internal cohesion (Sjöstedt, 1997, p. 15). As we shall see, issues of internal cohesion retain their salience for any contemporary discussion of EU actorness.

In addition to these behavioural criteria, legal factors are inevitably also of significance to any discussion of EU actorness. Here it is noteworthy that the European Community (but not the Union) has been accorded legal personality in international law and has, accordingly, attained legally sanctioned actorness. However its formal status is that of an international organisation and it is entitled to act only in areas of legally established competence. In the context of external policy, competence is understood as 'the authority to undertake negotiations, conclude binding agreements and adopt implementation measures' (Macrory and Hession, 1996, p. 6).

In some external policy areas, notably trade in goods, the Community enjoys exclusive competence and the Commission is the sole negotiator in both bilateral and multilateral fora. In these areas the Community is widely acknowledged to be a formidable, frequently dominant actor. As one trade counsellor commented, it is not unusual for Commission negotiators to 'agree a position and push it down our throats' (Interview, Brussels

Mission, January 1996).[3] Even US officials admit that, when negotiating with the Commission, 'there are no free lunches' (Interview, US Mission, June 1996). However in other policy areas, for example 'new' trade issues and many aspects of environmental policy, competence is mixed (that is, shared between the Commission and the Member States), rests with the Member States or is disputed. The vexed issue of competence, coupled with the differences in international legal status of the Community/Union, can prove both a source of confusion to third parties and an impediment to actorness. This is not necessarily the case, however. Commission negotiators regularly use the complexity of the Union, and the ponderousness of its decision-making procedures, as a negotiating ploy when seeking to avoid granting concessions to third parties. As one Commissioner official commented,

> Negotiation is a three-card game. We don't tell third parties which articles are covered by Community competence and which by Member States. This allows us to wash our dirty linen in private (Interview, Commission, July 1997).

Despite the difficulties associated with its multiperspectival personality, the world role of the EU has undoubtedly grown considerably since Sjöstedt's 1977 analysis. This reflects, in part, the processes of widening and deepening which have occurred since that time. Of significance, also, has been the changing external policy environment, and hence the changing pattern of constraint and opportunity confronting the EU. Here a central assumption is that commitment to the development of a proactive external policy has been largely rhetorical, and that the EU's role in world politics has evolved, primarily, as a response to external expectations – and to the unfolding of events. Of enormous significance, here, has been the changing nature of the international, and increasingly global, system.

The creation of the Communities itself represented a response to the needs and opportunities of the post-Second World War period, while the failure to develop a proactive external role in the early years reflected both a preoccupation with internal construction and the realities of a bipolar world dominated by military superpowers. However, from the mid-1970s, following the collapse of the Bretton Woods system and the apparent decline in US economic power, the international system was increasingly perceived in terms of its (primarily economic) interdependence. In circumstances where the ability of individual states to govern effectively was questioned, the Community, a partially integrated regional policy system, appeared well placed to act on behalf of its members in the management of interdependence. It was in this context, during the *détente* period of the Cold War, that EC commitment to a more proactive external role became evident. Subsequent events have been conducive to the development of this role.

Firstly, the ending of the Cold War and the dissolution of the Soviet Union radically altered the external policy environment of the EC/EU – presenting an unprecedented, and unanticipated, range of challenges, demands and opportunities for actorness. Thus, in relation to its immediate neighbours to the East, the EU has played a proactive role as co-ordinator of international assistance and mentor during the transition process. In the Balkans, however, the outbreak of armed conflict in 1991 found the EU initially willing, but woefully ill equipped, to meet this new challenge.

Secondly, by the 1990s notions of interdependence had been largely superseded by an insistent discourse of globalisation, which depicts the state as increasingly incapable of regulating the activities of globally oriented economic actors or responding to global issues such as environmental change. Thus it is possible that, in an increasingly globalised system, regional organisations offer an 'optimal solution to collective action problems' (Hveem, 2000, p. 76). Globalisation, in this analysis, implies increased opportunities, indeed imperatives, for the EU to act externally on behalf of its members. Hence it might be concluded that 'the EU represents an unparalleled test of how government and politics can do more than simply react as other spheres go global' (Leonard, 1997, p. 19).

This chapter seeks to investigate the extent to which the EU has, indeed, moved beyond 'simply reacting'. The focus will be upon actorness, that is the extent to which the EU has developed the capacity to formulate purposes and make decisions, and hence to engage in purposive, externally oriented action. The potential for enhanced actorness in the future will also be considered, and here the emphasis will be upon the potential impact of EMU and the single currency. In examining the construction of EU actorness, and considering its future potential, a major focus will be upon the concept of presence as an indicator of latent actorness. However the related concept of capability will also be considered.

Presence conceptualises the relationship, in the construction of actorness, between the internal development of the EU and third party perceptions and expectations of the EU's role in world politics. Capability refers to the capacity to formulate and implement external policy, both in developing a proactive policy agenda and in order to respond effectively to external expectations, demands and opportunities.

Presence and the Construction of Actorness

Broadly following the usage of Allen and Smith (1990), presence refers to the ability to exert influence, to shape the perceptions and expectations of others. Presence does not connote purposive external action, rather it is a consequence, largely unintended, of internal policies and processes. Thus presence is a function of being rather than doing. Inevitably, presence is enhanced by the success of the European project – reflected in the implementation of internal measures such as the creation of the Single Market or the accession of new members. Important for the construction of actorness is the understanding that presence is 'not solely the property of "actors" centred on people and institutions, but can be a property of ideas, notions, expectations and imaginations' (Allen and Smith, 1990, p. 22).

Presence, then, plays an important role in the construction of actorness, indeed presence denotes latent actorness. The relationship between presence and actorness can be relatively direct, in that active responses from third parties generated by internal EU policy initiatives tend to produce, in turn, demands for action by the EU. The trade diversionary effects of the Common Agricultural Policy provide an obvious example here. Or presence may promote profound yet relatively subtle processes associated, for example, with the impact of the EU as a model – of regional economic integration,[4] or as a 'Community of security' in Europe (European Commission, 1997b, p. 27).

Trade and market access: foundations of presence

EU presence is today discernible in many areas of external policy, however its most fundamental aspect derives from the initial creation of the customs union. While the stimulation of trade, to promote internal economic growth, was the main reason for its establishment, the creation of the customs union had immediate impacts for third parties in terms of trade diversionary effects. The customs union brought about a reversal of the ratio between internal and external trade between the founding Member States, while the accession of new members automatically transferred trade from the category of external to internal. Enlargement, of course, greatly added to the presence of the Community in the world economy, both in terms of the size of its market and the extent of its participation in world trade. The accession in 1973 of the UK, with its high dependence on external trade and its extensive system of ex-imperial preference, was particularly significant in this respect.

The Community/Union is the world's largest trading entity, maintaining a share of global exports and imports of approximately 20 per cent. Inevitably the operation of its Common Commercial Policy has impacted upon, and drawn a response from, third parties in all parts of the globe.[5] Trade provides the primary explanation for the accreditation of 164 external Missions to the EU and, for many countries (117), the motivation for negotiating some form of preferential trade agreement. The initiation and content of successive rounds of multilateral GATT negotiations have also closely reflected the concern of prominent trading partners, particularly the United States, with evolving practice in the EU. Thus, in the words of the Chairperson of a WTO trade policy review meeting, 'the trade policies and actions of the EU do not leave any WTO member indifferent' (WTO, 1997, p. 8).

Perhaps the most objectionable aspect of EU presence, from the perspective of third parties, has been the impact of the Common Agricultural Policy upon trade in agricultural products. The success of the CAP in encouraging food production, coupled with market protection measures and use of export subsidies, ensured that the EU moved from being largely a food importer to the status of major exporter. Its share of the world wheat flour market, for example, increased by almost 40 per cent between 1964 and 1981, while the US share fell by 22 per cent in the same period (Paeman and Bensch, 1995, p. 24). The US subsequently retaliated and later insisted that agricultural products be included within the GATT framework. In this and other areas the EU has been obliged to act in response to external pressures.

Particularly significant as an indicator of presence is the level of dependence of trading partners on the EU market. For some European and African economies this can be very extensive indeed. Thus the 1995 average for Central and East European countries (CEEC) was 63 per cent, with Slovenia conducting 78.8 per cent of its trade with the EU (European Commission, 1997c, pp. 5-7). Comparable figures for Africa are Uganda 75 per cent, Mauretania 79 per cent and Equatorial Guinea 99 per cent (Commission, 1997d, pp. 56-7). High levels of dependence inevitably provide considerable scope for influence, and contemporary trade and 'association' agreements contain numerous conditionalities, in terms of human rights observance, 'good governance' and environmental protection. The content of such agreements, referred to by Commission officials as 'trade plus', exemplify the relationship between economic presence and the potential to act across a range of policy areas.

A highly significant boost to EU presence was provided by the Single Market programme, which was perceived by third parties as having enormous implications. In the case of the EFTA countries it led, in a process facilitated by the ending of the Cold War, to the accession of Austria, Finland and Sweden. In the US the reaction to completion of the Single Market – frequently referred to as 'fortress Europe' – was both excessive and politically significant. It led the US government to seize the initiative in seeking to extend and deepen the US-EU relationship – and hence to provide enhanced opportunities for US influence on EU policy – initially through the 1990 Transatlantic Declaration. Following entry into force of the Treaty on European Union, with the major policy deepening implied by Economic and Monetary Union and an explicit aspiration for an enhanced global role for the EU, the 'New Transatlantic Agenda' and 'Joint US-EU Action Plan', launched in 1995, sought to move the process beyond consultation. Thus, in the words of Stewart Eizenstat, then US Ambassador to the EU, the EU acquired a political force.

> Most importantly for the United States, the Agenda marks the first time we have dealt comprehensively with the European Union as a political force able to join with the United States as a full partner (*European Voice*, January 1996, p. 14).

Despite these efforts, however, the US-EU relationship has remained subject to intermittent, and intense, disputes on a range of specific trade issues from bananas and beef hormones in the late 1990s to steel and genetically modified foods in the new millennium.

The development of the EU, and in particular its economic presence, has significantly affected global politics. Indeed the EU is frequently characterised as an economic power on a par with the US and Japan.[6] Building upon this established presence, the implications of Economic and Monetary Union and the adoption of the Euro appear likely to have significance – in terms both of presence and of third-party expectations.

The single currency: enhancing presence, raising expectations?

Presence, it has been argued, is primarily a function of internal policy developments. Introduction of the Euro undoubtedly represented both an important symbol of political commitment to the European project on the part of key Member States, particularly Germany and France, and a major deepening of the integration process. Indeed, some commentators predicted that the single currency would initiate a significant, perhaps inevitable, process of federalisation (Feldstein, 1997; McKay, 1999). Should these prognoses ultimately prove correct, a federal European state equipped with the second largest currency after the US dollar would achieve a formidable presence. According to Cohen (2000a, p. 88),

> a position of prominence in the hierarchy of currencies plainly promotes the issuing state's overall reputation in world affairs. Broad international circulation tends to become an important source of status and prestige – a highly visible sign of elevated rank in the community of nations.

It might be anticipated that, just as the dominance of the US dollar has contributed to US political supremacy, such a status for the Euro would provide the EU with a major additional source of influence in world politics. It would also bring an expectation that the EU should assume responsibilities – in terms of ensuring the stability, and maintaining the credibility of the Euro, and readiness to act as a lender of last resort. Thus expectations of various forms of actorness on the part of the EU might be anticipated from third countries and international economic institutions.

In practice, however, in marked contrast to reactions to the introduction of the Single Market process in 1987, international response to the launch of the Euro in January 1999[7] was muted – despite warnings from commentators about its significance and (and, for some, distinctly malign) implications (Feldstein, 1997; Hosli, 1998).[8] There are several reasons for this. Firstly, of course, the project was beset by difficulties from the outset. Economic factors such as the exchange rate turbulence which affected several European currencies in 1992 and 1993, coupled with a widespread perception that various aspirant participants in the single currency would fail to meet the convergence criteria, convinced third parties that the project would 'never come into fruition' (Hosli, 1998, p. 165). Alongside these evident practical difficulties, high-profile controversies among economists and other commentators regarding the merits of, and prospects for, the single currency also influenced perceptions of its potential significance.

Even after the launch of the Euro, doomsayers continue to predict the 'degeneration' of the project in the medium term, 'when Europe is hit by the fiscal crises looming for the majority of the Euro zone's member countries' (Ferguson and Kitlokoff, 2000, p. 111).

Initial perceptions of the precariousness of the EMU project were strengthened by political factors, not least the difficult TEU ratification process in 1992/3, which was widely regarded as evidence of increasing scepticism among European publics. Related to popular Euro-scepticism, and of great significance to the current discussion, are the TEU opt-out provisions which allowed the UK and Denmark to remain outside the Euro zone. Subsequently, a number of factors have ensured that early perceptions of precariousness have persisted. These include the decision of Sweden (following accession in 1995) also to remain outside the Euro zone, the rejection of the Euro by the Danish people in a referendum in early 2001, and of the Nice Treaty by the Irish later that year.

Lack of enthusiasm for further integration in some Member States has become associated with an increasing discourse of differentiation and flexibility. Enshrined in the Amsterdam Treaty as 'closer co-operation' (TEU Art. 43), and compounded by the prospect of enlargement to include the transitional countries of Central and Eastern Europe, by the late 1990s flexibility had replaced federalism as the dominant discourse of European integration. During the French Presidency, in the latter half of 2000, this centred around a rhetoric of commitment to 'strengthen both the powers and profile of the [then] "Euro-11" group' (*The Guardian*, 5 July, 2000). Such efforts to enhance the presence of the Euro group, while doubtless intended to encourage participation by the non-members, inevitably contribute to external perceptions of divisions, and hence weakness, within the EU.

A discussion of the external impacts of monetary union must acknowledge the intimate relationship between presence and confidence. Indeed trust in the political stability and competence of the issuing authority is deemed to be a prerequisite for the use of an international currency (Eijffinger and De Haan, 2000, p. 170). Third-party perceptions of enduring internal divisions, coupled with the persistently gloomy predictions of some economists, have undoubtedly been reflected in the Euro's performance. This is neatly encapsulated by an article in *The Economist* (4 March 2000, pp. 106-7) entitled 'The quick and the dead', which contrasted the performance of the 'distinctly tired and old' Euro with the 'vibrant, youthful' US dollar. Despite the vicissitudes of the US economy, the dollar's continued strength relative to the Euro is a clear demonstration of the importance of confidence. Clearly there is 'a paradox in the dollar being seen as a safe haven when it is the US stock market which has been leading the way down' (*The Guardian*, 24 March 2001).

While it is important to highlight the significance of external perceptions, and hence confidence, for the development of the Euro as an international currency, presence, it has been argued, connotes *being*. The Euro now exists and, given the size of the Single Market and the significance of the EU's share of global trade, must be considered an important currency – although the potential significance of its impact is disputed between sceptics and enthusiasts.

For some enthusiasts, economic size is the principal determinant of a currency's status. This assumption forms the basis of the argument that the Euro will eventually rival the dollar as the world's leading currency. Thus Bergsten (1997) anticipated a shift of official reserves and private investment from the dollar to the Euro of between $500 billion and $1 trillion. Ultimately, he argued, 'the Euro's rough parity with the dollar is probably inevitable' (1997, p. 91). In order to avoid turbulence in international markets, and an increasingly conflictual US-EU relationship, Bergsten has advocated a co-operative arrangement between the EU and the US in managing the international monetary regime, in which Japan would remain a 'junior partner' (ibid.).

Bergsten's conclusions, however, assume rapid integration of European capital markets. For a number of reasons, including differences between Member States in tax regimes and financial regulation, this process has been slow to occur (Coffey, 2000). This is an important conclusion given that integration of capital markets is regarded, even by enthusiasts, as a prerequisite for an international role for the Euro. Indeed Portes and Rey (1998) argued that capital market integration was the most significant factor in promoting the Euro's use, since, by reducing transaction costs, it would make investment in the Euro attractive. Moreover, in order for the Euro to play a major role as an international currency, they considered that it would be necessary for the UK, with its well-developed capital markets, to enter the Euro zone.

While Coffey's focus is upon delays and impediments to capital market integration, more sceptical commentators consider that markets may remain segmented indefinitely.[9] This would reduce the attractiveness of the Euro by exacerbating the general lack of enthusiasm for novelty among central bankers and reinforcing the bias towards home markets of other investors.

In the medium term, then, it seems unlikely that the Euro will bring to the EU the presence associated with a major international currency; or that the US will perceive, and respond to, a significant challenge to the dominance of the dollar. There have been suggestions, nevertheless, of preparations to defend the position of the dollar if necessary – through, for example, the introduction of legislation which offers financial incentives to developing countries which agree formally to adopt the dollar as a replacement for their own currencies (Cohen, 2000b, p. 13). In recent years the Japanese government, too, has been actively promoting internationalisation of the yen and the development of a currency area of its own (ibid.). Such responses to the potential of the Euro on the part of the major players in the international system, if followed through, might contribute to the construction of EU actorness by provoking attempts at retaliation.

For economically weaker countries, a climate of competition between the major international currencies may encourage closer alignment, or pegging of currencies – either to the dollar (in the case of Latin American countries) or to the Euro in the case of African and Mediterranean countries exhibiting a high level of economic dependence upon the EU. This would extend the stabilising effect of a link to the Euro beyond the CFA (African Financial Community)[10] franc zone and could result, in time, in 'the emergence of two giant blocs dominating the monetary world, one centered on the US and the other on Europe' (Cohen, 2000b, p. 16). Clearly such an outcome would further increase the presence of the EU.

The performance of the Euro is likely, also, to impact indirectly upon third parties. Inevitably the countries having greatest sensitivity to economic conditions within the EU are those with the highest levels of dependence on exports to the EU market. In addition to the CEEC seeking EU membership, which constitute a special case, included in this category would be Mediterranean non-member countries in North Africa and the Middle East and those sub-Saharan African countries, particularly in the CFA franc zone, which trade overwhelmingly with Europe (Cohen, 2000b, p. 5). For these countries economic growth within the EU, promoted by introduction of the single currency, may provide additional export opportunities and hence growth by association. Conversely, however, the Euro may stimulate increased concentration of trade within the Euro zone, hence reducing opportunities for exporters. Thus, for export dependent countries, the Euro introduces new uncertainties rather than the prospect of assured, contingent growth. Ultimately this consequence of EU presence may require a policy response by the Union, not least in the context of the

EU's structured relationship with the ACP (African, Caribbean and Pacific) group, where the Cotonou Agreement governing this relationship declares poverty reduction to be its central objective (European Commission, 2000).

For Central and East European (CEE) aspirant members of the EU, the impacts of monetary union are more specific. All have indicated their intention of joining the Euro zone when they are able to meet the EMU criteria and most CEE governments have undertaken some preparatory action. The more economically advanced applicant countries (Czech Republic, Estonia, Hungary, Poland, Slovakia and Slovenia) have already linked their currencies to the Euro. Nevertheless the EMU convergence criteria in respect of inflation and public debt present a significant challenge even to those countries (Hungary and Slovenia) considered to be best prepared for membership (Palánkai, 2001). Consequently, transition periods of varying length may be necessary, following accession, to allow the new members' economies to adjust. Here, as elsewhere, the implications for presence are mixed. Evidently EMU and the introduction of the Euro have contributed to EU influence, and to the construction of EU actorness, in relation to CEEC. At the same, however, doubts about the timing, scale and implications of the Eastern enlargement, and in particular the ability of CEEC to fully cope with the economic requirements of membership, contribute to third-party perceptions of the fragility of the EMU project and, perhaps, of the integration process itself.

In summary, then, the significant presence of the EU in world politics has primarily economic foundations. The magnetic effect of the Single Market, together with the EU's important contribution to world trade, provide enormous influence and, in relations with economically dependent countries, potential dominance. If the Euro were to achieve an international status commensurate with this economic power, monetary union has the potential greatly to strengthen the EU's presence. Much depends, however, upon perceptions of and responses to the Euro by third parties. Here it is interesting to note a reaction from the USA, following circulation of Euro notes and coins in early 2002.

> Now that Europe has a common currency it has made it easier for Americans to accept the EU as a political force. When the US government is in negotiations with the EU the US public have a greater understanding of who is involved. The Euro has removed the 'Who are we talking to?' argument from US politicians when talking to the EU (Europe Union in the US, 2002, p. 3).

While such claims seem somewhat exaggerated, circulation of the currency has undoubtedly enhanced the presence of the EU. Nevertheless many questions remain concerning the willingness of the EU to promote the single currency's international role, and, more specifically, its capacity to act, whether proactively or in response to external pressures, should the Euro begin to realise its potential as a major international currency.

Actor Capability

In order to capitalise upon its formidable presence, the EU must possess a number of prerequisites for actor capability. These will be considered in general terms prior to discussion of factors of particular relevance in the context of EMU. They include the following:

- shared commitment to a set of overarching values and principles;
- the ability to identify priorities and to formulate coherent policies;
- the ability to negotiate effectively with third parties;
- availability of and capacity to utilise policy instruments.

The first of these prerequisites for effective actorness is unproblematic, in that the TEU sets out the values and principles to which the EU and the Member States are committed. They are frequently reiterated, for example in the extract from *Agenda 2000* that introduces this chapter.

Unproblematic, too, is the ability to identify priorities and formulate coherent policies – at least in principle. In practice, however, the extent to which this is realised varies considerably between policy sectors. Inevitably, as in any complex policy system, divergent interests generate controversies which impede policy formulation. Co-ordination of EU policy, however, is impeded by difficulties which flow from its unique character. These are commonly identified as the problems of coherence and consistency.

Consistency is of particular significance as it provides an indication of the degree of political commitment, at the highest level, to the development of a global role for the EU. Consistency denotes the extent to which the bilateral external policies of Member States are consistent with each other and complementary to those of the EU. Hence it is a measure both of Member State commitment to common policies and the overall external impact of the EU and its Member States. In areas such as trade in goods, where there is full Community competence and common policies are entrenched, consistency is not a significant issue.[11] While Member State governments continue to pursue bilateral trade/investment opportunities in third countries, the Community is well established in its various roles as an international trade actor. These include representation of the EU and its Member States in bilateral negotiations with third parties and in multilateral negotiations in the context of the World Trade Organisation (WTO).

In most other areas, however, consistency can be a problem. In relation to development policy, for example, the claim that the EU is the world's largest donor of assistance is based upon a calculation which amalgamates EC aid and Member States' bilateral aid – despite the fact that insufficient effort is made to ensure complementarity between the various overlapping or competing programmes (van Reisen, 1997, p. 175). The reluctance of Member State governments to abandon sources of bilateral influence is exemplified by the bizarre spectacle of ten Member States and the Commission simultaneously operating assistance programmes in Burkina Faso, despite the pressure on the administration of a very poor country obliged to deal with eleven separate donors (Interview, Council Secretariat, July 1997). Inevitably the determination of Member State governments to maintain bilateral links and a range of independent external policies undermines EU actorness.

Problems of coherence stem from the internal policy processes of the EU. Here the fragmentation of Community external policy between several externally oriented Directorates-General of the Commission (the relex DGs) is exacerbated by the Pillar structure, which formally separates the Community's external economic policy (Pillar I) from the Union's 'political' foreign policy (Pillar II). This latter, in the form of the Common Foreign and Security Policy (CFSP), remains outside the Community structure and is intergovernmental in character, so that the Commission is merely 'associated' with the process. The evident tensions and rivalries across the Pillars, and between relex DGs in Pillar I, are exacerbated by the absence of an effective mechanism for resolving disputes.[12] There is little evidence that Chris Patten, appointed in the 1999-2003 Commission as Commissioner for External Relations, has been effective in reducing coherence problems within the Commission, while the simultaneous appointment of Javier Solana as High Representative for the CFSP has tended to highlight inter-pillar divisions. Paradoxically, the arrival of these prominent appointees, who have joined the Presidency and the Commission President in claiming to represent the EC/EU, has served both to increase the international visibility of the EU and to draw attention to the incoherence of its external persona(e).

The third prerequisite, the ability to negotiate with other actors in the international system, is directly linked to coherence and consistency. It is also fundamental to actorness; in that it is a condition of entry to the international system, where decision making is largely a function of formal negotiation between legally recognised entities. Thus, in circumstances where EC competence pertains, accordance to the Community of legal personality provides a formal right of entry to the international system. For most explicitly Community external activity, whether in the multilateral setting of the WTO or in constructing bilateral association or co-operation agreements, negotiation is central. The issue, here, is not the right to negotiate on behalf of the Member States, but rather the effectiveness of the negotiators.

Here, as elsewhere in the EU system, formal procedures are of great importance. Prior to the start of a negotiation the Commission puts forward a proposed mandate to the Council, which makes its decision on the basis of qualified majority – unless a Member State declares that a specific national interest is in jeopardy, when it may exercise a veto. Due to the difficulty in reaching agreement between fifteen Member States, Commission negotiators tend to be given an inflexible mandate, and hence very little room for negotiation. Changes to the mandate have to be renegotiated with the Council and the outcome can be unpredictable. In some cases, including the negotiation of the early Europe Agreements with CEEC, problems in agreeing an amended mandate almost caused the breakdown of negotiations.

In many bilateral negotiations, however, the Community's structural inflexibility adds to the Commission's reputation as a formidable negotiator. Thus interlocutors of the Commission speak with dread of the familiar threat 'if you want one word different we will have to go back to the Council' (Interview, external Mission, January 1996). It would be inaccurate, nevertheless, to suggest that the Commission's reputation rests solely upon obduracy founded on the difficulty of persuading fifteen Member States to agree. In trade-related matters Commission officials have long experience of negotiation, and competence in every sense of the word.

Where issues fall outside exclusive Community competence, the situation is rather different. As the agenda of international politics has broadened to include, for example, environmental issues, Member States have been reluctant to transfer competence to the Community for issues considered politically sensitive, such as energy policy. Where there is little or no Community competence, as in the case of climate change negotiations, the EU position is presented by the Presidency – supported by the Commission and Member States having particular interest or expertise in the area under discussion. In the absence of a formal mandate, the effectiveness of this procedure has sometimes been impaired by lengthy controversies between the Member States over the conduct of negotiations. Despite these difficulties, however, the EU has succeeded in enhancing its role in global environmental politics. For example, the EU played a key role, during 2001 and 2002, in negotiating modifications to the Kyoto Protocol to the Climate Change Convention – thus ensuring the survival of the climate change regime in the face of US opposition.

When considering the fourth requirement for actorness, it is clear that, despite the development of a modest military capability in the form of the Rapid Reaction Force, the policy instruments available to the EU remain primarily economic. Routine use of economic presence in the pursuit of broad policy goals is evident *inter alia* from the increasingly intrusive conditionalities inserted into trade and aid agreements. Moreover non-compliance, or simply EU disapproval, has led in a number of cases to full or partial suspension of privileges. As Piening has observed (1997, p. 10), incurring EU displeasure can 'cost the offending country dearly in financial terms'. Nevertheless, use of economic instruments, including formal economic sanctions, has tended to be complicated by the EU's structural complexity. Thus the policy decision is taken by the Council, frequently as a CFSP Joint Action under Pillar II, while control of the means of implementation rests with the Commission. This has led to numerous inter-Pillar disputes, which have obstructed or delayed implementation.[13] However the maturation of CFSP since its inception in 1993 has been characterised by gradual institutionalisation of cross-Pillar co-operation in the use of economic instruments to achieve political objectives (Koutrakos, 2001).

While impediments remain to effective external action, it is clear that there has been a modest, yet steady, increase in actor capability since formal commitment, in the Treaty on European Union, to strengthen the EU's external role. How, then, does the introduction of the Euro contribute to this developing capability?

Monetary Union: Implications for Actor Capability?

In contrast to the policy areas discussed above, where commitment to exert influence in external affairs has frequently been reiterated, there is little evidence of an ambition for the EU to play a proactive role on the global financial stage. In particular there is no consensus, among politicians or central bankers, about the desirability of a major international role for the Euro. The ongoing controversy over this issue is not simply a matter of differing levels of Member State commitment, however. Divisions are evident among politicians and central bankers, both between and within Member States (this latter is perhaps most evident in Germany); in consequence they straddle consistency and coherence factors. While the processes through which actorness is socially constructed are considered important, and the presence of the Euro as the world's second largest currency will inevitably generate demands for action from third parties, there remains a need to discuss the extent to which there has been an *intention* to develop an international role for the Euro.

The opening statement of the Treaty provisions on monetary policy – 'The primary objective of the ESCB shall be to maintain price stability' (TEC Art.105[1]) – leaves no doubt that internal policy is to be prioritised, and that the primary function of monetary union is to complement the Single Market. Nevertheless, should doubts remain, subsequent Articles referring to exchange-rate policy (TEC Art.111 [1and 2]) emphasise that any such policy 'shall be without prejudice to the primary objective of the ESCB to maintain price stability'. These provisions clearly indicate a lack of enthusiasm for development of the Euro as an international currency – reflecting, perhaps, a desire to avoid the responsibilities which such a status would attract. The precedent here is the policy of the Bundesbank, during the 1980s and 1990s, in suppressing the international role of the mark for this reason (Eijffinger and De Haan, 2000, p. 170).

While most commentators agree that the primacy of price stability indicates limited commitment to an international role for the Euro, Cohen suggests (2000b, p. 12-13) that the ECB's decision to issue high denomination Euro notes is evidence of a desire to increase international use of the Euro. A similar conclusion might be drawn from the decision to include, among trade agreement conditionalities, a provision requiring partners to hold a percentage of their reserve assets in Euros (*The Guardian*, 4 April 1998).

Despite these apparent indications of proactive behaviour, there has been little evidence of effective development of external monetary policy. Moreover there have been many criticisms of failure to act in response to external crises and financial market volatilities. An exception, here, is the EU's response following the terrorist attacks on the United States in September 2001, which is deemed to have been 'limited, but not unimportant' (Gros, 2002, p. 13).[14] On other occasions when an EU intervention might have been expected, however, there has been a failure to act. Examples here include the financial crises in Turkey in 2000 and in Argentina in 2002. In both cases, albeit to varying extents, the EU has both well-developed political links and economic interests.

Doubtless failure reflects lack of will, but it is indicative, also, of lack of capacity to act. Monetary union has brought major additional complexities and sources of controversy to the EU's already convoluted and disputatious policy process. This has significant implications for coherence and consistency, and for the ability to negotiate effectively with third parties – which are considered to be key requirements for actor capability. These pertain whether there is an intention to act proactively or a need to respond to external pressures or events.

The implications of monetary union for overall EU consistency are immediately apparent. The initial launch of the Euro with eleven participating countries (twelve following the entry of Greece in January 2001) undoubtedly reflected lack of political commitment by the governments of the UK, Denmark and Sweden. Moreover, in the UK in particular, the largely negative and wholly lacklustre policy debate on this issue suggests little prospect of an early entry into the Euro zone. This reluctance is not only a response to a potentially unpopular policy choice, it also reflects fundamental misgivings about the longer-term federalising implications of EMU and the loss of the economic and political advantages attaching to a national currency. As Cohen has argued,

> it is the exceptional government that does not still seek to preserve, as best it can, an effective monopoly over the issue and management of money in its own territory....A government that does not control money is a limited government (2000a, p. 84).

Given the marked reluctance of Member State governments to relinquish control of sensitive policy areas, or to abandon bilateral sources of influence, it is perhaps surprising that so many are actually participating in the single currency. It is, in consequence, *un*surprising that management of the Euro system is highly decentralised, with national central banks (NCB) playing a very significant, if not dominant, role in the European System of Central Banks (ECSB) and holding a high proportion of seats on the Governing Council of the European Central Bank (and all of the ECB's capital). NCB also retain the ability to engage independently in activities unrelated to the Euro system. The system is thus very different from that operated by central banks in federal countries (Eijffinger and De Haan, 2000, p. 33).

In addition to ensuring a prominent role for NCB, the desire of Member State governments to retain influence has been evident from, for example, the intense and highly public controversy over the appointment of the ECB President, whose term of office and replacement remain a matter of dispute, and the insistence of the French government that the CFA franc's link to the Euro should be managed by the French Finance Ministry rather than the European Council (ibid., 74). These consistency issues doubtless impinge upon actor capability, in terms of the ability to formulate external monetary policies and, in particular, actively to promote the Euro as an international currency.

In examining issues of coherence, it must be noted that monetary union introduces new institutions and inter-institutional relationships into an already complex system, thus contributing to the existing climate of rivalry and misunderstanding. Indeed, according to Eijffinger and De Haan (2000, p. 18), the coherence problems in relation to monetary policy result from 'a major design flaw in the Maastricht Treaty', which introduces structural impediments to action. Thus the Treaty provides for formulation of external monetary policy, by the Council 'acting unanimously on a recommendation from the ECB or from the Commission, and after consulting the ECB in an endeavour to reach a consensus consistent with the objective of price stability' (TEC Art.111[1]).

While the Nice Treaty (entered into force on 1 February 2003) provides for introduction of QMV in the Council, difficulties in reaching agreement are likely to remain. Moreover the considerable independence, and restricted remit, accorded to the ECB (where there are also internal disagreements[15]) further reduce the potential for proactive policy making. Hence it is hardly surprising that external monetary policy has been slow to develop. This dilemma was neatly summed up in the *European Voice*.

Euro-zone politicians know that they mishandled much of the new currency's first 18 months of life. They also know they should 'do something', but how can they act without treading on the feet of the

European Central Bank, offending the sensibilities of the countries still outside the 11-nation currency area or imposing an *omertà* on powerful men? (22-28 June 2000, p. 12)

Compounding the effect of structural impediments to policy formulation, problems of representation in international negotiations also inhibit the development of an international role for the Euro. As in other areas falling outside Community competence, the Commission is merely 'associated' with negotiations and the Treaty, in more than usually Delphic language, provides that the Council 'shall decide the arrangements for the negotiation and for the conclusion of such agreements. These arrangements shall ensure that the Community expresses a single position' (TEC Art.111[3]). Moreover and, tellingly, representation at fora such as G7/8, the IMF and the OECD remains confined to states, despite the over-representation of Euro-zone members at G7/8.

From the outset the Commission (amongst others) has expressed concern about representation of the Euro zone and the need for effective prior co-ordination of negotiating positions, initially proposing for this purpose the creation of a 'trinity', comprising representatives of the Council, the Commission and the ECB (*The Economist*, 14 November 1998, p. 130). While this somewhat unwieldy proposal did not find favour, the Commission continues to believe that a formula must be reached to enable proper representation of the Euro zone (Interview, February 2000). For some commentators this should be achieved through appointment of a 'Mr. Euro' (Gros, 2002, p. 13) although this would add to the array of prominent spokespersons already claiming to represent the Union. Meantime there have been reports of a 'secret agreement' between Euro-zone ministers and the ECB which 'guarantees prior discussions' of positions to be taken at G7/8 (*European Voice*, 22-28 June 2000, p. 18). It is to be assumed that this modest arrangement is regarded as 'secret' because it will offend the Commission, which is excluded, and cause alarm to non-Euro-zone Member States fearful of being 'left in the slow lane of Europe' (*The Guardian*, 25 July 2000). This provides a nice example of the coherence, consistency and negotiations problems currently afflicting the EU.

Stronger and Weaker? EMU's Paradoxical Implications

As early as 1977 Gunnar Sjöstedt concluded that the European Community had become an actor in world politics. Since that time the role played by the EC/EU has grown and diversified. Today, in addition to trade-related issues such as development assistance, the EU aspires to a leadership role in global environmental politics and is a major contributor to humanitarian assistance efforts in all parts of the world. Aspirations also exist for a more effective role in regional conflict resolution, and the positive role played by the EU in the 2001 Macedonian crises indicate progress in this area too.

The development of these external roles owes much to a process of construction, in which the EU's increasingly formidable economic presence has generated external expectations and demands which have, in turn, necessitated a response from the EU. External events, particularly since the end of the Cold War, have assisted this process. Of particular significance have been demands for EU membership, or various forms of support, from neighbours to the East; and the evolving, frequently cantankerous relationship with the US.

Given this context, it might be expected that monetary union would greatly enhance the EU's presence in the international system; indeed many commentators predicted that the Euro would quickly rival the dollar as the foremost international currency. As was the case with the relatively successful Single Market process, the advantages and responsibilities attending such a status would inevitably contribute to the construction of EU actorness. It would be premature to suggest that these predictions were mistaken, and there is evidence that introduction of the Euro is impacting upon third parties having close economic links with the EU. Nevertheless it is clear that the contribution to the EU's presence of the single currency has not been as significant as anticipated, despite an increase in awareness about the Euro following the introduction of coins and notes in January 2002 (European Union in the US, 2002).

There are numerous reasons for this which, when combined, have contributed to a perception that the project is precarious. This, in turn, produces a lack of confidence in the credibility of the Euro. Prominent, here, are the problems of consistency, coherence and negotiation/representation discussed above. These are not new problems, but they were becoming increasingly evident prior to the launch of the Euro – as demonstrated, for example, by Member States' reluctance to entrust negotiation on new trade issues to the Commission during the 1986-93

GATT Uruguay Round. Introduction of the single currency, with its restricted initial membership and plethora of new and untried institutions, thus introduced new elements of uncertainty, and arenas for conflict, into a set of complex and already troubled relationships. The prospect of enlargement, with its own uncertainties and its implications for decision-making in old and new institutions, including ultimately the ECB, can only compound these current difficulties.

In the medium term there seems to be little prospect of resolving these difficulties, hence it must be concluded that 'for the time being the EU is simply not an actor on the global financial stage' (Gross, 2002, p. 13). However, successful enlargement would further increase the size and importance of the Single Market and of the Euro zone. If this were to be accompanied by full participation in the Euro by all existing Member States, the impacts of the EU's enhanced presence would be formidable. As these impacts were increasingly experienced by third parties, this would put into train the familiar processes by which actorness is constructed. Conversely, of course, should the enlargement process falter, and the UK, Denmark and Sweden remain outside the Euro zone, both internal capability and external expectations would diminish, resulting in a diminution of the EU's global role.

Notes

[1]   Henry Kissinger's (apocryphal) jibe concerning the telephone number of the EU is still frequently repeated, although US officials readily admit that they know precisely whom to contact on any issue which interests them. A more specific example, among many available, is provided in Richard Benedick's account of the negotiation of the Montreal Protocol (Benedick was the chief US negotiator). Benedick claims that the EC was responsible for most of the difficulties encountered during the negotiations (Benedick, 1991). This view is not shared by other participants (see McConnell, 1991).

[2]   For an overview of approaches to actorness in the literature, see Bretherton and Vogler (1999, pp. 15-35).

[3]   In the course of researching EU actorness (Bretherton and Vogler, 1999; 2000) a programme of interviews was undertaken, intermittently between January 1996 and July 2000, with Commission officials, members of the Council Secretariat, third country diplomats and representatives of non-governmental organisations. In addition to these Brussels-based interviews, representatives of the UK Foreign and Commonwealth Office were also interviewed. The generosity of those interviewed in giving their time is gratefully acknowledged; their insights proved invaluable. All information was provided in confidence and hence cannot be attributed to specific sources.

[4]   The significance of the EU as a model of regional integration is not, of course, solely a function of presence. The EU regularly proclaims itself to be 'a natural supporter of regional co-operation initiatives' (ACP-EC, 1997, p. 23) and has actively encouraged regional initiatives in Southern Africa, Latin America and elsewhere.

[5]   Article 133 of the Treaty Establishing the European Communities provides that: The common commercial policy shall be based on uniform principles, particularly in regard to changes in tariff rates, the conclusion of tariff and trade agreements, the achievement of uniformity in measures of liberalisation, export policy and measures to protect trade such as those to be taken in the event of dumping or subsidies.

[6]   See, for example, Currie and Vines (1992).

[7]   As from 1 January 1999 the currencies of all participating currencies (eleven at that time as Greece did not qualify until January 2001) became manifestations of the Euro. However physical circulation of coins and notes was delayed until 1 January 2002.

[8]   Feldstein foresaw a range of negative consequences flowing from the adoption of the Euro, not least the possibility of a future war between Russia and a federal EU.

[9]   See, for example, *The Economist*, 14 November 1998, p. 129.

[10]   The CFA (Communauté Financière Africaine or the African Financial Community) comprises Burkina Faso, Senegal, Guinea Bissau, Côte d'Ivoire, Togo, Benin, Equatorial Guinea, Gabon, Mali, Chad, the Central African Republic, Cameroon, the Congo, and the Comoro Islands.

[11]   The situation in respect of trade in services is rather more complex. Here Member States have been reluctant to cede full competence to the Commission but have opted to proceed on a case-by-case basis. The Treaty of Nice contains provisions which seek to address this issue (Galloway, 2001).

[12]   In the absence of procedures to facilitate adjudication when disputes arise, there has been a tendency for high-profile Commissioners to dominate their colleagues. This was very much the case in a number of trade/environment disputes during the Santer Presidency (Bretherton and Vogler, 2000).

[13]   An example here is the Council's (CFSP) proposal, in 1997, that relations with the Association of South-East Asian Nations should be interrupted to protest Burma's accession to that organisation. The Commission vigorously opposed this proposal on the grounds that severance of links would result in loss of influence.

[14]   The European Central Bank acted promptly, lowering interest rates and ensuring liquidity until markets stabilised.

[15]   See *Business Week* (2000) 'Who's in Charge of Europe's Money?' 27 March, pp. 24-8.

References

ACP-EC Development Finance Co-operation Committee (1997), *Report and Resolution*, ACP-CE, 2144/97, Brussels.

Allen, D. and Smith, M. (1990), 'Western Europe's presence in the contemporary international arena', *Review of International Studies*, 16 (1), pp. 19-37.

Benedick, R. E. (1991), *Ozone Diplomacy: New Directions in Safeguarding the Planet*, Harvard University Press, Cambridge, MA.

Bergsten, C. F. (1997), 'The Dollar and the Euro', *Foreign Affairs*, 76 (4), pp. 83-95.

Bretherton, C. and Vogler, J. (1999), *The European Union as a Global Actor*, Routledge, London.

Bretherton, C. and Vogler, J. (2000), 'The European Union as trade actor and environmental activist: contradictory roles?', *Journal of Economic Integration*, 15 (2), pp. 163-94.

Coffey, P (2000), 'Economic and Monetary Union and the Integration of Capital Markets', paper to *5th UACES Research Conference*, Budapest.

Cohen, B. (2000a), 'Money in a globalized world' in N. Woods (ed.) *The Political Economy of Globalisation*, Macmillan, Basingstoke, pp. 77-106.

Cohen, B. (2000b), 'EMU and the Developing Countries', paper to *ISA Annual Convention*, Los Angeles.

Currie, D. and Vines, D. (1992), 'A global economic policy agenda for the 1990s', *International Affairs*, 68 (4), pp. 585-602.

Eijffinger, S. W. C. and De Haan, J. (2000), *European Monetary and Fiscal Policy*, Oxford University Press, Oxford.

European Commission (1997a), 'For a stronger and wider Union', *Agenda 2000*, Vol. I, DOC(97)6, Strasbourg.

European Commission (1997b), 'Summary and conclusions of the Opinion of the Commission concerning the Applications for Membership to the European Union presented by the candidate countries', *Agenda 2000*, DOC(97)8, Strasbourg.

European Commission (1997c), *Towards Greater Economic Integration: the European Union's financial assistance, trade policy and investments for central and eastern Europe*, DGIA Evaluation Unit, Brussels.

European Commission (2000), *The New ACP-EU Agreement*, available at http://europa.eu.int/comm/ development/cotonou/overview. (Accessed 12 March 2001.)

European Union in the US (2002), *The Euro: Completing Economic Union*, available at http://www.eurunion.org.infores/euguide. (Accessed 17 April 2002.)

Feldstein, M. (1997), 'EMU and international conflict', *Foreign Affairs*, 76 (6), pp. 60-73.

Ferguson, N. and Kotlikoff, L. J. (2000), 'The degeneration of EMU', *Foreign Affairs*, 79 (2), pp. 110-21.

Galloway, D. (2001), *The Treaty of Nice and Beyond: Realities and Illusions of Power in the EU*, Sheffield Academic Press, Sheffield.

Gros, D. (2002), 'Time for Europe to grab more of the spotlight on world's financial stage', *European Voice*, 28 February-6 March, p. 13.

Hopkins, R. E. and Mansbach, R. W. (1973), *Structure and Process in International Politics*, Harper and Row, New York.

Hosli, M. O. (1998), 'The EMU and international monetary relations: What to expect for international actors?' in C. Rhodes (ed.) *The European Union in the World Community*, Lynne Reinner, Boulder, CO, pp. 165-91.

Hveem, H. (2000), 'Explaining the regional phenomenon in an era of globalization' in R. Stubbs and G. R. D. Underhill (eds), *Political Economy and the Changing Global Order*, Oxford University Press, Oxford, pp. 70-81.

Koutrakos, P. (2001), *Trade, Foreign Policy and Defence in EU Constitutional Law*, Hart Publishing, Oxford.

La Serre, F. de (1996), 'France: the impact of François Mitterand' in C. Hill (ed.) *Actors in Europe's Foreign Policy*, Routledge, London, pp. 19-39.

Leonard, M. (1997), *Politics without Frontiers*, Demos, London.

Macrory, R. and Hession, M. (1996), 'The European Community and climate change: the role of law and legal competence' in T. O'Riordan and J. Jäger (eds) *Politics of Climate Change: a European Perspective*, Routledge, London, pp. 106-54.

Mayes, D. (2000), 'Independence and Co-ordination – the Eurosystem', paper to *5th UACES Research Conference*, Budapest.

McConnell, F. (1991), Review of "Ozone Diplomacy"', *International Environmental Affairs*, 3 (4), pp. 318-20.

McKay, D. (1999), *Federalism and European Union: A Political Economy Perspective*, Oxford University Press, Oxford.

Paemen, H. and Bensch, A. (1995), *From the GATT to the WTO: the European Community in the Uruguay Round*, Leuven University Press, Leuven.

Palánkai, T. (2001), *What are the prospects for Euro-zone Membership for the Candidate Countries and what will be its impact on their respective economies?*, Cicero Foundation, Paris.

Piening, R. (1997), *Global Europe*, Lynne Reinner, Boulder CO.

Portes, R. and Rey, H. (1998), 'The emergence of the Euro as an international currency', *Economic Policy*, 26, pp. 307-43.

Ruggie, J. G. (1993), 'Territoriality and beyond: problematising modernity in international relations', *International Organization*, 47 (1), pp. 139-74.

Sjöstedt, G. (1977), *The External Role of the European Community*, Saxon House, Farnborough.

Taylor, P. (1996), *The European Union in the 1990s*, Oxford University Press, Oxford.

van Reisen, M. (1997), 'European Union' in J. Randel and T. German (eds) *The Reality of Aid*, Earthscan, London, pp. 160-78.

Wendt, A. (1994), 'Collective identity formation and the international state', *American Political Science Review*, 88 (2), pp. 384-96.

WTO Trade Policy Review Body (1997), *Review of the European Union's TRPB Evaluation*, available at http://www.wto.org/wto/reviews. (Accessed 23 June 2001.)

10 NATO and the Challenge of Security in a New Era

ANDREW COTTEY[1]

Introduction

On 12 September 2001, one day after the devastating terrorist attacks on the United States in New York and Washington DC, NATO activated for the first time in the Alliance's history the Article 5 security guarantee at the heart of its founding treaty. Article 5 of the 1949 Washington Treaty states that an armed attack against any NATO member 'in Europe or North America shall be considered an attack against them all' and commits the Alliance's members to provide assistance to the state so attacked. Following this dramatic political gesture, however, NATO played only a very marginal role in the US intervention in Afghanistan and has yet to take a significant part in the wider American-led 'war against terrorism'. Indeed there are significant divisions between the US and its European allies over how to respond to the challenge of terrorism in the wake of the events of 11 September 2001, as well as over wider global security issues. Against this background, some observers suggest that the Alliance is peripheral to the new security challenges of the twenty-first century – that NATO is even coming to stand for Now Almost Totally Obsolete.

This chapter analyses the on-going development of NATO in the context of the changing international security agenda. It explores how NATO underwent a fundamental transformation in the 1990s turning itself from a traditional collective defence alliance into a Europe-wide security organisation engaged in peacekeeping and co-operation with its former enemies to the east. This chapter, however, also shows that – despite the organisation's transformation during the 1990s – the longer-term future of NATO remains uncertain. The relevance of the Atlantic Alliance to new global security challenges, in particular international terrorism and the proliferation of weapons of mass destruction, is unclear. There are also major differences between the US and its European partners over how to address these and other key international security issues. These new global security challenges, further, are likely to pose difficult dilemmas for governments and publics in Europe and North America for years to come.

The Changing Security Agenda

The international security agenda has changed dramatically over the last decade. For forty years from the late 1940s to the late 1980s that agenda was dominated by the Cold War confrontation between East and West and the ever-present risk of escalation to all-out nuclear war between the two superpowers. In this context, NATO was a response to the perceived threat of a Soviet invasion or military intimidation of Western Europe: a military alliance designed to counter-balance and deter Soviet military power and link the US to Europe militarily in order to achieve that goal.

The end of the Cold War in 1989-91 altered the security agenda overnight. The 'Soviet threat' – NATO's central rationale – disappeared. The prospect of an all-encompassing war between the West and the Soviet Union's successor Russia fell away. Over the last decade, however, 'new' security challenges have emerged or gained much greater salience. The Gulf War of 1990-91 was a sharp reminder that major regional conflicts might still occur outside Europe – and threaten American and European interests. The outbreak of the war in Yugoslavia in summer 1991 and the subsequent horrors of 'ethnic cleansing' and 'concentration camps' highlighted the reality that most conflicts are now internal wars within states but may nevertheless demand an external international response. Evidence that Iraq had been developing nuclear, biological and chemical weapons before the Gulf War of 1990-91, fears that countries such as Iran and North Korea were doing likewise and India and Pakistan's 1998 nuclear weapons tests indicated that the proliferation of weapons of mass destruction (in the jargon, WMD) was a growing problem. The first attempt to destroy the New York World Trade Centre in 1993 and other actual or thwarted terrorist attacks on US targets led to growing concern in the US about the threat of 'catastrophic terrorism'. The events of 11 September 2001 indicated the reality of that threat. At the same time, some analysts argued that non-military problems – economic instability, mass migration, environmental degradation and the like – might pose serious security threats and should be at the heart of the security agenda, although no consensus has emerged on this issue (Buzan et al., 1998).

For the countries of Europe this changing security agenda has had contradictory implications. The risk of general war within Europe is probably lower than at any time in modern history. At the same time, however, new security challenges such as international terrorism and the proliferation of WMD may threaten European states or generate pressures for military responses. The Cold War both facilitated and hid a revolutionary development in Europe's international politics: the emergence of a 'security community' in Western Europe. A security community is a group of states amongst whom war is inconceivable (Adler and Barnett, 1998). For most of Europe's modern history, the prospect of war has been a norm and the use of military force has been a standard tool in states' repertoires. Since 1945 this has changed in Western Europe as a security community has emerged. While the origins of this security community remain debated, most observers would accept that today war between Britain, France, Germany and the other countries of Western Europe is inconceivable. With the end of the Cold War and the collapse of the Soviet bloc, this security community – institutionalised via the EU and NATO – has become the defining feature of international security relations *within* Europe.

Despite the conflicts in former Yugoslavia in the 1990s, further, there is evidence that this security community is extending into Central and Eastern Europe. Relations between Poland and Germany have undergone a rapprochement similar to that between France and Germany after 1945. The Czech Republic, Hungary and Poland joined NATO in 1999 and up to ten Central and South Eastern European states (the three new NATO members, plus Cyprus, Estonia, Latvia, Lithuania, Malta, Slovakia and Slovenia) may join the EU by 2004-05 or thereabouts. Although the collapse of communism in Central and Eastern Europe has resulted in the re-emergence of tensions over borders and minorities, outside former Yugoslavia these problems have generally not escalated to violence. For a growing core of European states, therefore, war is an increasingly remote possibility. War remains conceivable between Greece and Turkey, but this is the exception to the norm. The emergence of a 'Weimar Russia' dragging Europe into war as Germany did in the 1930s is not impossible, but a decade after the demise of the Soviet Union the prospect of such a scenario developing appears to be low (Lieven, 1999).

Reflecting on the emergence of the European security community, some observers were inclined to argue that with the end of the Cold War the countries of Western Europe were more secure than at any time in their modern history. The conflicts in the Persian Gulf, the former Yugoslavia and between Israel and the Palestinians, however, illustrate that war remains a very real possibility on Europe's periphery and beyond. Such conflicts may threaten perceived Western interests (such, for example, as access to oil supplies in the case of the 1990-91 Gulf War) or generate demands for 'humanitarian intervention' to end massive human suffering. Thus, the post-Cold War period has witnessed military intervention by the US and the other major Western powers in various parts of the world – from the former Yugoslavia in Europe to Somalia and Sierra Leone in Africa and from Haiti in the Americas to East Timor in Asia. As Lawrence Freedman has put it, these are wars of choice rather than of necessity for the West (Freedman, 1998, p. 34). These conflicts do not threaten the Western powers in an existential sense and they can therefore choose whether and when to intervene, resulting in a mixed pattern of intervention in some cases and non-intervention in others. Nevertheless, the combination of interests and humanitarianism is likely to continue to generate demands for military intervention at least in some circumstances. As the experience of the Yugoslav conflict demonstrates, such interventions are likely to continue to pose difficult ethical, political and military dilemmas.

While the risk of an all-out Cold War style ground invasion of or nuclear attack on Western Europe and the United States has dissipated, new direct military threats to the West have emerged in the form of the proliferation of WMD and international terrorism. As the events of 11 September 2001 illustrated, international terrorism and the proliferation of WMD pose the threat of massive destruction of human lives and physical infrastructure at the heart of Western societies.

The extent, nature and implications of these twin threats, however, remain controversial (Reiss and Litwak, 1994). While there is consensus that countries such as Iran, Iraq, Libya and North Korea are attempting to develop nuclear, biological and chemical weapons and the means to deliver them (in particular long-range ballistic missiles), Western intelligence agencies differ on how close these states are to deploying operational WMD arsenals. Equally importantly, there is much debate over the likelihood of these states actually using WMD, the circumstances in which such use might occur and the extent to which their leaders can be deterred from using such weapons. In the most extreme case, these states may develop the capability to attack the United States or Western Europe directly with nuclear or other WMD weapons. More credibly, at least in the short term, they may develop – or to some extent even already have – the capability to attack forward-deployed Western forces or allies such as Israel or Japan. In the US in particular this has led to the fear that the threat of WMD retaliation (especially against vulnerable forward-deployed troop concentrations) might in future be used to deter Western military intervention and thereby allow countries to successfully prosecute wars of aggression. There is evidence, for example, that Iraq tried to use chemical weapons during the 1990-91 Gulf War. Some US analysts argue that had Iraq had a credible nuclear weapons capability in 1990 the US might have been deterred from reversing its invasion of Kuwait.

All of this has resulted in intensifying debate about how the West should respond to the growing challenge of WMD proliferation. Aside from the more traditional tools of multilateral arms control, export controls and diplomatic and economic sanctions, attention has focused on two other strategies: the pre-emptive use of force to prevent states acquiring WMD (in particular nuclear weapons) and the deployment of missile defences to provide protection against WMD attack. In 1981 Israel undertook surprise airstrikes against Iraq's Osirak nuclear reactor in order to prevent that country obtaining nuclear weapons. In 1994 the Clinton Administration contemplated the possibility of using airstrikes to prevent North Korea acquiring nuclear weapons. More recently, the US-led intervention to secure the overthrow of Saddam Hussein was ostensibly motivated in significant part by the goal of preventing Iraq from developing its WMD arsenal. Assuming the proliferation threat continues to grow, there is likely to be growing debate about the legitimacy and utility of pre-emptive military action as a means of preventing WMD proliferation.

The likelihood that it will not be possible to entirely prevent the further spread of WMD, including nuclear weapons, has prompted parallel debate on the prospects for defence against WMD attack. During the 1990s support grew within the US for the deployment of a National Missile Defence (NMD) capable of defending the US from ballistic missile attack, as well as for Theatre Missiles Defences (TMD) capable of defending US allies and/or forces overseas. Notwithstanding doubts about the technical effectiveness of such defences and criticism that their deployment would risk undermining arms control and triggering new arms races, President George W. Bush's Administration came to power strongly committed to missile defences. In December 2001 the Bush Administration announced that the US would withdraw from the 1972 Anti-Ballistic Missile (ABM) Treaty, which had placed strict limits on American and Russian missile defences. During the 2000s therefore it appears likely that the US will deploy major missile defences, although detailed decisions on the nature and scope of those systems remain to be taken. For America's European allies, this will pose difficult dilemmas about how far to support US missile defence plans and whether to buy US-built missile defences for themselves (and seek integration into the wider US missile defence architecture), build independent European/national missile defences or forego such defences (as unnecessary, ineffective, counter-productive and/or too expensive). In January 2003, the British government decided to acquiesce to American use of the US early warning radar located at Fylingdales in the north of England as part of US missile defences.

Parallel to the debate on proliferation, there has since the early 1990s been growing debate within America over the threat posed by international terrorism (particularly by radical groups fundamentally opposed to the West and especially the US). The events of 11 September 2001 confirmed the reality of that threat. The Bush Administration responded by intervening in Afghanistan to destroy the Al Qaida terrorist network and overthrow the Taliban regime and declaring a wider 'war or terrorism'. The war on terrorism, further, seems set to become a – and perhaps *the* – central focus of US foreign policy at the beginning of the twenty-first century. Behind the apparent consensus within US and international declarations of support, however, lie a host of contentious issues and difficult dilemmas. First, the extent and nature of the terrorist threat remain difficult to gauge. While there have been understandable fears that the attacks of 11 September 2001 may presage a wider long-term terrorist campaign, the extent to which Al Qaida or other groups have the capability to undertake or sustain such a campaign is unclear. As the Chief of the British Defence Staff, Admiral Sir Michael Boyle, has put it, 'the threshold for terrorist activity may have changed for ever, but on the other hand, it may subside to close to its historical norm' (Boyle, 10 December 2001). Second, the legitimacy, utility and costs of military intervention to disrupt terrorist networks will remain a matter of debate. Third, while the focus of attention has initially been on military action to disrupt terrorist networks, the longer-term questions of what 'causes' terrorism and how one should seek to address such deeper 'causes' will remain. Former US President Bill Clinton has argued that 'we in the wealthy countries have to spread the benefits of the twenty-first-century world and reduce the risks so we can make more partners and fewer terrorists in the future' (Clinton, 14 December 2001).

Adding to this already complex security agenda, is the issue of what are sometimes referred to as 'soft' or non-military security challenges. Since the 1980s there has been a growing recognition that non-military problems may pose serious threats to the well-being and even survival of both individuals and societies as a whole. International climate change (global warming), for example, may in coming decades cause flooding of low-lying coastal areas, radically alter patterns of agricultural production and trigger increasing migration flows. The dramatic collapse of the South-East Asian economies in 1997-98 highlighted both the vulnerability of national economies in an era of globally mobile finance and the way in which economic problems can trigger violent social and political disruption. The extent to which these and other non-military challenges should be considered security problems, however, remains contentious. Such problems can in some circumstances pose existential challenges to the stability and survival of societies and states. Such problems can also be important causes of violent conflict and warfare – there is, for example, convincing evidence that environmental degradation and resource scarcity can trigger or exacerbate violence in vulnerable countries. Critics, however, counter that widening the definition of security to include non-military issues risks making security an all-embracing and virtually meaningless concept. It may also risk importing traditional security dynamics – the tendency to think in zero-sum balance of power terms or to seek military solutions – into areas where they are at best irrelevant and at worst deeply counterproductive. There is unlikely to be any consensus on what does and does not constitute security. Economic, environmental and other non-military problems and the linkage between these challenges and the more traditional security problems of war and peace, however, will surely remain a key part of the wider international context of security in the early twenty-first century.

The international security agenda and especially the role of military force is also facing significant change as a consequence of the information technology revolution. The application of information technology to armed forces is producing a so-called Revolution in Military Affairs (RMA) (Freedman, 1998). The combination of advanced sensors, increasingly accurate weapons and long-range power projection is enabling the Western powers, in particular the US, to project military power with great accuracy over very long distances with relatively low risks of casualties amongst their own soldiers. Where Western interests are limited and intolerance of casualties is growing, further, the prospect of relatively low-risk military intervention is likely to be appealing to political leaders. In these circumstances, some argue that 'information dominance' (the ability to control communications and intelligence over a large combined ground/air/sea/space battle area) may be the key to future warfare. The significance of the RMA has, however, yet to be fully tested and may be exaggerated. While the RMA may allow states to strike from great distance with great accuracy, it may not overcome the need to deploy vulnerable ground forces in order to secure control of territory. The RMA may also result in 'asymmetrical warfare' with less technologically advanced foes fighting back through the use of WMD, terrorism or a greater willingness to sacrifice soldiers or civilians.

NATO's Transformation during the 1990s

The rapidly changing international security agenda has posed fundamental challenges to NATO. As the Cold War division of Europe crumbled in 1989-90, an Alliance based on forward defence of Germany's eastern border and nuclear deterrence of the Soviet Union looked increasingly outdated. Western governments argued that NATO was still vital – as a means of maintaining a security link between the US and Europe, integrating a re-uniting Germany into European security structures and counter-balancing a Russia that remained Europe's largest military power. It became increasingly clear, however, that if NATO was to survive it would have to help its members meet the new security challenges they faced. This view was best expressed by the influential US Senator Richard Lugar who argued that NATO had to go 'out of area', that is, take on new responsibilities beyond its traditional role of defending its members territory – or risk going out of business.

The most immediate challenge facing NATO was relations with its former enemies to the east. With the collapse of communism the new democracies in Central Europe were demanding to 'return to Europe' by joining Western organisations. Russia, meanwhile, was seeking a new post-confrontational relationship with the West. NATO's initial response was relatively cautious. Diplomatic contacts with the former Soviet bloc countries were expanded, NATO began to reduce its conventional and nuclear forces and pan-European frameworks (in particular the Conference on Security and Co-operation in Europe, CSCE, and the 1990 Conventional Armed Forces in Europe, CFE, arms control treaty) were developed – but all of this hardly amounted to a response adequate to the revolutionary change in the east. At the end of 1991 NATO adopted a new 'Strategic Concept' that defined the Alliance as having four key roles: acting as a foundation for a stable security environment in Europe; providing a transatlantic forum for consultations amongst the Allies; deterring and defending against the threat of aggression against its members; and preserving the strategic balance within Europe (NATO, 1991, 27). At the same time NATO agreed to establish a new North Atlantic Co-operation Council (NACC) as a framework for enhanced co-operation with its new eastern partners. Incorporating all the NATO countries and the former eastern bloc states, however, it rapidly became clear that the NACC amounted to not much more than a talking shop.

Meanwhile, in Central and Eastern Europe pressure was building for a more radical approach. After the January 1991 Soviet intervention in the Baltic states and attempted coup in Moscow by hard-liners in August of that year, Czechoslovakia, Hungary and Poland began to press for full membership of NATO – as a means of integrating themselves into the West, consolidating their democracies and providing reassurance against Russian revanchism. NATO's members were uncertain how to respond: while there was sympathy for the Central Europeans' desire to 'return to Europe', these countries faced no military threat and there was fear that premature enlargement of NATO's membership might weaken the Alliance or provoke renewed confrontation with Moscow. The result was the Partnership for Peace (PfP), established in January 1994. The PfP offered each partner an individual relationship with NATO, tailored to its own needs and including not only political discussions but also practical military co-operation. The PfP resulted in rapidly growing co-operation with the countries of Central and Eastern Europe, with NATO assuming a key role in helping these states to reform their militaries and joint exercises and training with these states. Within a few years, co-operation with the eastern partners through the PfP had become a key part of NATO activities.

Despite the success of the PfP, NATO still faced a difficult dilemma over whether to take in new members from Central Europe. While welcoming the PfP, the Central European states continued to press hard for full membership of the Alliance. Russian leaders, however, remained deeply opposed to NATO's enlargement, with President Boris Yeltsin warning of a new 'Cold Peace'. Within the West, supporters of enlargement argued that leaving the Central Europeans permanently outside the Alliance risked creating a dangerous security vacuum at Europe's heart and undermining the new democracies – integration in NATO could promote peace for Europe's east in the same way it had for Europe's west after 1945 (Allin, 1995). Critics argued that NATO enlargement was unnecessary since the Central Europeans faced no immediate military threat and risked strengthening hard-liners in Moscow and undermining hard-won arms control agreements. In the worst case, enlargement could be a strategic mistake of historic proportions, provoking a new Cold War with Russia (Gaddis, 1998). By the mid-1990s enlargement was the most controversial issue facing the Alliance – and not one it could postpone indefinitely.

Led by the Clinton Administration, NATO set about trying to square the circle of extending its membership into Central Europe while maintaining a co-operative relationship with Russia and reassuring states left outside the Alliance. In July 1997 NATO invited the Czech Republic, Hungary and Poland to join the Alliance. At the same time, a Founding Act on Mutual Relations, Co-operation and Security was agreed with Russia, a new NATO-Russia Permanent Joint Council (PJC) was established and the Alliance confirmed that it had no intention to deploy nuclear weapons or large concentrations of conventional forces on the territory of new Central European members. NATO also committed itself to an 'open door' policy on membership for other Central and Eastern European states and offered them enhanced co-operation through the PfP. In March 1999, only a decade after the collapse of communism and the withdrawal of Soviet troops from their territory, the three Central European states formally joined NATO. Despite warnings of a new Cold War, Russia – perhaps faced with few credible alternatives – chose to learn to live with NATO's enlargement, while none of the other Central and Eastern European states was seriously destabilised by exclusion from the Alliance. NATO's first post-Cold War enlargement was both a remarkable development and a considerable diplomatic success for the Alliance, especially the Clinton Administration (Goldgeier, 1999).

The successful management of NATO enlargement in 1997-99, however, did not resolve the Alliance's eastern dilemmas. Most of the other states lying between NATO and Russia continued to press for full membership of the Alliance. Moscow remained opposed to NATO's further enlargement, while the long-term direction of the Russia-NATO relationship was still uncertain. The new NATO-Russia relationship embodied in the Founding Act and the PJC was described by supporters as giving Russia 'a voice but not veto' in the Alliance's affairs, since it gave Moscow a forum for dialogue with NATO but not a role in the Alliance's decision making. This left the Russians dissatisfied. Moreover, serious differences remained between Russia and the West over intervention in the former Yugoslavia and missile defences. When NATO intervened in Kosovo in 1999, Russia strongly opposed the Alliance's action. At the end of the Kosovo war in June Russia unexpectedly rushed forces from Bosnia to Pristina, generating a tense stand-off with NATO and the risk of direct military confrontation with the Alliance (although the situation was eventually defused). Following the down-turn in relations with NATO at the end of the 1990s, however, Russian President Vladimir Putin used the aftermath of the September 2001 terrorist attack on the US as an opportunity to re-build relations with the West, offering strong support to the US (including accepting the deployment of American troops in Russia's Central Asian backyard). NATO responded to this by offering to establish a new NATO-Russia Council that would give Moscow a stronger voice in Alliance affairs. Nevertheless, President Putin faced significant domestic criticism of his new friendliness towards NATO and the West, while NATO was no more likely to offer Russia a veto over its decision-making than in the mid 1990s. The long term future of the NATO-Russia relationship therefore remains uncertain.

Having committed itself to an open door policy when it took in the first Central European states in 1997-99, NATO also faced continuing dilemmas over enlargement. Aside from continuing fears of antagonising Russia, there were also concerns within NATO about overstretching the Alliance by taking in too many new members and about the military preparedness of the candidates. By early 2002, however, NATO was effectively committed to inviting further Central and Eastern European states to join the Alliance. And at its Prague summit in November 2002, seven states (Bulgaria, Estonia, Latvia, Lithuania, Romania, Slovakia and Slovenia) were formally invited to join NATO. President Putin's post-September 2001 détente with NATO suggested that Russia might learn to live with further NATO enlargement, that included the Baltic states (which directly border Russia, had been part of the Soviet Union and, in the cases of Estonia and Latvia, have large ethnic Russian minority populations). By the mid 2000s therefore there is every likelihood that the Cold War Western Europe NATO of sixteen states will have become an alliance of perhaps twenty-six members incorporating most of Central and Eastern Europe.

The second major challenge that NATO faced in the 1990s was the conflict in former Yugoslavia. In the early 1990s there was reluctance within NATO to transform the Alliance from a collective defence organisation to a wider peacekeeping/enforcement body. George Bush senior's Administration, further, argued that the US did not have any important interests in Yugoslavia. In 1991-92 the then European Community and the United Nations (UN) took the lead in efforts to manage the Yugoslav wars, with Western European states supplying the bulk of a UN peacekeeping force. A number of factors, however, gradually drew NATO into the conflict. First, the Western Europeans, the EC/EU and the UN proved unable to end the conflict, with cease-fires negotiated and promptly broken and UN peacekeepers unable to halt the worsening violence. Second, as the war escalated, pressure grew within the US for more robust action to end the bloodshed. In particular, when the Clinton Administration came to power in 1993 it was committed to taking a more forceful approach. Third, the on-going conflict was increasingly viewed as undermining the credibility of NATO as a whole: if NATO could not address this, the key European security challenge of the 1990s, what was the Alliance for?

Bitter disputes, however, emerged within NATO over how to respond to the Yugoslav conflict. Many Americans argued that the European approach of diplomacy backed up only by traditional peacekeeping (which requires the consent of the parties to the conflict) was only encouraging aggression and amounted to appeasement of Serbia and the Bosnian Serbs. Europeans argued that American reluctance to deploy its own troops on the ground meant that the forceful use of airpower by NATO would put European troops at risk while only escalating the conflict. Participants described these as perhaps the worst intra-Alliance disputes in NATO's history. At times in 1993-94 the very future of NATO appeared to be a stake.

A series of shifts in 1994-95 eventually produced a more robust NATO response. Further escalation of the conflict, in particular a series of atrocities by the Bosnian Serbs (culminating in the July 1995 Srebrenica massacre in which more than 6,000 unarmed Muslim men were murdered), galvanised opinion within the West. The situation on the ground was altered by the strengthening of the Croatian and Bosnian Croatian and Muslim armed forces. UN peacekeepers were withdrawn from vulnerable forward locations and re-inforced with artillery. After a series of episodes in which NATO had threatened airstrikes and the Bosnian Serbs had called the Alliance's bluff, the shelling of Sarajevo marketplace in August 1995 produced a stronger reaction from the Alliance. NATO launched Operation Deliberate Force, a series of airstrikes against Bosnian Serb military targets. At the same time, Croatia and the Bosnian Croatian and Muslim forces initiated a ground offensive against Serbian positions in Croatia and Bosnia, forcing a rapid series of withdrawals. The Bosnian Serbs were forced to the negotiating table and the US was able to broker the Dayton peace agreement (named after Dayton in Ohio where it was negotiated). A 60,000 strong NATO-led Implementation Force (IFOR, later re-named the Stabilisation Force or SFOR) was deployed to enforce the settlement.

Less than four years later NATO found itself at war again in Yugoslavia in even more controversial circumstances. With its ninety per cent ethnic Albanian population facing escalating repression by the Serb-dominated Yugoslav authorities from the late 1980s, Kosovo was widely recognised as a potential flashpoint. In the late 1990s a Kosovar Albanian guerrilla resistance movement – the Kosovo Liberation Army – emerged, triggering an intensifying Yugoslav/Serb military response. By late 1998 and early 1999 the conflict appeared on the verge of a major escalation. NATO threatened airstrikes against Yugoslavia if it did not cease its military action. Peace talks between the Yugoslav authorities and the Kosovar Albanians broke down in controversial circumstances in March 1999 and the Yugoslavs escalated their military action in Kosovo. On 24 March NATO responded by launching Operation Allied Force, a sustained air campaign against Yugoslav military and infrastructure targets. NATO's action was particularly controversial because it was an unambiguous case of military intervention in another state's internal affairs (violating the norm of state sovereignty) and NATO acted without explicit UN Security Council authorisation (which Russia and China, as permanent members of the Security Council, would have vetoed).

Instead of backing down as Western leaders had hoped, Yugoslav leader Slobodan Milosevic responded by dramatically escalating military action on the ground against the Kosovar Albanians – causing the population to flee en masse to neighbouring Albania and Macedonia. By April and May 1999 NATO appeared to face the choice of acquiescing in Milosevic's victory – with potentially very destabilising consequences for the region and the Alliance itself – or preparing for a risky ground invasion of Kosovo. With its member states, and in particular the US, reluctant to consider a ground invasion, NATO escalated the air war against Yugoslavia (attacking a growing range of military, infrastructure and economic targets). In June, under Russian diplomatic pressure, Milosevic cracked and agreed to withdraw Yugoslav military and police forces. A 50,000-strong NATO led Kosovo Force (KFOR) was then deployed to enforce the settlement and provide security.

By the end of the 1990s NATO had used force to impose peace in Bosnia and Kosovo – the first such use of force in the Alliance's history – and had tens of thousands of troops on the ground enforcing peace settlements. In summer 2001, further, NATO deployed a small force into Macedonia to help facilitate disarmament in the context of a peace agreement between the Macedonian government and ethnic Albanian rebels. NATO's interventions in Bosnia and Kosovo also resulted in close military co-operation with neighbouring states, in particular Hungary, Albania, Macedonia, Bulgaria and Romania.

NATO also underwent significant internal reforms in the 1990s, reflecting its changing roles. Its members' conventional and nuclear forces levels were reduced radically and various European members initiated transitions from conscript to largely professional militaries. NATO's command structure was reformed, moving from one based on Cold War plans for defence of national territory to one designed for a range of different military operations. In 1994 NATO introduced the concept of Combined Joint Task Forces (CJTFs) as a framework for intervention or peacekeeping operations involving 'coalitions of the willing'. A process of 'Europeanising' the Alliance was also initiated, providing for the possibility of European military operations in which the US would not take part but which might use NATO's planning and command and control infrastructure. During the early and mid-1990s these plans centred on the Western European Union (WEU – the organisation bringing together the Western European members of NATO) and were relatively limited in scope. In 1997-98, however, 'New Labour' abandoned Britain's previous opposition to the EU developing a defence role. As a consequence, consensus emerged within the EU that the Union should for the first time in its history develop a military role and agreement was reached on the establishment of an EU rapid reaction capability (based on voluntary contributions from the EU member states' national armed forces). Although the EU's defence role remains embryonic, this is nevertheless a potentially revolutionary development, creating the possibility that for the first time since the Second World War European countries may develop the capacity to undertake collective military operations independently of the US (although current plans envisage the EU relying on some NATO or US assets, for example NATO's military planning structures and US intelligence satellites, for the foreseeable future). It appears likely that over the next few years the EU might take over some of the peacekeeping operations in the former Yugoslavia currently run by NATO. While the details – and the relative success and failure – of the EU's new defence role remain to be seen, the very fact of its development suggests that the EU, rather than NATO, may begin to take greater responsibility for military aspects of European security.

Continuing Uncertainty

Despite NATO's transformation during the 1990s, the long-term future of the Alliance remains uncertain. Significant differences in strategic outlook exist between the US and its European allies and these differences have led many observers to question the longer-term prospects for transatlantic co-operation and NATO (Daalder, 2001). These differences relate to some of the key security challenges facing the world, and especially the leading Western states, in the early twenty-first century. Since the early 1990s the US has been markedly more concerned than its European allies about the prospect and implications of the proliferation of WMD. This reflects the US's status as the world's only superpower: the US is the most likely candidate for WMD retaliation by belligerent states, has the largest forward military presence in the Persian Gulf, East Asia and elsewhere and its foreign policy choices may be greatly affected by proliferation. In contrast, European governments have been more sanguine about the prospect of proliferation, playing down both the extent of the problem and its possible implications. Similarly, and not withstanding the general international support for the US after the attacks of 11 September 2001, there are important European-American differences on terrorism. The US and American bases, embassies and personnel overseas have been the primary targets of international terrorism in the 1990s. While the European allies supported the US intervention in Afghanistan in 2001, they have been more wary of the extension of military action to other states and regions. European political leaders have also been more willing to think in terms of addressing the 'causes' of terrorism (for example, in viewing the Palestinian question as a driver behind Muslim resentment of the West).

There are arguably also more fundamental differences of strategic culture between the US and its European allies, which have grown during the 1990s. Over the last decade the US has increasingly come to reject multilateral agreements and treaties, especially those that might constrain US freedom of action. It has rejected the Kyoto agreement to limit global warming, the International Criminal Court and the Comprehensive Test

Ban Treaty on nuclear weapons. In contrast, European governments generally remain strongly committed to multilateral frameworks for international action and willing to accept the constraints that these impose on them. These differences in strategic culture again reflect America and Europe's different circumstances. As a global superpower, the US has less need (at least in the short term) to depend on multilateral frameworks, while its freedom of manoeuvre might be constrained by them. In contrast, European states have less power and freedom of manoeuvre in the first place and perhaps more to gain from multilateral constraints on others' power. The experience of being deeply embedded in the multilateral EU may reinforce this tendency.

These dynamics have also led to a shift in US attitudes towards NATO in recent years. During the Cold War, NATO was central to addressing the perceived core challenge to US national security – the 'Soviet threat'. If the core threats to US national security today are proliferation and terrorism – a perspective strongly reinforced within the US by the events of 11 September 2001 – NATO as currently constituted is at best marginal to addressing those threats. The experience of the 1999 Kosovo War, where the US faced the difficulty of working with eighteen other allies, has also made American officials (and especially the US military) wary of 'war by committee'. The Bush Administration made clear from the start that the intervention in Afghanistan would be undertaken very much on US terms, with allies playing a limited role and given no veto over US decisions. There is also growing discussion about the possibility of at least a limited withdrawal of US forces from the NATO peacekeeping operations in the Balkans. The changing US attitudes to NATO can be seen when even a mainstream figure such as Senator John Warner, the senior Republican on the Senate Armed Services Committee, argues that it may be time to 'consider proudly retiring the colours of NATO and start over again' (Wolffe, 1 March 2002).

These European-American differences are exacerbated by military technological divergences relating to the RMA. The US has invested heavily in the RMA and power projection capabilities, something facilitated by its large size and relatively high level of defence spending. European states have generally invested less in the RMA and power projection capabilities, a tendency re-inforced by the duplications inherent in the maintenance of national armed forces and defence budgets. In Kosovo and elsewhere this has led to growing arguments that the European allies are increasingly unable to operate effectively alongside the US military.

Since the mid-1990s some analysts have argued that if NATO is to remain relevant to the security needs of both the US and Europe the Alliance must adopt a global role. In particular, there have been proposals for a new strategic bargain between the US and Europe, whereby the US would commit itself to European security in return for a European commitment to support the US in managing global security challenges (Asmus, Blackwill and Larrabee, 1996). Similarly, in the wake of the September 2001 attacks on the US, Senator Lugar has argued that the campaign against terrorism must become a 'central NATO mission' (Lugar, 4 March 2002). A number of factors, however, militate against the development of a global role for NATO. European governments have been reluctant to move in this direction, fearing that the globalisation of NATO's responsibilities might drag them into US military interventions over which they may have little influence, generate tensions with countries outside Europe and undermine NATO's role within Europe. Despite the recent steps towards an EU military role, the European allies lack the military capabilities to contribute in a major way to US-led operations outside Europe. Whether the aftermath of 11 September 2001 will alter these dynamics and lead NATO to play a greater role in addressing the global challenges of terrorism and proliferation remains to be seen.

Conclusion

NATO's transformation during the 1990s was truly remarkable. At the beginning of the 1990s few if any predicted that the Alliance would have tens of thousands of troops on the ground as peacekeepers in Yugoslavia, that three former Warsaw Pact states would have joined NATO with more states queuing behind them or that NATO would have developed extensive political and military co-operation with Russia and the other former eastern bloc states. By the end of the 1990s NATO could claim to have successfully transformed itself from a Cold War defence alliance to a pan-European security organisation. At the same time, NATO remained an essentially European-focused organisation, dealing with security challenges within Europe, not beyond it.

Despite NATO's transformation, doubts about the long-term future of the Alliance have persisted. Such doubts have grown since 11 September

2001. These doubts reflect the reality that, while Europeans and Americans share common democratic values and common general security interests, their strategic outlooks differ significantly. The US is the world's only superpower, with a global perspective and a willingness to use its power, including military power, assertively. While recognising the importance of global security problems, European governments and the EU as a whole remain more focused on immediate security concerns on Europe's periphery. Europeans are also more inclined to seek multilateral solutions to international problems and more cautious than the US about the use of military force. These differences, further, relate to fundamental political questions about the nature of and prospects for international order and the role of force in world politics.

In the wider international context, NATO is only one security policy tool available to the governments of Europe and North America. The key question facing the Alliance is how far it will remain a core framework for the co-ordination of security policies amongst its members and in what circumstances and ways they may seek to use the Alliance. A number of possibilities exist. Notwithstanding the differences between Europe and America, the US may be willing to maintain its commitment to NATO and European security and NATO may remain an essentially European-focused organisation. If NATO is increasingly seen as marginal to core US national security concerns, however, American interest in and commitment to the Alliance may decline. Within the next decade, for example, American troops could be withdrawn from the Balkans and the EU could take over these peacekeeping operations. Alternatively, America's European allies could gradually come to play a greater role alongside the US in addressing global security challenges, with NATO adopting an increasingly global role. The first chapter of NATO's post-Cold War development was completed in the 1990s. The next chapters in the story remain to be written.

Note

[1] This chapter was received before the recent (2003) US-led military action against Iraq commenced, but the divisions over the war are very much in line with its analysis.

References

Adler, E. and Barnett, M. (eds) (1998), *Security Communities*, Cambridge University Press, Cambridge.

Allin, D. H. (1995), 'Can containment work again?', *Survival*, 37 (1), pp. 53-65.

Asmus, R. D., Blackwill, R. D. and Larrabee, F. S. (1996), 'Can NATO survive?', *The Washington Quarterly*, 19 (2), pp. 79-101.

Boyle, M. (10 December 2001), 'RUSI speech UK strategic choices following SDR and 11th September', available at http://news/mod.uk/news/press/news_press_notice.asp?newsItem_id=1262. (Accessed 8 January 2002.)

Buzan, B., de Wilde, J. and Waever, O. (1998), *Security: A New Framework for Analysis*, Lynne Rienner Publishers, Boulder/London.

Clinton, B. (14 December 2001), 'The struggle for the soul of the 21st century', The Dimbleby Lecture 2001, available at http://www.bbc.co.uk/arts/news_comments/dimbleby/print_clinton.shtml. (Accessed 10 January 2002.)

Daalder, I. (2001), 'Are the United States and Europe heading for divorce?' *International Affairs*, 77 (3), pp. 553-67.

Freedman, L. (1998), *The Revolution in Strategic Affairs*, Adelphi Paper 318, Oxford University Press for The International Institute for Strategic Studies, Oxford.

Gaddis, J. L. (1998), 'History, grand strategy and NATO enlargement', *Survival*, 40 (1), pp. 145-51.

Goldgeier, J. M. (1999), *Not Whether But When: the US decision to enlarge NATO*, Brookings Institution Press, Washington DC.

Lieven, A. (1999), 'The weakness of Russian nationalism', *Survival*, 41 (2), pp. 53-70.

Lugar, R. G., Senator (R) (4 March 2002), Speech 'NATO after 9/11: crisis or opportunity?', available at http://www.senate.gov/-lugar/030402.html. (Accessed 8 March 2002.)

NATO (1991), 'The Alliance's new strategic concept. Agreed by the Heads of State and Government participating in the meeting of the North Atlantic Council in Rome on 7-8 November 1991', *NATO Review*, 39 (6), pp. 25-32.

Reiss, M. and Litwak, R. S. (eds) (1994), *Nuclear Proliferation After the Cold War*, The Woodrow Wilson Center Press, Washington DC.

Wolffe, R. (2002), 'Republicans hit out at NATO expansion', *The Financial Times* (1 March).

11 Globalisation and Third World Poverty

BRIAN VALE

Introduction

The global capitalist system, through its use of neo-liberal economic policies, economic globalisation, free trade, deregulation, privatisation, the opening up of local markets in the Third World to transnational corporations, structural adjustments through the International Monetary Fund and World Bank and the cutting back of social welfare subsidies, is having profound effects on poverty in the Third World, especially sub-Saharan Africa. It is estimated that 1.2 billion people live on less than $1 a day. In a world where rich nations provide the agenda for international meetings, for example on affordable drugs, debt reduction or pollution, this is leading not just to moral and humanitarian questions but also to a possible rationale for terrorism. This author accepts that there is a debate on globalisation, but his personal beliefs are those of a 'pessimistic Transformationalist'. In other words economic globalisation has widened and deepened, reaching across the globe, but is having negative effects on Third World poverty. It is the poor who are having to pay the price for this transformation. In this chapter I start by outlining some of the varying definitions and aspects of economic globalisation. This is important because the concept of globalisation has been one of the most contested concepts in the field of social scientific research over recent years. I then briefly discuss globalisation in other areas of life, before focusing on the neo-liberal ideology which currently pervades the IMF and the World Bank, the major institutional aspects of globalisation seen from the Third World. I conclude by arguing that their policies have exacerbated poverty since around 1980.

The Concept of Globalisation

Globalisation is, however, a contested concept. According to Held and McGrew 'no single universally agreed definition of globalisation exists. As with all core concepts in the social sciences its precise meaning remains contested' (2001, p. 3). They say that globalisation has been conceived as 'action at a distance' (whereby the action of social agents in one locale can come to have significant consequences for 'distant others'), time-space compression (as referring to the way in which instantaneous electronic communication erodes the constraints of distance and time on social organisation and interaction) to accelerating interdependence (the intensification of enmeshment among national economies and societies such that events in one country impact directly on others), and a shrinking world (the erosion of borders and geographical barriers to socio-economic activity) and among the other concepts, global integration, the reordering of inter-regional power relations, consciousness of global conditions and the intensification of inter-regional interconnectedness. For Held and McGrew,

> globalisation denotes the expanding scale, growing magnitude, speeding up and deepening impact of inter-regional flows and patterns of social interaction. It refers to a shift or transformation in the scale of human social organisation that links distant communities and expands the reach of power relations across the world's major regions and continents (2001, p. 4).

For McGrew globalisation can be defined as a growing global interconnectedness. It implies that social political and economic activities are becoming 'stretched' across national frontiers such that events, decisions and activities in one part of the world come to have immediate significance for individuals and communities in distant parts of the globe (1997, p. 7). It also involves an intensification or increasing density in the flows and patterns of interaction or interconnectedness which transcends states and societies, and also a blurring between what is local and what is global. Alongside the stretching goes a 'deepening' such that even though 'everyone has a local life, phenomenal worlds for the most part are truly global' (Giddens, 1990, p. 187).

Growing interconnectedness generates a host of transnational problems, from the proliferation of weapons of mass destruction to global trafficking in narcotics, which cannot be solved by an individual country but only through international co-operation. Globalisation for McGrew 'stimulates the growth of international organisations and multilateral mechanisms for regulating areas of transnational activity' (1997, p. 7). This involves multiple webs of relationships between states, and international institutions, non-governmental organisations and multinational corporations which make up the global system and which generate constraints upon not only their activities but their autonomy.

For Goldblatt globalisation denotes 'a significant shift in the spatial form of human social organisation and activity to transcontinental or inter-regional patterns of relations, interaction and the exercise of power' (1997, p. 8). This implies more than simply flows and connections across nation states and national boundaries and 'advertises the fundamental historical shift in the scale of contemporary social and economic organisation which globalisation entails,' (McGrew, 1997, p. 8). Globalisation involves the organisation and exercise of social power on a transnational and intercontinental scale. 'In an increasingly interconnected global system the exercise of power through the decisions, actions or inaction of agencies on one continent can have significant consequences for nations, communities and households on other continents' (McGrew, 1997, p. 8).

Globalisation is associated with a 'stretching of power relations such that sites of power and the exercise of power become increasingly distant from the subjects or localities which experience its consequences. Consequently, 'inequality and hierarchy are deeply inscribed in the very process of globalisation' (McGrew, 1997, p. 8).

According to Held et al. (1999, pp. 149-50), the emergence of global free trade provides the basis for open worldwide markets. For such markets to emerge requires networks between regions and countries. Trade has become much more extensive than ever before, as a worldwide network of trading relations between regions and countries has developed. Trade globalisation entails more than exchange of goods and services between separate economies, since it suggests the emergence of worldwide markets for traded goods and services. Of course this does not presume that all countries trade with each other; rather it assumes existence of a trading system in which trade activity between any two countries may affect trade relations between the rest. More specifically trade globalisation implies the existence of significant levels of inter-regional trade such that markets for traded goods function at a global rather than primarily at an inter-regional level. Global trade therefore entails a system of regularised exchange of goods and services at the inter-regional level.

For Hurrell and Woods, 'states, communities and nations are differentially enmeshed in global and transnational flows and networks'

(1995, quoted in McGrew, 1997, p. 9); whilst for Johnson '[p]atterns of hierarchy and stratification mediate access to sites of power whilst the consequences of globalisation are unevenly experienced' (1995, quoted in McGrew, 1997, p. 9). 'Moreover, the unevenness of globalisation simultaneously stimulates the process of global fragmentation and global integration.' (McGrew, 1997, p. 9). The rich, powerful and wealthy have much greater control over global networks than do the poor.

For Waters, there has been a form of globalisation in progress throughout history. In the modern period it has been an outcome of capitalism: it is 'the product of the disorganised capital, of post industrialism and post modernity' (1995, quoted in Beynon and Dunkerley, 2000, p. 4). Giddens and Wallerstein are both ambivalent about any long-term benefit that globalisation may hold for the human race. Giddens sees a world market for capital, commodities, labour and communications as having developed, 'with deadly weaponry and sophisticated surveillance techniques truly global in their reach' (1990, quoted in Beynon and Dunkerley, 2000, p. 4). For Wallerstein, globalisation presents a world increasingly dominated by capital controlled by the West. However, for Jameson, given its complexity, it is not yet possible to come up with anything like the comprehensive definition of globalisation. For Chomsky, it is the paradox of globalisation that although capitalism is centralising in character nevertheless 'all around the world there is much more involvement in grassroots organisations, regionalism and moves towards developing more local autonomy' (1996, quoted in Beynon and Dunkerley, 2000, p. 4).

For Beynon and Dunkerley, 'it is this contradictory character that makes defining the ongoing globalisation so perilous, along with the factor that it crosses the boundaries of conventional academic disciplines' (2000, p. 4). For Jameson, globalisation is 'that intellectual property of no particular field yet seems to concern politics and economics in an immediate way, but just as immediately culture and sociology, not to speak of information and the media, or ecology or consumption and daily life' (1998, quoted in Beynon and Dunkerley, 2000, p. 4). Beck attempts to distinguish between globality, globalism and globalisation:

> globality, refers to the fact that we are increasingly living in a world society in the sense that the notion of closed spaces has become illusory... From now on nothing which happens on the planet is only a limited local event ...globalism is the view that the world market is now powerful enough to supplant (local and national) political action...globalisation is the blanket

term to describe the processes through which sovereign national states are criss-crossed and undermined by transnational actors with varying prospects of power, orientations, identities and networks (1992, quoted in Beynon and Dunkerley, 2000, p. 4).

For Waters, globalisation

> is a social process in which the constraints of geography on social and cultural arrangements recede and in which people become increasingly aware that they are receding, [and in which] territoriality will disappear as an organising principle for social and cultural life... It will be a society without borders or spatial boundaries. In a globalised world we will be unable to predict social practices and preferences on the basis of geographical location (1995, quoted in Beynon and Dunkerley, 2000, p. 5).

Waters believes that globalisation has the following features,

> increasing speed and volume (speed of movement and volume of goods, messages and symbols have massively increased), 'shrinking space' (space is increasingly expressed in time of travel or communication and appears to shrink as travel and communication time decreases – this appears as 'global shrinkage' and the 'phenomenological elimination of space and the generalisation of time' (1995, quoted in Beynon and Dunkerley, 2000, p. 6).

Increasingly, he thinks, borders are permeable (political and geographical boundaries have been rendered permeable with greatly increased relations whether through trade, tourism and or electronically. The degree of interconnectedness between all nation states and the wider world is increasing. Total national autonomy or isolation is almost impossible to maintain. Economic political and cultural change is now beyond the control of any national government) (1995, summarised in Beynon and Dunkerley, 2000, p. 6).

However, Hirst and Thompson are sceptical of the concept of globalisation and contest the notion of a truly global economy. They believe that the present international economy is not unprecedented. It is one of a number of distinct conjunctures or states of the international economy that have existed since an economy based on modern industrial technology began to be generalised from the 1860s. In some respects the current international economy is less open and integrated than the regime that prevailed from 1870 to 1914. They point out that genuinely transnational companies appear to be rare, and most companies are based nationally and trade multinationally on the strength of location of assets, production and sales. Capital mobility, they say is not producing a massive shift of investment and employment from the advanced to the developing countries. Rather, foreign direct investment is highly concentrated among the advanced industrial economies. The Third World remains marginal in both investment and trade. Rather than being truly global, trade and investment are concentrated in the triad of Europe, North America and Japan. Although their view serves as a corrective to some of the more extreme claims made by the theorists of globalisation, Thompson and Hirst do not provide evidence to refute the present writer's claim that globalisation in its neo-liberal form has dramatic and adverse effects on Third World countries.

Non-Economic Globalisation

For Held, Goldblatt and Perraton (1999, p. 88), military globalisation

> can be conceived very crudely as a process which embodies the growing extent and intensity of military relations among the political units of the world system. Understood as such, it reflects both the expanding network of worldwide military ties and relations as well as the impact of key military technological innovations, which, over time, have reconstituted the world into a single geo-strategic space.

This process of the time-space compression has brought centres of military power into closer proximity and potential conflict, as the capability to project enormous power across vast distances has proliferated. Military globalisation has resulted in permanent preparation for war becoming an integral feature of modern social life, due to the shrinkage in military decision and reaction time.

> Various quantitative indicators may be utilised to help map the spatio-temporal and organisational dimensions of military globalisation. These include: the reach of imperial expansion; foreign military presence; military and diplomatic representation; the arms trade; arms expenditure; defence expenditure; alliance membership; military co-operation agreements; defence – industrial linkages; the incidence of military intervention and patterns of military assistance (Held et al., 1999, p. 89).

Contemporary military globalisation is contributing to the reconstitution of sovereignty, autonomy and democracy, that is, to the reconstitution of the modern nation state.

For Held et al. (1999, p. 341), contemporary cultural globalisation is associated with several developments:

> New global infrastructures are of an unprecedented scale, generating an enormous capacity for cross-border penetration and a decline in their cost of use; an increase in the intensity, volume and speed of cultural exchange and communication of all kinds; the rise of Western popular culture and inter-business communication as the primary content of global control interaction; the dominance of culture industry multinationals in the creation and ownership of infrastructure and organisation for the production and distribution of cultural goods; and shift in the geography of global cultural interaction departing in some significant way from the geography of the pre-Second World War global order.

Globalisation and Neo-Liberalism

Economic neo-liberalism is the pervasive doctrine of the main economic institutions of globalisation. A general characteristic of neo-liberalism is the desire to intensify and expand the market, by intensifying the number, frequency, repeatability and formalisation of transactions. The ultimate goal of neo-liberalism is a universe where every action of every being is a market transaction, conducted in competition with every other being and with every other transaction, influencing every other transaction, with transactions occurring in an infinitely short term, and repeated at infinitely fast rate.

According to Gill (1995, p. 406), the neo-liberal concept of 'globalisation' suggests

> that the privatisation and transnationalisation of capital are either inevitable or desirable from a broad social viewpoint... A positive aspect is the equation of free competition and free exchange (global capital mobility) with economic efficiency, welfare and democracy and a myth of virtually unlimited social progress as represented in the World Bank and IMF reports. A negative aspect is how neo-liberal market forces are often said to have marginalised non-market alternatives.

For Kiely, neo-liberalism consists of a limited government intervention in the economy, a low level of price distortion in the economy, and an outward orientated strategy of export promotion. These principles formed the basis of structural adjustment and stabilisation programmes in the developing world in the 1980s and 1990s. Structural adjustment can be defined as a set of policies designed to promote economic growth through the opening up of economies to competitive market forces. Stabilisation policies, more closely associated with the IMF, are designed to alleviate short-term balance of payments deficits.

Policies include the removal of obstacles such as state subsidies to industry, minimum wage and price controls. Combined with a competitive exchange rate, prices are said to reflect the laws of supply and demand and so investors and consumers can respond to the correct price signals that, in turn, facilitate high levels of economic growth.

For Williamson, neo-liberalism comprises fiscal discipline, a change in public expenditure priorities that reduces subsidies for special interests; tax reform that includes cutting marginal tax rates specifically on overseas investments; financial liberalisation; unified exchange rate; trade liberalisation; increase of foreign direct investment; privatisation of state enterprises; deregulation and the abolition of regulatory barriers to entry for all industries; and guarantees of secure property rights (1993, pp. 1329-36).

Panitch talks of attempts to 'constitutionalise neo-liberalism' through 'interstate treaties designed to legally enforce upon future governments general adherence to the discipline of the capital market' (1996, p. 213). For Haque (1999, p. 203), neo-liberalism

> is an ideological position based on strong beliefs in the promotion of the general good by following the principles of the free-market and open competition, limited state intervention and welfare, individualistic self-interest, rational utility maximisation and comparative advantage in free trade.

One of the most prominent features of the neo-liberal thinking is its emphasis on maximising the role of the market and minimising the interventionist role of the state. This involves private property and the free market at every level of society from individuals to the global economy. For neo-liberals 'the market is the optimal space for the production and distribution of wealth and as the optimal vehicle for social mobility' (Haque, 1999, p. 203). In the case of developing countries, neo-liberal ideology requires the replacement of the interventionist developmental state by a more non-interventionist state, and encourages the expansion of market forces by undertaking various market-friendly policies. Related to this relatively anti-state and pro-market position is the neo-liberal advocacy of policies such as deregulation and privatisation. Under the dominant neo-liberal ideological persuasion, almost all nations have been engaged in selling state enterprises, deregulating the agricultural and industrial sectors and contracting out government services. Neo-liberals believe in the principles of comparative advantage and free trade, while opposing protectionist policies for domestic industry and tying economic growth more closely to export expansion. They believe in the liberalisation of trade, facilitation of foreign investment and elimination of export controls and import licensing and have an overwhelming emphasis on economic growth, in some instances even endorsing inequality as a prerequisite for growth. This preference for economic productivity and growth, with a disregard for issues such as income distribution and equality, is evident in policy preferences for reducing welfare subsidises and abolishing anti-poverty programmes. Neo-liberalism thus wishes not only to revive market forces, but to dismantle the basic economic and welfare rights of citizens such as education, economic security and health provisions.

Neo-liberals believe in market principles, a minimalist state, comparative advantage and economic growth. This is evident in the privatisation of state enterprises, and deregulation of state controls, liberalisation of trade, elimination of import restrictions, and encouragement of foreign investment, withdrawal of subsidies and reduction of welfare programmes.

The World Bank and IMF have applied structural adjustment of debtor economies along neo-liberal lines and imposed austerity plans as a condition of debt reduction and of further loans. Structural adjustment had the following requirements: privatisation of publicly owned industries, especially oil, power, telephone, ports and railways; slashing of public services with massive lay-offs, reduction of social welfare, closure of hospitals, libraries and schools; removal of wage and price protections and laws for workers' rights; removal of barriers to foreign investment and ownership, and abolition of tariffs on imports; allowing the currency to float, or devaluing the currency to stimulate exports.

According to Haque, under the influence of the IMF and World Bank 'most of the current regimes in Asia, Africa and Latin America have adopted so-called structural adjustment programmes derived from neo-liberal theories' (Haque, p. 204). The neo-liberal foundation of these programmes is visible in their central policy of contracting out government enterprises and services; the weakening of the state's economic management by deregulating controls over pricing, marketing, investment and finance; and the liberalisation of trade and investment by reducing import tariffs, subsidising export-led production, attracting foreign investments and exempting foreign companies from taxes and labour codes. The scope of privatisation transactions encompasses a variety of sectors such as telecommunications, power, water supply, railways and ports, airlines, hotels, shipping companies, natural gas; the oil industry and petrochemicals. Most regimes in developing countries, due to the IMF and the World Bank, have liberalised trade specifically by withdrawing a considerable percentage of import tariffs and by financing export-led industries. There is an increasing participation of foreign investors in privatisation transactions, and in extending foreign ownership of privatised assets in developing countries. In addition developing countries have reduced state subsidies, withdrawn welfare programmes and introduced fees for various services. Provisions for education and health care for the poor have been cut back.

Neo-Liberal Policies and Poverty

In what follows I have neither attempted to define poverty, nor to compare the definitions used by different authors. While this would be necessary in a longer piece of work, it seems obvious to me that an income of under two dollars a day, malnutrition, or a lack of basic housing, sanitation and safe drinking water are such stark indicators as to be matters of the highest concern whatever one's benchmarks.

According to Haque neo-liberalism and structural adjustment programmes have resulted in a decline of government expenditures in sub-Saharan Africa in health. The expenditure for primary school education has fallen in 21 out of 23 countries. Between 1980 and 1985 government spending on social welfare declined by 26 per cent for the region and there have been severe cuts in health and education expenditure and food subsidies in Zimbabwe, Zaire, Swaziland, Lesotho and Uganda.

> More importantly, under the neo-liberal states, as the role of the state in anti-poverty programmes and welfare subsidies has diminished, there have been worsening conditions of poverty and inequality in many developing countries and these negative changes have had an adverse effects on the

environment and on sustainability. Poverty often leads to various forms of environmental destruction... because the rural poor often have no choice but to use forests for food and firewood and over-cultivate crop land. At the same time increases in the urban poor cause overcrowding and the contamination of water (Haque, 1999, p. 206).

Many of these effects are directly attributable to neo-liberal policies of stabilisation and structural adjustment, under which governments adopt austerity measures, reduce subsidies, lay off workers and mature welfare benefits.

Between 1980 and 1992, a period when neo-liberal policies were in ascendance, the number of people in poverty in Latin America rose from 136 million to 266 million, while in Africa the number increased from 270 million in 1986 to 335 million in 1990. Even in the economically 'successful' Asian countries the extent of poverty remains quite significant. The overall standards of living have dropped in most African and Latin American countries due to adjustment related reductions in social services, increases in food prices, decline in real wages and reduced access to health and education facilities. In the developing world as a whole, more than 25 per cent of the population today lives in poverty and almost 34 per cent lives on an income of less than one US dollar per day (Haque, 1999, p. 207).

In addition, reductions in subsidies and the withdrawal of welfare and anti-poverty programmes have increased inequalities among various income groups, which has worsened the poverty situation even further. Beyond poverty, economic inequality implies the expansion and further enrichment of the more affluent classes, which leads to excessive consumption and environmental degradation. In Latin America after a decade of neo-liberal policies the top 20 per cent of the population earns 20 times the amount earned by the poorest 20 per cent. According to Haque in Chile, one of the earliest followers of neo-liberalism, the income of the richest 10 per cent of households increased from 36 per cent to 47 per cent, the income of the poorest 40 per cent of households decreased from 19 per cent to 13 per cent during 1979 to 1989. Trade liberalisation has also contributed to increased international economic inequality between advanced capitalist nations and developing countries. By 1992 the average per capita income of the 23 high-income countries reached US $22,160 while 1.3 billion people in the developing world had an average income of less than US $310. This increasing international inequality is not isolated from neo-liberal policies. Trade liberalisation in particular has led to a massive transfer of resources from developing countries to advanced capitalist nations.

> This international inequality implies that while people in affluent industrial nations expand their over consumption even further, people in low income countries suffer from poverty and hunger, thereby increasing negative pressures on the environment at both ends of the development spectrum (Haque, 1999, p. 209).

According to Weller, Scott and Hersh (2001), despite economic integration, reductions in poverty and income inequality remain elusive in most parts of the world. Moreover, greater integration of deregulated trade and capital flows over the last two decades has undermined efforts to raise living standards for the world's poor. In 1980 median income in the richest 10 per cent of countries was 77 times greater than in the poorest 10 per cent. By 1999 the gap had grown to 122 times. Inequality has also increased within many countries. Over the same period any gains in poverty reduction have been relatively small and geographically isolated. The number of poor people rose from 1987 to 1998 and the percentage of poor people increased in many countries. In 1998 close to half the population were considered poor in many parts of the world. In 1980 the world's poorest 10 per cent or 400 million people lived on 72¢ per day or less. The same number of people had 79¢ (nominally) per day in 1990 and 78¢ in 1999.

The evidence shows that unregulated capital and trade flows contribute to rising inequality and impede progress in poverty reduction. Trade liberalisation leads to more import competition and to a growing use of the threat to move production to lower wage locales, thereby depressing wages. Deregulated international capital flows have led to rapid increases in short-term capital flows and more frequent economic crises while simultaneously limiting the ability of governments to cope with crises (Weller et al., 2001).

Economic upheavals disproportionately harm the poor and thus lead to lack of success in poverty reduction and to rising income inequality. The world's poor may stand to gain from global integration but not under the unregulated version currently promoted by the World Bank and others. According to the World Bank, 'the long-term trends of rising global inequality and rising numbers of people in absolute poverty have been halted and perhaps even reversed due to greater globalisation' (World Bank, 2001).

However, for Weller et al. (2001), the purported success in poverty reduction is elusive: the number of poor people is on the rise, the proportion of people in relative poverty remains high in many parts of the world, and is rising in many regions. The World Bank ignores regional or country-by-country differences and underestimates the proportion of people living in poverty. They estimate that an additional 14 per cent of the population should be considered poor compared to the figures provided by the World Bank. In 1998 the proportion of the population in poverty remained very high in some regions: over 40 per cent in the South Asian and over 50 per cent in sub-Saharan Africa and Latin America. Since 1987 the proportion of poor people has stayed relatively constant in sub-Saharan Africa and Latin America but has more than tripled in Eastern Europe and Central Asia.

Table 3 Proportion of People Living Below the Poverty Line (%)

Location	1987	1998
Sub-Saharan Africa	51.09	50.49
East Asia (excluding China)	45.06	24.55
Eastern Europe and Central Asia	7.54	25.60
Latin America	50.20	51.35
South Asia	45.20	40.20

According to Weller, Scott and Hersh (2001), the poorest 10 per cent of the world population in 1980 consisted of about 400 million people and lived on a nominal 72¢ a day. This rose to 79¢ a day in 1990, fell to 84¢ in 1996 and to 78¢ in 1999. In other words income of the world's poorest people did not even keep up with inflation. Clearly the economic burden worsened for a large number of people in the 1990s, and this does not include the full impact of the crisis in Asia, Latin America and Russia. They also point out that, although the World Bank claims that 'between countries globalisation is mostly reducing inequality' (World Bank, 2001, p. 1), the IMF states that 'the relative gap between the richest and poorest countries has continued to widen in the 1990s' (IMF 2000, p. 1). Rich countries have become richer and poor countries have become poorer. 'The median per-capita income of the world's richest 10 per cent of countries was 76.8 times that of the poorest 10 per cent of countries in 1980, 119.6 times greater in 1990 and 121.8 times greater in 1999' (Weller et al., 2001, p. 1).

When comparing world income across people rather than countries, the richest 10 per cent of the world's population had an income, on average, 79.8 times higher than those of the poorest 10 per cent in 1980, 119.7 times higher in 1990 and 117.7 times higher in 1999. According to the World Trade Organisation (1999, p. 1) the number of people in the world living on less than $1 a day in 1987 was 1.183 billion (28.3 per cent), in 1998 it was 1.199 billion (24 per cent), and the organisation estimates that in 2008 the number will have increased to 1.242 billion (22 per cent). The number of people in the world living on less than $2 a day in 1987 was 2.549 billion (61 per cent), in 1998 it was 2.801 billion (56 per cent) and it was estimated that in 2008 the number will have decreased to 2.722 billion (48 per cent).

It is an empirical fact that the income gap between the poor and rich countries has increased in recent decades. Only a handful of developing countries - primarily in East Asia - have been able to grow out of poverty so far... If anything, richer countries have been growing faster on average than poorer countries, thereby increasing global income disparity... Some of the poorest countries have become poorer still (World Trade Organisation, 1999, p. 1).

According to *Social Policy and Development*:

The marked slowing of the pace of economic growth after 1980, specifically in middle and many low income developing countries, has limited the scope for poverty reduction. In many cases, slower growth has been exacerbated by growing income inequalities within countries, which have increased the incidence of absolute poverty... The absolute decline in per capita income has for more than half of all low income developing countries from 1970 to 1995 increased disparities in income levels and increased the level of poverty within those countries... The incidence of poverty has increased in those low income countries, especially the poorest countries in sub-Saharan Africa, that suffered from a general economic decline during the past quarter century (1997, p. 1).

This pattern of depressing economic statistics was reinforced by the United Nations Development Programme (1998). It highlighted that 841 million people worldwide were malnourished; the richest three individuals in the world had assets that exceeded the combined GDP of the 48 least developed countries, and a total of 358 people owned as much wealth as 2.5 billion people together – nearly half the world's population. Among the 4.4

billion people in developing countries around the world, three-fifths of them lived in communities lacking basic sanitation; one-third went without safe drinking water, a quarter lacked adequate housing; a fifth were undernourished and 1.3 billion lived on at less than $1 per day.

According to Kacowicz (2001, p. 15), globalisation simply exacerbates world poverty levels through the process of 'creative destruction'.

> Globalisation requires economies and societies to adapt since economies almost never succeed equally, some nations will grow faster than others, so that globalisation would increase inequality... Poverty is directly related to the affluence and exploitation by the rich nations. The very structure and processes of globalisation perpetuate and reproduce the unequal relations and exchange between the 'core' of the international economic system and its periphery... Globalisation has increased inequality by having significant effects on various types of social stratification, including class, country, gender, race, the urban/rural divide, and age both between and especially within nations... globalisation has tended on the whole to widen the gaps in life chances.

Kacowicz (2001, p. 16) adds that the

> adoption of the liberal ideology of globalisation and the restructuring of the world economy under the guidance of the Bretton Woods institutions [the World Bank and the IMF] increasingly deny developing countries the possibility of building their national economies. Thus the internationalisation of macro-economic policies transforms poor countries into open economic territories and their national economies into 'reserves' of cheap labour and natural resources. For instance, since the early 1980s, the macro-economic stabilisation and 'structural adjustment' programmes negotiated among the IMF and World Bank have led to the impoverishment of hundreds of millions of people. In addition the multinational corporations, as carriers of technology, capital and skilled labour between states, have reinforced the negative effects of foreign capital penetration, enlarging the gap between the rich and poor.

At least 45 per cent of Africans live in poverty, average life expectancy in 1999 was 52 years, 34 per cent of African children under the age of five suffer from malnutrition and 43 per cent of the adults were illiterate. Accordingly, 'compared to other regions of the world, sub-Saharan Africa has been marginalised in terms of its participation in the global economy' (Kacowicz, 2001, p. 21).

According to Berg and Krueger (2002), one of the most common criticisms of trade liberalisation and globalisation, particularly in developed countries, is that it drives down wages and exports jobs to low wage economies. Critics see the creation of a global sweatshop economy in which corporations pit workers around the world against each other in a race to the bottom to see who will accept the lowest wages and benefits.

However Berg and Krueger claim that over the past 20 years the proportion of extremely poor people in the world, those living on less than $2 a day, has fallen sharply from 38 per cent in 1978 to 19 per cent in 1998. On the other hand, according to Denny and Elliot (2002, p. 1),

> more than 100 million people in the world's poorest countries will be dragged below the basic subsistence level of a dollar a day by 2015 as they become ensnared in globalisation's poverty trap... the current form of globalisation is tightening rather than loosening the international poverty trap.

The African Church Information Service states that over 300 million people in Africa live in poverty. Moreover,

> market liberalisation, market-based pricing, privatisation of state industries and trade liberalisation have had disastrous effects on the fledgling African economies. Capital market liberalisation which is designed to allow investment capital to flow in and out of countries has had the effect of draining national reserves. Capital can be shifted to any part of the globe and African governments are powerless to stop it exiting from their countries (2002, p. 1).

Conclusion

There can be little doubt that the current neo-liberal version of economic globalisation is exacerbating poverty in most of the Third World. The role of the state in alleviating poverty through education or health programmes has been eroded; wages have tended to decline while food has become more expensive; environmental degradation has accelerated. Neo-liberal policies have also been implemented in many of the advanced countries, worsening relative poverty and widening inequalities in income and wealth.

A whole series of interesting questions remain. Would economic globalisation which implemented a different set of policies help to alleviate

Third World poverty? Who has an interest in the current neo-liberal policies, outside of a small circle of extremely rich people in the advanced countries? Is it possible to devise a form of politics, perhaps based on social democracy, perhaps based on the ideas of the anti-globalisation protesters, which would have a decent chance of altering the current policies? Why has a small group of countries managed to flourish, and so reduce poverty, in current conditions? China has recently been admitted to the World Trade Organisation, which also pushes neo-liberal policies. One-fifth of the world's population lives in China, and many of them are poor. Will China be able to emulate the success of the small group of countries that have managed to benefit from economic globalisation?

References

African Church Information Service (2002), *Globalisation Casts Millions into Poverty*, Global Policy, New York.

Beck, U. (1992), *Risk Society: Towards a New Modernity*, Sage, London.

Berg, A. and Krueger, F. (2002), *Lifting All Boats: Why Openness Helps Curb Poverty*, Global Policy, New York.

Beynon, J. and Dunkerley, D. (eds) (2000), *Globalisation: the Reader*, Routledge, New York.

Chomsky, N. (1996), *Global-local Cultural Production and the Transnational Imagery*, Duke University Press, London.

Denny, C. and Elliott, L. (2002), *100 Million More Must Survive on Less Than $1 a Day*, Global Policy, New York.

Giddens, A. (1990), *The Consequence of Modernity*, Polity, Cambridge.

Gill, S. (1995), 'Globalisation, market globalisation and disciplinary neo-liberalism', *Millennium, Journal of International Studies*, 24 (3), pp. 399-423.

Haque, M. (1999), 'The fate of sustainable development under neo-liberal regimes in developing countries' *International Political Science Review*, 20 (2), pp. 197- 218.

Held, D., Goldblatt, N., Perraton, J. (1999), *Global Transformations*, Polity, Cambridge.

Held, D. and McGrew, A. (ed.) (2001), *The Global Transformation Reader*, Polity, Cambridge.

Hirst, P. and Thompson, G. (2001), 'Globalisation: a necessary myth' in D. Held and A. McGrew *The Global Transformation Reader*, Polity, Cambridge.

International Monetary Fund (2000), *World Economic Outlook*.

Jameson, F. (1998), *The Cultures of Globalisation*, Duke University Press, London.

Johnson, R. J. (ed.) (1995), *Geographies of Global Change*, Blackwell, Oxford.

Kacowicz, A. (2001), *The Dark Side of the Moon: Globalisation and Poverty as a Global Problem*, Hebrew University of Jerusalem, Jerusalem.

Kieley, R. (1998), 'Neo-liberalism revisited', *International Journal of Health Services*, 28 (4), pp. 683-702.

McGrew, A. (1997), *The Transformation of Democracy*, Polity, Cambridge.

Panitch, L. (1996), *Rethinking The Role of the State in Globalisation - Critical Reflections*, Lynne Rienner, London.

Social Policy and Development (1997), *Report on the World Social Situation, Part 2: Core Issues*.

Wallerstein, I. (1979), *Limits of the Capitalist World Economy*, Cambridge University Press, Cambridge.

Waters, M. (1995), *Globalisation*, Routledge, London.

Weller, C., Scott, R., and Hersh, A. (2001), 'The unremarkable record of liberalised trade', *EPI Briefing Paper*.

Williamson, J. (1993), 'Democracy and the Washington consensus', *World Development*, 21 (8), pp. 1329-1336.

World Bank (2001), *Draft Policy Research Report: Globalisation, Growth and Poverty: Facts Fear and an Agenda for Action*, World Bank, USA.

World Trade Organisation (1999), *Trade, Income Disparity and Poverty*.

Index